KILLER ROBOTS

Killer Robots
Legality and Ethicality of Autonomous Weapons

ARMIN KRISHNAN
University of Texas at El Paso, USA

ASHGATE

Published by
Ashgate Publishing Limited
Wey Court East
Union Road
Farnham
Surrey, GU9 7PT
England

Ashgate Publishing Company
Suite 420
101 Cherry Street
Burlington
VT 05401-4405
USA

www.ashgate.com

British Library Cataloguing in Publication Data
Krishnan, Armin, 1975-
    Killer robots : legality and ethicality of autonomous
    weapons
    1. Robotics - Military applications 2. Artificial
    intelligence - Military applications 3. Military robots -
    Moral and ethical aspects 4. Arms control
    I. Title
    623'.04

Library of Congress Cataloging-in-Publication Data
Krishnan, Armin, 1975-
    Killer robots : legality and ethicality of autonomous weapons / by Armin Krishnan.
        p. cm.
    Includes bibliographical references and index.
    ISBN 978-0-7546-7726-0 -- ISBN 978-0-7546-9442-7 (ebook)
    1. Military robots--Moral and ethical aspects. I. Title.

    UG479.K75 2009
    355.8'2--dc22

2009002113

ISBN: 978-0-7546-7726-0 (Hb)
ISBN: 978-0-7546-9442-7 (Ebook)

Mixed Sources
Product group from well-managed
forests and other controlled sources
www.fsc.org Cert no. SA-COC-1565
© 1996 Forest Stewardship Council
FSC

Printed and bound in Great Britain by
MPG Books Ltd, Bodmin, Cornwall.

Contents

List of Tables

Acknowledgements

The idea for this book developed five years ago when I had to prepare a presentation for a seminar at the University of Salford. I was surprised about the great interest in the topic of 'killer robots' and also about the many emotional responses I got from students and colleagues there. Though I was initially quite sceptical of the notion that future wars could be fought by machines only, I was nevertheless drawn strongly towards it. Now it is no longer speculation whether or not lethal autonomous military robots or 'killer robots' are technically feasible, as military robotics projects advance at breakneck speed. The question whether such machines should be developed and used in war, or maybe how they should be used, becomes ever more urgent. Thus I felt that the topic deserved a lengthier treatment. This book is, in part, based on an article published in the journal, *Contemporary Security Policy*. I am greatly indebted to all the people who helped me to shape my view over the years through critical comments. I want to thank my former colleagues at the University of Salford, in particular Caroline Baker for allowing me to present my ideas at her seminar in December 2007. I also want to thank Ian Pericevic and Simao Marques for reading my manuscript and for their willingness to discuss killer robots on many occasions. I am particularly indebted to Ian Pericevic for taking the trouble to proofread and correct the manuscript. More than anybody else, I have to thank Dr. Larry Valero from the University of Texas at El Paso for everything he did for me. Of course, all errors remaining in the book are entirely my fault. Finally, I have to thank all the people who supported me over the last year and who enabled me to complete this book despite numerous obstacles. My sincere thanks to Dr. Tamara Tulaikova and my mother, Christine Krishnan. Special thanks to Svetlana for keeping my spirits high and giving me the strength to bring this book to a successful conclusion.

List of Abbreviations

ABL	airborne laser
ADS	active denial system
AI	artificial intelligence
ALV	autonomous land vehicle
APC	armored personnel carrier
ASAT	anti-satellite
ATL	advanced tactical laser
ATR	automatic target recognition
AW	autonomous weapons
BVR	beyond visible range
C4ISR	command, control, communications, computers, intelligence, surveillance and reconnaissance
CAV	common aero vehicle
COA	course of action
DARPA	Defense Advanced Projects Agency
DEW	directed energy weapons
DoD (US)	Department of Defense
EMP	electromagnetic pulse
EOD	explosive ordnance disposal
FCS	Future Combat Systems
GPS	global positioning system
HCV	hypersonic cruise vehicle
ICBM	intercontinental ballistic missile
ICC	International Criminal Court
ICJ	International Court of Justice
IED	improvised explosive device
IR	infrared
IT	information technology

JDAM   Joint Direct Attack Munition
J-UCAS   joint unmanned combat air system

LADAR   laser detection and ranging
LCS   littoral combat ship
LOCAAS   Low Cost Autonomous Attack System

MARV   micro autonomous robot vehicle
MAV   micro aerial vehicle
MDARS   mobile detection assessment response system
MEMS   micro electromechanical systems
MEPAC   Marine Exoskeletal Augmentation Program
MNT   molecular nanotechnology
MoD (UK)   Ministry of Defence
MULE   multifunction utility/logistics and equipment

NCW   network-centric warfare
NT   nanotechnology

ODS   Operation Desert Storm

PGM   precision-guided munitions
PMC   private military company
PTSD   post-traumatic stress disorder

RAF (UK)   Royal Air Force
RMA   Revolution in Military Affairs
RPV   remotely piloted vehicle

SAM   surface-to-air missile
SCI   Strategic Computing Initiative
SDI   Strategic Defense Initiative

TAC   tactical autonomous combatant

UAV   unmanned aerial vehicle
UCAV   unmanned combat aerial vehicle
UGV   unmanned ground vehicle
USAF   United States Air Force
USV   unmanned surface vehicle
UUV   unmanned underwater vehicle

WMD   weapons of mass destruction

Introduction

Killer robots seem to be everywhere. They have made it to the headlines of major newspapers and Hollywood has been busy turning out killer robot movies for years. The roboticist Daniel Wilson writes in his humoristic handbook *How to Survive a Robot Uprising*: 'If popular culture has taught us anything, it is that someday mankind must face and destroy the growing robot menace. In print and on the big screen we have been deluged with scenarios of robot malfunction, misuse, and outright rebellion' (Wilson 2005, 10). He asks rhetorically – 'How could so many Hollywood scripts be wrong?' – just to carry on with his science- and science-fiction-inspired analysis of how to defeat our future robotic enemies.

First indications for a rebellion of military robots have been spotted by the media. In October 2007 it was reported on some websites that a 'robot cannon' malfunctioned, killing nine soldiers in South Africa (e.g. Shachtman 2007d). This resulted in some rebuttals that the mentioned cannon was 'not a robotic weapon' and that the failure was mechanical (Simonite 2007). Some time later in April 2008 there were several stories about an armed ground robot making 'unintended movements' in Iraq (e.g. Sofge 2008c). Again, further clarifications showed that this was no incident of a robot turning on its human masters (Weinberger 2008c).

It is quite easy to make jokes about people who predict the machine Armageddon and who are scared of robot armies that will soon be going on a rampage. There is a growing fear that 'Terminators' could soon roam the earth in search of human prey. Of course, much of the beginning public debate on military robotics sounds just far-fetched and taken straight out of a science fiction story. Everybody who knows at least something about military history and the current reality of war will naturally be very skeptical about even the possibility of robot soldiers fighting our future wars. A book that aims to investigate more seriously the issue of 'killer robots' risks becoming the target of ridicule or, at the very least, criticism.

So it is important to start with an obvious observation. Killer robots in the sense of lethal autonomous military robots do not exist. The military robots that do exist are largely remote-controlled machines, which in rare cases carry weapons. They are so far away from the Terminator as a calculator is from the fictional computer HAL 9000 in *2001: A Space Odyssey*. Current robots have no brains to speak of and are highly dependent on human operators for carrying out their narrow functions, which are mainly reconnaissance, explosive ordnance disposal, logistics (mainly warehouse robots) and base security. Nothing of this does appear to be very threatening or would indicate a need for an investigation into the legality and ethicality of autonomous weapons (AW).

However, it is also true that the number of military robots has increased very rapidly over the last decade. There are currently more than 11,000 robots enlisted in the US military, with much more to come in the next five years. They are becoming more and more sophisticated and autonomous. Though real military robots might never resemble those of science fiction, they will still be largely capable of autonomously carrying out a great variety of military missions with little need of constant human supervision. From this point of view, AW that can search for and pick targets by themselves, in other words 'killer robots', are no longer far-fetched, but could relatively soon become a reality.

Why are the armed forces currently so keen to develop robotic and increasingly autonomous systems? There are many answers to this question. The main reason is probably that the manpower pool for military recruitment is getting smaller, while the requirements for military service continue to grow. The armed forces in many technologically advanced countries already experience serious difficulties in terms of recruiting and retaining personnel (Coker 2002, 59). It is no surprise that Western armed forces are getting smaller and smaller. If they wish to retain their current military advantage in the long term they will need to increasingly substitute soldiers with technology, i.e. robots. The use of robots is also – similar to the use of mercenaries – politically convenient. Casualties are usually politically difficult to justify and governments that wish to intervene militarily in far away places have to keep the risks for their soldiers low in order to sustain the political will for such an intervention (Shaw 2005, 79–80). In addition, there are important economic factors that encourage the development and use of military robots and other automated systems. Robotic platforms are believed to cost far less than manned platforms, as they can be made smaller, do not have to accommodate human operators and can be left less protected (Belin and Chapman 1987, 76). Military robots are also cheaper over their lifetime compared with human soldiers. A human soldier costs the Pentagon over their lifetime about $4 million. A robot would cost less than 10 percent of that and a robot can be scrapped once it is damaged or obsolete. Tim Weiner writes that personnel-related costs will become a major worry for the Department of Defense in the future, as the 'Pentagon owes its soldiers $653 billion in future retirement benefits that it cannot pay' (Weiner 2005b). Defense budgets will get tighter in the US and in Europe and the economic pressures for rationalization and automation in the military sphere will become inevitably bigger and bigger.

If current trends continue, it is foreseeable that once military robots become more common on the battlefield, they will gradually also become more and more capable and more autonomous. At the moment, humans remain in the loop at least wherever the use of force is involved. However, weapons developers and high-ranking military officers feel confident that the technology for truly autonomous weapons will in the medium term (after 2025) be available. Gordon Johnson, who is a member of the Pentagon's Joint Forces Command and its Alpha group studying future war, is quite confident about the future of military robots: 'They don't get hungry. They're not afraid. They don't forget their orders. They don't care if the

guy next to them has just been shot. Will they do a better job than humans? Yes'
(Weiner 2005b).

The investigation will show that it is quite difficult to define AW and to delineate
them clearly from other types of weapons and systems. AW can be based on a wide
range of technologies, which includes information technology, biotechnology,
robotics, artificial intelligence and nanotechnology. All of these technology
areas have begun to converge in the sense that progress in one field (or lack of
it) affects progress in other fields as well. A breakthrough in computing through
nanotechnology (quantum computing), for example, could lead to a breakthrough
in artificial intelligence and in the design of robots. Looking further ahead, it might
be quite difficult to speak of bio-weapons, or robotic weapons, or nanotech-weapons
as distinct classes of weapons, as future weapons could incorporate all of these
different technologies. Jürgen Altmann uses the term 'military nanotechnology'
to summarize very different types of military weapons systems such as artificial
intelligence, armed autonomous systems, mini/micro-robots, distributed sensors
and small satellites because they would be likely to incorporate some aspects of
nanotechnology (Altmann 2006). Although his suggestion makes some sense with
respect to finding an effective leverage point for future regulation, it also obscures
the fact that AW, which seem to be his main concern anyway, existed long before
the age of nanotechnology. Additionally, the term nanotechnology itself has
become such a generic catch-all phrase for a 'miscellany of technologies' that it is
almost meaningless (Shelley 2006, 15–16).

AW are distinct in the sense of the general approach to war that they represent:
they aim to eliminate the human operator, either in part or completely. AW can be
defined as weapons, which are programmable, which are activated or released into
the environment, and which from then on no longer require human intervention for
selecting or attacking targets. Different to other types of weapons, AW are in some
form 'intelligent' with respect to their design and/or their ability to choose targets.

This definition would include a great number of very different systems like
some types of mines, cruise missiles, armed autonomous robots, weaponized
micro-systems and automated air and missile defense systems. Weapons of
mass destruction (WMD) would not fall under this definition because they are
not programmable or intelligent. However, biological weapons that could be
genetically engineered to target specific groups or individuals would count as AW.
The focus of the study will be on robotics rather than military biotechnology or
military nanotechnology simply because autonomous military robots are much
closer to actual deployment than, for example, genetically engineered bio-weapons
or nano-scale weapons, which are much more speculative.

Some academics are already very concerned about future conventional
weapons that could turn war into little more than massacre. For example, Paul
Hirst fears that:

> Developments in computer miniaturisation, robotics and nanotechnology will
> combine to make entirely new weapons possible. Weapons and sensors will fuse,

creating a decentralised network of intelligent automatic killers. Small remotely piloted aircraft will be able to carry huge numbers of micro devices that will find their way into any space – making bunkers or tanks death traps. Something like a 'Terminator' may be possible: a robot capable of fighting in jungles and cities, capable of making decisions on the basis of its sensors, and allowing advanced armies to kill at low cost to themselves. (Hirst 2001b)

Roboticist Noel Sharkey even speaks of a 'threat to humanity' and recommends some immediate action aimed at addressing the danger of armed forces feeling compelled to deploy 'dumb' AW in an accelerating technological arms race (AFP 2008).

However, alarmism and exaggerating the dangers of AW would be as wrong as putting one's head in the sand in the face of the immense ethical challenges ahead that result from technological progress. In this book it is argued that AW can be both: a progress toward humanizing war and an unprecedented danger to humanity. It will largely depend on an effective regulation with respect to what aspect will eventually prevail. Machines will never absolve us from our responsibility of making ethical decisions in peace and war. It is the author's belief that it would be really up to us to make the right choices about how the technology will eventually be used and with what kind of outcomes.

The book is divided into six chapters. Chapter 1 summarizes the history of autonomous weapons from ancient times to the current occupation of Iraq. It is shown that autonomous weapons have already been used in war with varying success and that technological progress may eventually lead to far more effective types of AW than have been possible before. Chapter 2 explains the military advantages that can be gained from AW and describes some of the technologies that may enable them. In Chapter 3 there is an overview of weapons systems currently under development and a look at some possible technological futures of warfare. Chapter 4 analyzes the compatibility of AW with international law and the conventions of war. Chapter 5 discusses the ethical positions and issues concerning AW and military robotics in general. Chapter 6 investigates dangerous futures resulting from the rise of robotic warfare. It is argued that arms control for AW would be desirable and the chapter outlines some options for future regulation.

As many terms in the discussion of military robotics are not very well defined, it would be important to offer some definitions of key terms. These terms are used throughout the book in the way they are defined below:

- **Robot:** a machine that is programmable, that can sense its environment and that can manipulate its environment. Robots can have all shapes and sizes and can be designed for a great variety of functions. A machine needs at least some minimal autonomy to be called a robot.
- **Autonomy:** capability of a machine (usually a robot) for unsupervised operation. The smaller the need for human supervision and intervention, the greater the autonomy of the machine.

- **Robotic weapon:** a computerized weapon equipped with sensors, which may be tele-operated or autonomous. For example, smart munitions are 'robotic', as they have sensors that guide them to their target.
- **Autonomous weapon:** a computerized weapon that does not require any human input for carrying out its core mission. Normally this would include the capability of a weapon to independently identify targets and to trigger itself.
- **Unmanned system:** a robotic sensor or weapons platform, which is reusable and thus not destroyed through its use. An unmanned aerial vehicle (UAV) would count as an unmanned system, but a cruise missile would not.
- **Microsystem (also micro-machine and microelectromechanical system):** a machine of a size between one millimeter and one micron. Autonomous mini-robots of a size of less than one centimeter have already been built and molecular-size robots (nanobots) may be possible after 2030.
- **Artificial intelligence (AI):** software that equips a computerized system (e.g. a robot) with some, usually very specific, human-like capabilities such as pattern recognition, text parsing and planning/problem-solving. This form of AI is already being utilized in many everyday applications (e.g. word processing). The term 'strong artificial intelligence' refers to machine intelligence at, or above, the human level and is a distant long-term research goal. According to most estimates, strong AI may arrive after 2030.

Chapter 1

The Rise of Military Robotics

Some people say that the age of robotic warfare began with the attack on a moving car occupied by four terrorists in Yemen in November 2002 (Weed 2002). The attack was carried out by CIA operators with a modified *Predator* UAV (unmanned aerial vehicle), which fired a *Hellfire* missile at the car, killing all of the occupants. Although the UAV was flown by a human pilot (from a remote location), who also launched the missile, the incidence gave a glimpse of things to come: the possibility of the complete removal of the human soldier from the battlefield and, at least potentially, also the exclusion of humans from the decision-making loop. Finally – the lethal military robot has appeared on the world stage and had killed its first prey. At least so it seemed. In reality, military robots have been around for a long time and have been used in various guises ever since the First World War (Shaker and Wise 1988, 21–39). The difference is only that the technology is now maturing and that intelligent weapons that can operate successfully with little need for human supervision are now technically possible. The armed *Predator* drones are only an indication of this general trend and also proof that robots have now reached the point where they can be actually militarily useful (Weiner 2005a).

Robots have aroused human fascination and fantasies for a long time. They have appeared in uncounted science fiction novels and movies. Although much of the present reality of robots is still that of huge computer-controlled arms putting together cars in factory halls rather than the fantastic machines of science fiction, it is also true that the military affinity with 'robotic' weapons goes back a long way. Robots always seemed somehow destined to enter military service and to become one day the ultimate weapon: a weapon that no longer requires a human warrior to wield it. In a sense, the military robot could be the perfect warrior: superior in strength and skills and completely obedient. At the moment, we are still far away from robot soldiers, but there is no doubt that robotic systems have proliferated rapidly in the modern armed forces around the world, with much more to come in the next decade. Robotic warfare seems to be just around the corner (Brzezinski 2003).

What Is a Robot?

Great confusion exists about what exactly a robot is. At different times a self-steered steamship, an animated puppet and a computer-controlled arm have all been called robots or robotic machines (G. Chapman 1987). The computer scientist Gary Chapman has pointed out that 'there is no logical explanation why certain devices are called robots and others are not' (G. Chapman 1987). The main problem is that the idea of the automaton that can do things a human can do is very old, while the term 'robot' only appeared in the early 1920s. From then on any automaton, in particular those imitating humans or animals, could be called a robot. At the same time, science fiction authors were creating the image of the robot as an artificial man that is in many respects equal, if not superior, to a human being. So the term 'robot' was attributed to anything from the simple clockwork automaton to the convincing human duplicate of science fiction, with industrial robots occupying the middle ground. The main idea behind robots is that of a useful artificial worker that can free humans of the burden of work. A robot is therefore simply a machine, but it is also a very special machine in the minds of many people, as it is a machine that comes closest to being 'alive' or life-like.

In contrast to other machines, which are merely automata, robots are often attributed agency or intent, as they are able to interact with, or even compete with, humans. Sometimes robots are talked about as if they had emotions like desires, or good or bad intentions toward humans. This human uneasiness toward possible robot intentions is indicated by the public response to the first lethal accident involving a repairman being crushed by a robotic arm in Japan in 1981, which received a lot of media attention around the world. The incident was not treated as just another industrial accident, but as a special kind of accident because it involved a robot and not any other ordinary machine. In fact, it was portrayed by the press like a homicide committed by a machine capable of evil intentions (Dennet 1997, 351). Of course, from a purely technical point of view this was hardly a possibility.

So there is this interesting tension in the popular image of the 'robot' of being an automaton – a machine that is completely predictable and completely controllable and obedient – and the concept of an artificial man with own intentions and desires and therefore equipped with an inherent capability of unexpected behavior, disobedience and even rebellion. Science fiction authors have skillfully played with this double meaning of the term 'robot', portraying them sometimes as obedient machines following the commands of humans mindlessly to the extent that it is even detrimental for themselves and their human masters; and sometimes portraying them as machines that can become self-aware and can suddenly decide to follow their own interests. This double image of the robot created by science fiction writers since the 1920s still affects popular conceptions of what robots are, or might be in the future.

Not surprisingly, there are many relevant definitions of what a 'robot' is today, some of which include a greater variety of machines, while others are more restrictive. The *Encyclopaedia Britannica* defines a robot as 'any automatically operated machine that replaces human effort, though it may not resemble human beings in appearance or perform functions in a humanlike manner' (*Encyclopaedia Britannica Online* 2008). Daniel Ichbiah, who is a renowned robotics expert and enthusiast, suggests that a robot in the early twenty-first century 'is a very powerful computer with equally powerful software housed in a mobile body and able to act rationally on its perception of the world around it' (Ichbiah 2005, 9).

Generally speaking and for the purpose of this book, a robot can be defined as a machine, which is able to sense its environment, which is programmed and which is able to manipulate or interact with its environment. It therefore reproduces the general human abilities of perceiving, thinking and acting. So strictly speaking a simple remote-controlled device is not a robot. A robot must exhibit some degree of autonomy, even if it is only very limited autonomy.

Currently there are two basic types of 'robotic' machines that are in use by the armed forces: they can be remotely controlled (tele-operated) or self-directed (autonomous) (Bongard and Sayers 2002, 299). In the case of tele-operated machines, the human operator takes over the tasks of perception and thinking for the machine and is in full control of its actions. However, normally a robot would have to carry out at least some functions autonomously, even when generally tele-operated, in order to deserve the label 'robot'. In other words, they need to be in some form programmable and in some situations able to act without direct control of the operator. This is indeed usually the case with current military robots, although it might be just a 'return home' function in case they lose communication with their operator. In the future robots will become more intelligent and more capable of making their own decisions, for example which route to choose or how best to achieve a given objective. But that might also be the point where the similarity with humans stops. In general, robots do not have to be humanoid or possess intelligence similar or even comparable to humans.

In fact, robots can be all sizes and shapes and are at present hardly more capable than fulfilling a rather narrow function for which they were originally designed and programmed. This means that machine intelligence is likely to remain very specific to the task for which a machine was originally designed and not to be as universal as human intelligence (Ratner and Ratner 2004, 59). But the dream of roboticists, however, is indeed the development of a truly universal robot, which could be easily reprogrammed for a great variety of tasks – in other words, make a robot less of an automaton and more of an artificial man. Roboticist Hans Moravec, for example, believes that the eventual development of robotics will be in the direction of universal robots that could rival and even exceed humans in terms of general abilities and versatility (Moravec 1999, 110).

In the future, the meaning of the term 'robot' could even become more diverse and confusing than it already is. The director of the Pentagon's Alpha analysis group on military robotics, Gordon Johnson, has pointed out in an interview that:

> The robots [under development by the Pentagon] will take on a wide variety of forms, probably none of which will look like humans ... Thus, don't envision androids like those seen in movies. The robots will take on forms that will optimize their use for the roles and missions they will perform. Some will look like vehicles. Some will look like airplanes. Some will look like insects or animals or other objects in an attempt to camouflage or to deceive the adversary. Some will have no physical form – software intelligent agents or cyberbots. (US Joint Forces Command 2003)

The robots of the future will, like the robots of the present, therefore be quite different from the popular conception of robots and will be more astonishing than the robots of the past. The numbers and variety of robots used by the military are growing and they could change warfare forever. Of course, much of this is speculation, but there are already very clear trends that indicate the growing importance of automation and robotics in many areas of society, not just in warfare. Robots have already become viable in the manufacturing industries and they are now spreading to the services industries. If Alvin and Heidi Toffler are correct in their assumption that 'the way we make wealth is … the way we make war' (Toffler and Toffler 1995, 80), then robots will have a major influence on the conduct of war within the next two decades.

The following investigation sticks to the above definition of robots as programmable and sensor-controlled machines and will therefore include a wider range of military systems than are usually discussed in the context of military robotics. The term robot is therefore a description of a particular type of AW (e.g. the autonomous land vehicle), as well as a figurative term for any programmed or autonomous weapon. Another term that is frequently used in the literature on military robotics is 'unmanned system'. The term usually refers to mobile platforms like aerial vehicles, spacecraft, ground vehicles, or naval vehicles. This means not all robotic systems are unmanned systems (only if they are platforms for weapons or sensors). At the same time, 'unmanned' would usually imply robotic and robotic could mean remotely controlled or autonomous. For example, a cruise missile would not be called an unmanned system, as it is not designed to return from a mission (compare US DoD 2005b, 1), but it is clearly a robotic weapon, as it is programmable. The exact meaning of autonomy is discussed in more detail in Chapter 2.

The Current Robotics Revolution of Warfare

There is little doubt that the interest in developing robotic weapons has substantially grown over the last couple of years. The technology is maturing and the costs are dropping, making military robotics both more viable and affordable for many nations. Robotic systems, especially UAVs, have already proven their effectiveness in recent conflicts, such as the Kosovo air campaign in 1999 and the wars in Afghanistan and Iraq. Their numbers in the US armed forces have risen so dramatically since 2000 that even several years ago few military analysts saw it coming. The number of the Pentagon's unmanned air systems shot up from 50 to over 5,000 (Gates 2008) and the number of unmanned ground vehicles (UGVs) recently surpassed 6,000 (Nowak 2008a). The bulk of the literature on the Revolution in Military Affairs (RMA) that has been produced since the early 1990s therefore hardly mentions military robots, including some newer titles such as Tim Benbow's *The Magic Bullet*, published in 2004. Military robotics is still, in terms of military/strategic thought, in unknown territory. Technological progress is once again outpacing the development of doctrine. With regard to finding effective ways of using the new technology, much currently happens in the field through a process of trial and error.

In particular, the US military will soon be transformed by the current robotics revolution of warfare. US Congress already mandated in 2001 that by 2010 one-third of all combat aircraft shall be unmanned and that by 2015 one-third of all ground vehicles shall be unmanned (US Congress 2001, S.2549, Sec. 217). Furthermore, the 2006 Quadrennial Defense Review states that '45% of the future long-range strike force will be unmanned' (US DoD 2006a, 46). The Department of Defense (DoD) has also recently published a report called 'Unmanned Systems Roadmap 2007–2032', indicating a long-term commitment to military robotics. According to this report, the US DoD plans to spend more than $24 billion on unmanned systems in the years 2007 to 2013 (US DoD 2007, 10). Its biggest project involving robotics is currently the $300 billion *Future Combat Systems* program, which relies so heavily on military robotics that some people call it an attempt to field a robot army (Sparrow 2007b, 64).

The robotics professor Noel Sharkey from the University of Sheffield claims that the arms race for developing and fielding military robots is already well under way (Minkel 2008). It has been reported that more than 40 nations are currently developing robotic weapons (Boot 2006b, 23). This includes first and foremost the US, but also the UK, France, Italy, Canada, Germany, Japan, Sweden, Singapore, Iran, South Korea, South Africa and Israel. They are working on UAVs, unmanned combat aerial vehicles (UCAVs), UGVs, stationary sentry robots, unmanned underwater vehicles (UUVs) and micro and nanorobots. About 90 nations are believed to have UAVs in their arsenals and about 600 different types are produced worldwide (Conetta 2005, 17). A growing number of states have somewhat less advanced (or less autonomous) robotic weapons, such as cruise missiles and anti-ship missiles. After all, a cruise missile is nothing but a robot plane that is not expected to come back. A report to the US Congress claims that already 75 nations are believed to have such weapons in their arsenals (Feikert 2005).

Most efforts and money are presently directed toward the development of UAVs and UCAVs, which are the type of autonomous robotic weapons system that is closest to actual deployment. UAVs/UCAVs are technologically at least 10 years ahead of UGVs and there are many types either already in the field or in an advanced stage of development. For example, between 1998 and 2006 Boeing developed the *X-45* UCAV, of which several prototypes flew successfully. The *X-45* was designed to operate autonomously as a reconnaissance and strike platform with the ability to take off, refuel mid-air, respond dynamically to threats, carry out its mission and return to base – all by itself or with minimal human supervision (Tirpak 2005). The US is by no means the only state developing UCAVs; Europe is not too far behind in this field.

The current European UCAV projects include the *Taranis* and *Mantis* (UK/BAE Systems), the *nEuron* (France/DGA) and the *Barracuda* (Germany/EADS), all of which are expected to enter service in some form or shape in the years 2010 to 2020.

Even Russia is trying to catch up in the development of UCAVs with at least two prototypes under development by MiG and Sukhoi (Komarov and Barrie 2008). John Pike sees an expanding role for military robots and contends that 'we are probably seeing the last manned tactical fighter being built now, and in a few years there will be no manned tanks or artillery'; he also argues that the era of robotic warfare is approaching 'faster than many people think' (*Arizona Star* 2007). So it can be claimed safely that lethal military robots will be introduced in larger numbers by the most technologically advanced armed forces within the next five to ten years. Their exact roles, autonomy, functions and doctrine are still undetermined. Sooner or later military organizations will have to figure out what they want to do with ever more capable unmanned systems and how to use them most effectively.

Table 1.1 gives an overview of military robotics research in 20 countries around the world.

Military robotics is still in its infancy, but it is developing at an incredibly rapid speed. This can be seen in the progress that has been made in developing autonomous ground vehicles over the last few years. In 2004 the Defense Advanced Projects Agency (DARPA) held a competition called *Grand Challenge* in which autonomous vehicles had to race over a distance of 142 miles. None of the 15 vehicles managed to get further than eight miles (Hallinan 2004), but just one year later in *Grand Challenge 2005* there were five finishers. In late 2007 DARPA held the *Urban Challenge* competition in which robotic vehicles had to drive alongside human-driven cars in an urban environment. There were 11 finalists on the 2.8-mile course and only one crash (US DARPA 2007b). At the very least the three competitions prove the rapid progress in autonomous vehicle technology and may indicate that the autopilot for cars is not far off (Lee 2008). Similar military robotics competitions have been organized in some other countries around the world in recent years.[1] This gives good evidence for the military's interest in unmanned systems and of the rapid development in this area.

However, building military UGVs, which can move as quickly and intelligently over difficult terrain as human-driven vehicles in all weather conditions, evading obstacles and enemy fire while being able to autonomously engage suitable targets, is a lot more difficult than getting autonomous vehicles to obey traffic rules. But few experts doubt that it could be done in principle. So it might be reasonable not to have exaggerated expectations about military robots in the near term, while acknowledging the truly transformational potential of robotics on warfare in the medium to the long term. The autonomous killer robot is not yet here, but there are no technical reasons why it should not arrive in a fairly short time measured in historical terms.

Despite the recent hype surrounding robotics and military robots in particular, it is quite surprising how old the idea of the war robot and robotic weapons actually

---

1   For example, the German *European Land Robot* (Elrob) competition, which was held in 2006 and 2008, or the British MoD *Grand Challenge* held in August 2008, and Singapore's *TechX Challenge*, also held in August 2008.

Table 1.1   Worldwide military robotics research

Country	UAVs	Cruise missiles/ anti-ship missiles	UCAVs	Automated air and missile defense	UGVs/ armed stationary robots	USVs	UUVs	Robotic microsystems	NT-based/ enabled weapons
Australia	yes	yes	–	yes	yes	yes	yes	–	–
Canada	yes	yes	–	yes	yes	–	yes	–	–
China	yes	yes	–	?	?	?	?	?	?
France	yes	yes	yes	yes	yes	–	yes	–	?
Germany	yes	yes	yes	yes	yes	–	yes	–	–
India	yes	yes	?	?	yes	?	?	?	?
Iran	yes	yes	–	–	–	–	–	–	?
Israel	yes	yes	?	yes	yes	yes	?	yes	yes
Italy	yes	yes	yes	yes	yes	–	–	–	–
Japan	yes	yes	–	yes	yes	–	yes	yes	?
Russia	yes	yes	yes	yes	?	–	yes	?	?
Singapore	yes	yes	?	?	yes	yes	?	?	?
South Africa	yes	yes	–	yes	yes	–	–	–	?
South Korea	yes	yes	yes	yes	yes	–	–	yes	–
Spain	yes	yes	yes	–	–	–	–	–	–
Sweden	yes	yes	yes	yes	–	–	yes	–	–
Taiwan	yes	yes	–	yes	?	–	?	?	–
UK	yes	yes	yes	yes	yes	yes	yes	yes	yes
US	yes	yes	yes	yes	yes	yes	yes	yes	yes

are. The following section gives a brief historical overview of military robotics, from ancient times to the occupation of Iraq.

The Early History of Military Robotics

The robots that became prominent in the modern science fiction writing of Karel Čapek, Isaac Asimov and Arthur C. Clarke symbolize the ancient dream of creating an artificial man – however, an artificial man that is far from being considered equal to man. The word 'robota' is Czech and means slave laborer – and that is exactly what robots are meant to be. But no man wants to be a slave and to live in fear of their own master. The relationship of man and robot, or creator and creation, has therefore always been seen as a potentially very problematic one.

Robots of Ancient and Pre-modern Times

Creatures appear in many Greek myths that are very similar to our modern understanding of robots. The myths already point at the weaknesses and dangers of robots, which may still be relevant today. There are, for example, the legends of Cadmus and the Argonauts, according to which dragon teeth sowed on the ground transformed into soldiers or fierce warriors, who could be easily defeated by throwing a stone amongst them. Not knowing who threw the stone, they would fight against each other. Similar is the myth of the Greek god of war Hephaistos who, according to Homer's *Iliad*, created mechanical female servants out of gold, which he alone could control. The legend tells that Hephaistos once created for Minos of Crete a bronze statue (forged with the help of the Cyclopes) and brought it to life. The animated bronze statue was called Talos or Talon, whose function was to guard the goddess Europa in Crete. Unfortunately, Talon had a weak spot, a nail that protected his neck, which led to his destruction. Medea used some trickery to remove the nail and Talon was slain. Other robot-like creatures of ancient legends are the so-called Myrmidons, who were originally highly skilled and ruthless warriors commanded by Achilles during the siege of Troy. The term 'Myrmidon' later acquired the meaning of completely obedient ant-like soldiers, similar to our understanding of robots, or maybe rather similar to the clone soldiers that appear in the *Star Wars* movie series. A theme that goes through all of these ancient myths of artificial beings is that they are always portrayed as somewhat deficient compared with humans. They might be faster and stronger than humans, but they are easily confused or have weak spots that make it easy for smarter humans to defeat them.

The ancients did not have to rely on their imagination alone for creating the idea of robots or artificial slave laborers or soldiers, but even built themselves some sophisticated automata. The first primitive water-powered clocks appeared around 3500 BC in Egypt. Around AD 100 Hero of Alexandria built several automata that used wind and water power. For example, he invented the first vending machine that released water when a coin was inserted. He even constructed a primitive steam engine (the 'aeolopile') and some pneumatically operated human forms – in other words, the first humanoid robots (Brooks 2002, 13).

The Renaissance thinkers eventually rediscovered many of the ancient texts and ideas. The greatest genius of his time was Leonardo da Vinci, who also developed a keen interest in automata. It can be assumed that Leonardo was inspired by the ancients, and particularly by the writings of Hero of Alexandria, when he worked on the design of anthropomorphic clockwork automata or humanoid robots. Unfortunately, few of his inventions survived and many of his blueprints for his automata remain incomplete. Among other automata, Leonardo designed a mechanical knight that could carry out complex movements like a human, controlled with strings and pulleys. It is also possible that the movements of the mechanical robot could be triggered and powered by a sophisticated clock mechanism. The robot could move its arms and could stand up or sit down. However, the most likely purpose of this robot knight was to scare and entertain the visitors of the owner (Rosheim 2006, 112). Leonardo was not able to find funding for actually building the robot knight.

Leonardo's clockwork robots were not entirely forgotten, and in the eighteenth century humanoid clockwork automata were rediscovered. It was 'the golden age of the automaton' in which people like the French engineer Jaques de Vaucanson built (among other things) a mechanical duck that could eat and drink (Ichbiah, 2005, 16–17). Such 'animatronics' became quite fashionable among the upper class in Europe during that time and led to the development of quite sophisticated mechanical clockwork automata.

Later in the nineteenth century Charles Babbage tried to build an analytical engine, which was a mechanical computer that could be programmed with punch cards. It was the first programmable digital computer ever to be conceived. Unfortunately, Babbage did not succeed in making it work and it took almost 70 years before the first programmable electromechanical computer was built by Konrad Zuse in 1939. The programmable computer opened up entirely new and unprecedented possibilities for actually creating something that we now call a robot. Thus the foundations for the development of modern-day robots were laid in the nineteenth century. Technology eventually caught up with the ancient dreams in the early twentieth century.

Remote-control Weapons before the Second World War

One of the first to build a remote-controlled machine that can be vaguely called a robot was the famous Serb inventor Nikola Tesla. He can be considered the father of modern smart weapons, which are guided to their targets. In 1898 Nikola Tesla built an electric boat that could be remotely controlled by radio. He demonstrated his invention in an indoor pool in New York's Madison Square Garden. Tesla considered the use of remote-controlled boats as a weapon and thought that they could carry warheads and be guided by operators to enemy ships (Tesla and Leland 1998). In other words, he invented the modern torpedo. Tesla called the new technology 'The Art of Teleautomatics' and offered it to the American Government. The inventor was so convinced of the tremendous impact 'teleautomatics' would have on warfare that he wrote in his autobiography: 'At that time I really thought that it would abolish war, because of its unlimited destructiveness and exclusion of the personal element of combat' (Matthews 1973, 35). But Tesla was so much ahead of his time that the American armed forces simply did not yet recognize the potential military value of this invention. As Telsa could not find funding for it elsewhere and as the discipline of 'teleautomatics' created little general interest amongst the military and weapons developers, it was almost forgotten.

However, Telsa's remote-controlled weapons were eventually developed further and used during the First World War, which provided a better climate for the experimentation with radically new concepts. The German Navy experimented with remote-controlled torpedoes and used them in attacks on enemy ships, but they were not very successful. Another early application of remote-control technology was in the field of emerging aerial warfare. Only 13 years after the first aircraft flew in 1903, the development of an 'aerial torpedo' was proposed by H.P. Folland and Professor A.M. Low in Britain. A first prototype was demonstrated to British generals on 21 March 1917 (Werrell 1985, 8). Before the First World

War was over, a remotely piloted aircraft flew and was developed as a primitive cruise missile. In America the US Navy started to experiment with a catapult-launched unmanned aircraft based on the Curtiss *N-9* plane, but its performance as a 'flying bomb' was so poor that the Navy did not manage to iron out the problems before the end of the war. The US Army was not much more successful: Charles Kettering, Vice President of General Motors, designed and built a small unmanned biplane that was supposed to deliver a 300-pound warhead to a target. It carried a gyroscope for keeping the aircraft on its flight path and had a simple mechanism that caused the wings to fold up after a certain time and the unmanned aircraft to drop on a target. The 'Kettering bug aerial torpedo', as it was called, was intended to be mass produced by Ford Motor Company at the price of $400–$500 each. But the war ended before the 'bug' could see combat. After the armistice no large orders were placed, which is not surprising considering its poor results in tests (McDaid and Oliver 1997, 11). There were only eight successful launches out of 36 attempts (Werrell 1985, 17).

Nevertheless, the development of unmanned aircraft continued and several types were built in the US and Britain, mainly for target practice. In 1937 the US Navy developed a pilotless aircraft, the Curtiss *N2C-2*, which could be remote-controlled by a pilot in another aircraft over a distance of 20 miles. In April 1942 the US Navy showed in a demonstration that a torpedo carrying a *TG-2* drone with TV and remote-controlled from another aircraft 20 miles away was able to find a destroyer and to successfully attack it with a torpedo (Werrell 1985, 24). Britain also continued working on remote-control weapons. In 1927 there were three different missile projects sponsored by the Royal Air Force: 'a mechanically-controlled "flying bomb," a radio-controlled missile, and an air defence missile to break up enemy aircraft formations.' In the end, the RAF did not pursue the flying bomb concept further because of high unit costs and low accuracy (Werrell 1985, 20).

Military Robots of the Second World War

During the Second World War Germany eventually managed to take the lead in the development of robotic weapons with its Fieseler *Fi-103*, or the so-called 'retaliation weapon one': *V-1*. In 1943, when it became increasingly obvious that Germany was about to lose the war, the Führer put his hope in the development of 'wonder weapons' (Wunderwaffen), which could turn around the war again. Germany developed a whole range of secret weapons, which included the first jet fighter aircraft (*Me 262*) and the first military ballistic missile (*V-2*). Although the *V-2* is rightly considered as the greater technological achievement because it had a direct impact on American and Soviet ballistic missile programs *after* the war, it was the *V-1* which was at that time by far the more dangerous weapon. The *V-1* was the first robotic weapon in history to be used on a massive scale, causing considerable damage amongst the enemy. Its example is quite instructive.

The *V-1* was a far more advanced flying bomb than older models like the *Kettering bug*. It was equipped with a jet engine that propelled it to a speed of over 400mph and it could carry a 2,000-pound warhead over an average distance of 150 miles. The *V-1* was therefore slightly faster than many manned aircraft of the war. The *V-1* could be carried under the wings of a bomber, or could be launched from the ground with a steam catapult launching system. The first attack on Britain with *V-1*s occurred just after the Normandy landing on 13 June 1944. Germany built more than 30,000 *V-1*s and successfully launched 8,000 of them, of which almost 6,000 fell on Britain and the rest on the continent (mainly Liege and Antwerp). Although the *V-1*s killed altogether more than 4,700 people (947 in Britain) and injured 35,000, the flying bomb had little impact on the war. The *V-1* (and later the *V-2*) was just a terror weapon aimed at demoralizing the British population, but it utterly failed in achieving that goal. In addition, the guidance system was very crude and it was only possible to target a large area such as the London metropolitan area. Even so, most *V-1*s failed to hit London, as the average miss distance was still almost five miles (Hambling 2005, 60). Additionally, the British employed deception by using captured German double agents (the so-called Double Cross System) to make the Germans shorten the range of the *V-1* (Keegan 2003, 530). As the Germans lacked aerial reconnaissance for bomb damage assessment, they did not know where exactly the *V-1*s came down and were therefore successfully deceived by the British. Aware of this massive inaccuracy of the *V-1*, the Germans developed at the very end of the war a manned version of it (*Fi-103 R* or Reichenberg) for which a suicide pilot would function as a guidance system. It was never operationally used (Zaloga 2005, 39). However, in purely economic terms the *V-1* was a success: it was much cheaper than a manned bomber and did cause the Allies about three times the damage it cost the Germans to produce it (even considering the tremendous losses of *V-1*s due to Allied bombing). Kenneth Werrell concludes that 'although advanced technically, tactically, and economically, it was just too far ahead of its time' (Werrell 1985, 61–2).

The Germans also developed a small, remotely controlled tracked vehicle called *Goliath* for delivering explosives to the enemy. The original *Goliath* was a copy of a French prototype, which was found by German forces in 1940. *Goliath* was powered by an electric motor, weighed about 815lbs and could carry a 130lb. explosive charge over a distance of 1 mile (Bongard and Sayers 2002, 301). Later models used a more reliable gasoline engine and could carry 165–220lbs of high explosives. From early 1942 onwards German forces deployed *Goliath* in all theatres in larger numbers and about 7,500 were built altogether. During the Normandy landing greater numbers of *Goliaths* were deployed as anti-tank weapons (Shaker and Wise 1988, 16–17). But the unmanned vehicle was not considered a success because it was too expensive, too vulnerable and too impractical. The vehicle moved very slowly at 5.9mph and the operator, using a joystick, had to be in a line of sight to the vehicle because it did not have a TV camera. The control cable could get entangled or could get severed by the enemy. Very few *Goliaths* were actually used in combat (there were still almost 4,000 of them waiting for action in 1945) (Hahn 1987, 100).

There was also a heavy version of the *Goliath*, weighing 1.5 tons (4 tons for a later version), which could deliver an explosive charge of 1,100lbs; it entered service in April 1942. It was designated *B IV* vehicle and was in many respects far more sophisticated than the better known *Goliath*. *B IV* could be driven by a human driver or be remote-controlled by radio. It was armored, could reach a speed of 25mph, and travel a maximum distance of 75 miles. Later versions were supposed to be equipped with a TV camera, but tests were not completed before the end of the war. Similar to *Goliath*, the *B IV* was produced in significant numbers in various versions (altogether 1,178), but very few of them actually reached the frontline (397 remained unused by the end of the war) (Hahn 1987, 98–9).

During the Second World War the Japanese also fielded several remote-control weapons that were quite similar to German designs. Between 1934 and 1945 the Japanese converted the small *Nagayama* tanks, based on the American Ford agricultural tractor, to remote-controlled demolition devices reminiscent of the *Goliath*. Japan even produced two prototypes of a remote-controlled tank. The operator could change the direction of the tank and could remotely control the tank gun, which was able to reload automatically (Hahn 1987, 101).

The Japanese also developed some primitive cruise missiles that were based on the German design of the *V-1*. They were called *Baka* (fool) and *Ohka* (cherry blossom) and were used in some rather unsuccessful attacks on US ships. As it is widely known, the Japanese did eventually use suicide pilots or 'kamikaze' as manned cruise missiles. The Japanese could simply not solve the problem of accuracy in any other way, as their targets were Allied ships and, as such, quite small compared with the area targets the Germans tried to hit. The *Ohka* was designed as such a manned cruise missile and was dropped from a *G4M Betty* bomber. In the final approach the *Ohka* pilot would ignite the rocket engine and guide it to the target. About 750 of them were built and they sank at least three Allied ships. Through kamikaze attacks with all kinds of aircraft (modified fighters, dive bombers and purpose-built kamikaze planes) the Japanese managed to sink overall a significant number of Allied ships, but they ran out of fuel and aircraft before the kamikaze could make a difference.[2]

It is apparent that other great powers, namely the US and Britain, did not make great efforts with respect to deploying unmanned platforms. In part they simply did not need to, as German and Japanese remote-control weapons arrived too late in the war and could not affect its outcome. In the Pacific theatre Admiral Chester Nimitz was decidedly against remotely piloted vehicles (RPVs). 'Why deploy an untried weapon when carrier aviation seemed to do everything better?' (Werrell 1985, 25). The US Army aviation was similarly dispositioned against drones and only funded a few smaller research programs. One was an air-launched RPV with a TV sensor for guidance, which could be carried by a *B-25* bomber and which was later canceled because of high development costs. The US Army Air Force eventually deployed a 'flying bomb' in August 1944, code-named *Aphrodite*. Modified *B-17* and *B-24* bombers were loaded with 9 tons of bombs and guided

---

2 Estimates of the number of US ships sunk or damaged beyond repair by kamikaze differ widely and range from 34 (US Navy estimate) to 81 (official Japanese estimate).

by remote control towards German targets, but all of them seemed to have either crashed or were shot down before they reached their targets.

In August 1945 the war eventually ended quite dramatically with the detonation of two nuclear bombs in Hiroshima and Nagasaki. The development of robotic weapons in the Second World War came to a temporary end, while the nuclear and missile age dawned on mankind.

Military Robotics since the Second World War

US Air Force General Hap Arnold was one of the few supporters of the American drone programs and he predicted in 1945 that 'the next war may be fought by airplanes with no men in them at all' (Shaker and Wise 1988, 87). From then on the vision (or nightmare) of an automated war machine periodically reappeared in various versions. In the 1950s nuclear weapons and ballistic missiles threatened to render conventional (human) forces obsolete and irrelevant. The destructive power of nuclear weapons is simply so great that they can hardly be even compared with conventional munitions. Through the push of a button whole nations could be obliterated, making nuclear weapons pure instruments of mass murder rather than weapons of war (Van Creveld 1991, 19).

However, the new prevalence of low-intensity conflicts and the strategic conventional threat to western Europe required the US and other major military powers to maintain old-fashioned conventional forces throughout the Cold War. The research into the improvement of conventional weapons and platforms continued largely independently from the development of nuclear weapons (Hacker 2005, 255). Conventional weapons became much more sophisticated than their Second World War counterparts. In the 1960s the concept of the electronic battlefield was developed, aimed at the exploitation of the electromagnetic spectrum for command and control, as well as the tracking of enemy forces.

Vietnam and the Advent of the Electronic Battlefield

The Vietnam War became a testing ground for electronic warfare and automated command and sensor networks, or for what was later called the 'automated battlefield' (Hacker 2005, 274). The Soviets called it 'reconnaissance-strike complexes' (Krepinevich 2002, 6). It was therefore probably no coincidence that it was the former commander of the US Military Assistance Corps Vietnam (MACV) General Westmoreland who made the following prediction in 1967:

> On the battlefield of the future enemy forces will be located, tracked and targeted almost instantaneously through the use of data-links, computer-assisted intelligence evaluation and automated fire control. With first-round kill probabilities approaching certainty, and with surveillance devices that can

continuously track the enemy, the need for large forces to fix the opposition physically will be less important. (Barnaby 1986, 1)

In this spirit the JASON Committee of the US Department of Defense suggested in 1966 the construction of an anti-intrusion line along the borders of South Vietnam – a concept that later became known as the 'McNamara Line'. The line would consist of a sensor network of seismic and acoustic sensors, photoreconnaissance and land mines. Any attempt of the Viet Cong crossing the border would be blocked through air-delivered mines and bombing. What was particularly notable about the McNamara Line was that 'the plan required virtually no ground forces: it was executed predominantly from the air' (Youngblood 2006, 148). For this purpose, the Americans developed several types of sensor-triggered and air-dropped anti-personnel mines, among them the *Gravel* and *Dragontooth* mines. The *Dragontooth* mine dispenser held 4,800 small mines that were spread from the air over a wide area. The *Gravel* mine was a simple canvas-covered charge. The plan emphasized the use of anti-personnel weapons so heavily that it was estimated that there would be a *monthly* consumption of 20 million *Gravel* mines and 20,000 cluster bombs (Prokosch 1995, 109). The plan for the McNamara Line was only partially implemented because of high costs, technical problems with the sensors and because of the political controversy connected to the proposed massive use of air-delivered anti-personnel mines.

In the early 1970s the first precision munitions or smart weapons appeared. This meant that weapons became robotic in the sense that the terminal guidance of these weapons (missiles and guided bombs) became automated. At the very end of the Vietnam War the first laser-guided bombs were used, which can find their targets by following a laser beam that is pointed at a target, either by the launching platform or by troops on the ground. Laser-guided bombs proved during the Linebacker raids to be much more accurate than simple freefall bombs (Friedman and Friedman 1996, 114). While the effectiveness of laser-guided bombs still depends largely on human operators, smart weapons that were even more automated also made their first appearance in the Vietnam era. These were so-called 'fire-and-forget' weapons that, once launched, no longer required any attention or action on the part of the operator. This reduces the time a soldier or firing platform is exposed to enemy fire and allows them to take evasive action (disengage, seek cover) or engage other targets immediately after the weapon is launched. The guidance system of the weapon takes over and the weapon will pursue the target autonomously.

Fire-and-forget weapons of the 1960s and 1970s like the *Shrike* anti-radiation missile or the Soviet *Styx* anti-ship missile did not have a particularly high success rate. It was estimated to be less than 20 percent. However, stand-off fire-and-forget missiles were constantly improved over time. The newer air-to-surface missiles and air-to-air missiles (mid-1970s onwards) have an over-the-horizon attack capability, which means they can be launched over a distance of 30 (or more) miles away from a target without any visual contact. For example, the *Phoenix* missile was developed for fleet defense and allows a single *F-14* to engage six aerial targets at a time and to control an airspace of 40,000 square miles (Barnaby 1986, 58). Modern anti-ship missiles like the French *Exocet* missile only need to be launched in the direction of the enemy fleet from a distance of 30 miles and they can then find and attack their targets by themselves. During the Falklands War four of the six *Exocet* missiles launched by Argentinian aircraft hit their targets (Ismat 2001).

The smart weapons and sensors of the Vietnam era were generally not AWs in the sense that they could be automatically launched at targets, but they were already quite autonomous with respect to finding and attacking targets once they were launched by a human operator. In some cases, such as anti-radiation missiles (e.g. the *Shrike*), they were able to choose their own targets *after* they were launched. As they were designed as stand-off weapons, they could be fired over a great distance to the target. So the decision of the human operator to launch a weapon is often not based on a visual identification of a target, but is rather based on radar or other sensor data. For example, in modern air-to-air combat a pilot might fire a missile simply at a dot on a radar screen without ever actually seeing the opponent, which was the most frequent mode of air-to-air combat during the 1991 Gulf War (Nichols 1998, 5). A research report from the US Air University thus concludes: 'Future technology will continue to provide the ability to obtain long range contact on the enemy, and employ BVR [beyond visible range] weapons. That capability, coupled with our radar evading stealth technology might make the classic dogfight obsolete' (Nichols 1998, 15). The implication is that a human pilot might be in most cases no better (maybe even worse) in determining which targets to engage than a computer, as both would rely on the same sensor data.

Although sensors, mines and smart weapons seem to have little in common with the killer robots of popular fiction, they have at least some characteristics of robots: they are automated or programmed and they use sensors to direct them to their targets. Smart weapons are therefore an important evolutionary step toward the development of AW and of military robots that are closer to those envisioned by science fiction authors.

Experimental Robots and Space Exploration

One area of military/civilian research that contributed immensely to the eventual development of more-autonomous robots was the aim of space exploration and the subsequent militarization of space. The near-earth space became militarized because it offered unprecedented possibilities for collecting photointelligence of denied territories and because it allowed military units and bases around the world to be connected to a global communications network. The numbers and sophistication of earth-orbiting satellites, or 'space robots', have grown rapidly since the late 1950s.

But the American and Soviet ambition was to go beyond near-earth space and to explore our solar system. From the beginning it was obvious that it was unlikely that humans could conquer space without the help of robots. So the conceptualization of unmanned space exploration began even before the era of manned spaceflight. The physicist and computer pioneer John von Neumann developed in the 1950s the idea of self-replicating automata, which could be sent into space and which could explore and populate our solar system, and later our galaxy, speedily, as their numbers could grow exponentially. The so-called 'von Neumann automata' would consist of three parts: a factory placed in a sea of raw materials, which it can use to assemble new parts; a duplicator that could read and copy instructions; and finally a brain or control mechanism for the automaton (Levy 1992, 38). Von Neumann proved that such self-replicating automata would be possible in theory and the interest in building them has never really ceased.

However, in the particular climate of the Cold War, the overruling rationale for conquering space was not just exploration, but national security combined with the desire to beat the other side in terms of prestige. It was deemed to be more prestigious to put humans into space and on the moon rather than using mere machines for these tasks. So a great deal of effort and money went into sending the first human to the moon. Unfortunately, the moon itself proved to be not very interesting scientifically and militarily. The unsurprising result was that the *Apollo* program was soon discontinued once the original goal was achieved and manned spaceflight suffered a backlash.

On the positive side, after *Apollo* NASA concentrated more on sending probes and robots into space, which increased the scientific efforts of developing autonomous robots. Important milestones were the *Viking* missions to Mars in 1975. The probes reached Mars in 1976 and were able to map the planet, to land on the surface and analyze soil samples, and to transmit the results back to earth. Daniel Ichbiah writes that 'the Vikings were the most advanced craft of their time. They cost around one billion dollars and were the fruit of 10,000 space scientists in the US' (Ichbiah 2005, 268). Since then many other probes and robots have reached Mars, most recently *Sojourner* in 1997 and *Spirit* and *Opportunity* in 2004.

NASA rediscovered the von Neumann automata in 1980 in a landmark study called *Advanced Automation for Space Missions*, which NASA conducted 'because of an increasing realization of the major role that advanced automatic and robotic devices, using machine intelligence, must play in future space missions' (Freitas and Gilbreath 1980). In 1989 Rodney Brooks from the MIT AI Lab suggested sending large numbers of small and less sophisticated robots into space instead of a few big and expensive ones to speed up exploration (Brooks and Flynn 1989, 478–85). Brooks later developed a range of small autonomous robots for this general purpose.

In the 1990s there was a revival of the interest in manned spaceflight, despite the *Challenger* disaster in 1987. The Russians gained valuable experiences with long space missions thanks to their space station *Mir*, which was kept in operation for more than 15 years until 2001. International cooperation allowed astronauts from many countries to visit *Mir* and to spend extended periods in space. The success of *Mir* eventually led to the decision to build the *International Space Station* (ISS) in 1998. However, the value of a long-term human presence in space is highly debatable. It costs about $100 million to keep a human for one year in space (Kelly 1995, 200) and there is little they can do that could not either be done by a robot, or by a human on earth (Rees 2003, 172–3). Outer space is an extremely dangerous environment to live in and the human body is simply not adjusted to living in conditions of constant zero gravitation and continuous exposure to radiation. It seems highly likely that space will have to be explored by robots rather than humans and that human presence in space will always remain small, unless a new race of space-humans is created that is much better adapted to living in space.

The space missions resulted in the development of lots of spin-off technologies and technology adaptations to different settings. For example, the technology of space robots could be applied to 'terrestrial hazardous settings, such as under the ocean, in nuclear power plants, or on the battlefield' (Shaker and Wise 1988, 146). Amitai Etzioni claims that 'although rarely discussed … the greatest achievement of the space program – whether by NASA, the military, or the private sector – have been the result of unmanned vehicles and instruments' (DeGroot 2008, 258). NASA's successful robot programs of the 1960s and 1970s enabled, or at least encouraged, the robotics upsurge of the 1980s.

The Military Robotics Upsurge of the 1980s

By the 1980s there was a significant shift in US and NATO strategy for countering the Soviet threat to western Europe. The Soviets had gained a quantitative advantage of about 2–3:1 over NATO forces deployed in Europe and they threatened to simply overrun western Europe in a fast surprise attack ('the bolt from the blue'). In the previous decades NATO believed that the only way of stopping a Warsaw Pact attack on western Europe was to retaliate with nuclear weapons (Betts 1985, 153). The Strategic Defense Initiative (SDI) changed the picture insofar as it aimed at neutralizing nuclear weapons, thus making it more likely that a military conflict with the Warsaw Pact could stay below the nuclear threshold. Reliance on nuclear retaliation was seen as an unsatisfactory solution, 'since it destroys the very country one is trying to defend' (G. Chapman 1985).

In the 1980s NATO was aiming to be able to stop the Soviets with conventional weapons alone. As a result, the US military became more interested in high-tech weapons. This was part of US Secretary of Defense Harold Brown's earlier 'offset strategy', which aimed at gaining a qualitative advantage over the Soviets (Sloan 2002, 25). It would have allowed NATO forces to stop the Warsaw Pact before they could wreak havoc inside NATO territory. The new NATO strategy was called Follow-On-Forces-Attack (named so because NATO forces would go after the second and third echelons of Soviet forces) and was officially adopted by NATO in 1984 (Miller 2001, 30). The concept relied heavily on the development and use of new robotic types of weapons, such as RPVs, robotic artillery and smart munitions for the defense of western Europe.

At the forefront of the technological development was DARPA. In 1983 DARPA started its Strategic Computing Initiative (SCI), which aimed to achieve 'real' artificial intelligence within a decade. DARPA spent an additional one billion dollars between 1983 and 1993 to speed up the development of intelligent machines that could be used for fighting wars entirely by themselves. In a 1983 document DARPA declared its overly ambitious goals, which called for the virtual elimination of the human soldier from the battlefield:

> Instead of fielding simple guided missiles or remotely piloted vehicles, we might launch completely autonomous land, sea, and air vehicles capable of complex, far-ranging reconnaissance and attack missions ... Using this new technology [of artificial intelligence], machines will perform complex tasks with little human intervention, or even with complete autonomy ... The possibilities are quite startling, and could fundamentally change the nature of human conflicts.'
> (quoted from Belin and Chapman 1987, 171)

DARPA announced three large research projects in October 1983 to realize these goals: the development of an all-purpose autonomous land vehicle (ALV), the development of a 'pilot's associate' that would assist human pilots in flying military jets, and the development of a battle management system for aircraft carrier task forces.

During this time AI seemed to be just around the corner. Lots of new companies aimed at building 'machines that think' were founded in Silicon Valley and Boston with DARPA money. Although SCI produced some tangible results in advances of computer technology, the ultimate aims of developing truly autonomous weapons were obviously not achieved. Nevertheless, a whole range of new robotic weapons were developed and fielded, most importantly the cruise missile, several automated air defense systems (*Phalanx*, *Aegis*, *Patriot*) and automated rocket artillery (*MLRS*). These weapons were part of the US Army modernization program of the 1980s, which also replaced the older *M60 Patton* tank with the modern *M1 Abrams* tank. In addition, the Pentagon funded numerous smaller robotic weapons programs, such as the Grumman *Robotic Ranger*, which allowed the remote firing of anti-tank missiles (Gage 1995, 4).

The revolutionary *Assault Breaker* program, which was a new type of stand-off precision munition that integrated reconnaissance and strike capability, had great potential. It had a range of 60 miles and was designed to identify and track Soviet armor columns and attack each single tank with submunitions (Kopp 1984). According to the strategist Colin Gray, 'The Soviet General Staff realized that NATO's conventional ET [emerging technologies], most particularly the US "Assault Breaker" technology development programme, was rendering obsolete their entire strategy for the rapid conquest of Europe' (C.S. Gray 2005, 107). In the end, the *Assault Breaker* program was prematurely halted by Congress in 1983 and split up into different capabilities and programs, of which some were successfully developed and deployed (JSTARS and the Army Tactical Missile) (Van Atta et al. 2003, 4).

After the Cold War

When the Cold War ended in 1991 much of the funding for military robotics projects dried up because of decreasing defense budgets (Shukman 1996, 190). There was a public expectation of a 'peace dividend' in the sense that part of the overblown Western defense budgets could now be made available for welfare, as the greatest military threat that preoccupied Western defense establishments for more than 40 years simply disappeared. The development of military robots, which just a few years before were believed to be the ideal solution to the expected high lethality of the central European conventional battlefield, were no longer a priority for Western defense establishments. In part this was due to the slow progress in AI and computer perception, in part because military robots did not seem to be very useful for the kind of peacekeeping and stability operations that became the primary focus of Western armed forces during the 1990s.

These new peacekeeping operations turned out to be a great challenge for modern armed forces. Increasingly, Western governments became unwilling to intervene in ongoing conflicts in the Third World. The failed international intervention in Somalia and the American aborted attempt to arrest the warlord Mohammed Aideed in October 1993 was seen as an important turning point in US foreign policy and military strategy (Shawcross 2000, 101). From then on Western governments avoided sending their soldiers to conduct risky peacekeeping operations in Africa and other places. This particular situation of the 1990s – which combined a breakout of numerous conflicts that were previously contained by the superpowers during the Cold War and a reluctance by the US, Russia and other great powers to intervene in these conflicts – created a business opportunity for mercenaries and private military companies (PMCs), which quickly filled the void (Singer 2003, 49–60).

At the same time, there was the hope that US defense planners would take advantage of a so-called 'Revolution in Military Affairs' (RMA), which was 'glimpsed' during the 1991 Gulf War (Krepinevich 2002). The American-led coalition thoroughly defeated the Iraqi military – which at one point was described by the Pentagon as the fourth biggest in the world (Freedman and Karsh 1993, 279) – in just six weeks of air campaign and four days of ground combat while suffering very few casualties. Many military analysts concluded that the RMA that had begun in the late 1970s with the development of new types of sensors and precision weapons finally had shown its potency. It was also argued that the new weapons and tactics used in the 1991 Gulf War were just the beginning of an even more far-reaching revolution to arrive shortly.

The RMA was extensively discussed and questioned by military thinkers throughout the 1990s, who have produced a great number of definitions for it. The broadest and maybe one of the most useful definitions is the one by the military historian Clifford Rogers, who wrote: 'To my mind, an RMA is simply a revolutionary change in how war is fought – a change that can often be recognised by the ease with which "participating" armed forces can defeat "nonparticipating" ones' (Rogers 2000, 22). What exactly this new quality is that can help defeat future enemies with relative ease with regard to a possible current RMA is highly disputed.

However, a unifying theme of almost all of the RMA literature is the element of information (Leonhard 1998, 219). The argument made by people like Admiral William Owens is that superior information on the enemy (strength, location, status) and all other factors that influence the course of battle would give a decisive advantage to the side that enjoys 'dominant battlefield knowledge' or 'information superiority' (Owens and Offley 2000, 100–102). Advanced sensors and information processing technology would eventually 'lift the fog of war' and would help to overcome 'friction', or those limiting and inhibiting factors that distinguish war on paper from war in the real world.

The key to realizing the revolution in full would be the military adaptation of advanced information technology. In particular, it would require the development of a 'system of systems' that collects and exchanges information in real time for 'immediate and complete battle assessment'. The sharing of information amongst all units and decision-makers would allow a high degree of coordination in an increasingly complex operating environment, but would also vastly increase the speed of military operations. It would allow completely new tactics, such as to 'conduct prompt, sustained, and synchronized operations with combinations of forces tailored to specific situations and with access to and freedom to operate in all domains – space, sea, land, air, and information' (US DoD 2000a, Ch. 3) causing an effect of 'shock and awe' amongst the enemy that paralyses and makes the enemy incapable of resistance (Ullman and Wade 1996, xxv). Altogether, this will supposedly allow 'to do more with less', so that fewer forces are needed for defeating a much bigger opposing force.

New technologies such as directed energy weapons (e.g. lasers) or nanotechnology and robotics could potentially trigger 'a revolution within the revolution' or a 'successor revolution' that could take the RMA much further than many of its original proponents envisioned (Vickers and Martinage 2004, 63–8). What particularly surprised military analysts was the recent growth of military robotics. The vision of 'unmanned combat' is now becoming more plausible than ever before in history.

Robotics and 'the Revolution within the Revolution'

Although the IT-based RMA that began in the late 1970s and took shape in the 1990s led to impressive new capabilities, such as precision-guided munitions (PGMs) with near 100 percent kill probability and stealth aircraft undetectable to radar, observers were surprised how little had actually changed in the 2003 Iraq War and how much of Clausewitz still remained valid (Murray and Scales 2003, 237–41). The war in 2003 was certainly no simple repetition of the 1991 Gulf War, but the way the campaign was conducted was not radically new either. It is true that the 'system of systems' has not been created yet and that the digitalization of the armed forces down to the individual soldier is still many years in the future. So the Iraq War is not really an indication that the RMA or transformation has been accomplished, or even that the RMA will help modern armed forces to prevail in all kinds of conflict. However, the most interesting feature of the Iraq War was the growing role of unmanned systems, mainly for reconnaissance, but also for other functions such as clearing the way for the attack with manned systems.

Aerial Drones and UAVs

During the 1990s UAVs used for battlefield reconnaissance were identified as one defining element of the RMA because they could become important nodes in military information networks. The American experience with reconnaissance drones in the 1991 Gulf War had the greatest influence on the development and proliferation of UAVs during the 1990s. The drone used by the Americans in the Gulf was the Israeli-developed *Pioneer* UAV. It could be launched from battleships or from truck-mounted catapults and could collect real-time battlefield intelligence for target acquisition and bomb damage assessment. At the beginning of Operation Desert Storm it flew 300 reconnaissance sorties. It was later used in Bosnia, Somalia, Kosovo and Iraq. Although a greater number of UAVs were shot down in these conflicts, they still proved to be highly suitable for the continuous surveillance of the battlefield.

In the 2003 Iraq War UAVs played a major role with respect to intelligence collection and defeating the Iraqi air defenses. The Coalition used no fewer than 10 different types of altogether 50 drones, which could continuously observe Iraqi troop movements (Krane 2003a, 2003b). In addition, *Firebee* UAVs were used for laying a chaff corridor for manned aircraft or cruise missiles in order to make it harder for the Iraqi air defenses to target them (Blackmore 2005, 159). The Israelis had already pioneered the use of drones for defeating air defense systems during the Lebanon conflict in 1982 (McDaid and Oliver 1997, 51). The Americans followed the Israeli example and even armed some UAVs. On one occasion a *Predator* armed with a *Stinger* missile attacked an Iraqi *MiG-25*, but the drone was eventually shot down by the *MiG*, as its missile missed the target (Bone and Bolkcom 2003, 16). A *Predator* 'pilot' of the squadron that engaged in the unusual dogfight commented: 'If it happens again, the Predator will come out on top' (Krane 2003a, 2003b).

The *Lear* jet size *Global Hawk* UAV proved to have been particularly effective in collecting battlefield intelligence. The UAV can remain airborne for 24 hours at a time, has an intercontinental range and can survey an area of 38,000 square miles. It operated out of the Gulf states and was 'flown' by Northrop Grumman technicians more than 4,300 miles away at Beale AFB, California, via satellite link. At the time of the Iraq War there were only about eight *Global Hawk* prototypes available and they suffered from frequent technical problems. Nevertheless, *Global Hawk*:

flew 3% of all aircraft imagery-collection sorties and only 5% of all high-altitude reconnaissance missions, but it collected information on 55% of the air defense related time-sensitive targets. *Global Hawk*'s score card included locating more than 13 full surface-to-air missile [SAM] batteries, 50 SAM launchers, 300 canisters and 70 missile transporters. The UAV also found 300 tanks, which amounted to about 38% of Iraq's known armor.' (Wall and Fulghum 2003, 62–3)

The future of unmanned aircraft seems bright and their numbers are soaring. In 2008 the US Air Force already had more than 5,000 UAVs, which would be a 25-fold increase since 2001. Their roles have already expanded from tactical reconnaissance to strike and combat missions. With regard to aerial warfare, important precedents have been set in terms of developing unmanned combat. No doubt, the current US experience in Iraq has greatly increased the interest in military robotics and Iraq is already a big testing ground for military robots of all kinds. Ground robots also have seen an unexpected revival and are now used with great effectiveness in the occupation of Iraq.

Unmanned Ground Vehicles in the Iraq War

The current American/British experience in Iraq is characterized by low-intensity insurgent warfare with the insurgents' weapon of choice being self-made bombs or improvised explosive devices (IEDs). IEDs have already greatly influenced the development of military robotics and robotic warfare concepts (*Space Daily* 2006). Robots have been used for decades for bomb disposal, but since the intervention in Afghanistan that began in 2001, the demand for explosive ordnance disposal (EOD) robots has literally exploded. About 1,782 soldiers have been killed by IEDs so far (May 2008), with many more injured and maimed. They were described as 'the No 1 killer in the region at that time' (Isenberg 2007). Hence, great numbers of EOD robots are needed to safely search for and remove IEDs.

The US military uses thousands of EOD robots in Iraq and Afghanistan (probably more than 6,000). Most of them are Foster-Miller *Talon* robots (97lb) or iRobots *PackBots* (42lb), Mesa-Robotics *Matilda* (66lb), EOD Performance *Vanguard* (115lb) and Northrop Grumman *Mini-Andros*, which are all relatively small and manportable. The Marine Corps uses even smaller models like the 15lb *Dragon Runner*, which can be used as a 'throwbot': they can be tossed over walls or in windows and used for looking inside buildings or around corners. All of these robots are tele-operated and require a human operator for carrying out their functions. The operator usually controls the robot from a remote location with the help of a small computer and a joystick.

Particularly successful and capable is the *Talon* robot. Foster-Miller recently delivered its 2,000th robot of this model to the US forces and produces the model at a rate of 100 per month (Quinn 2008). The US soldiers in the field in Iraq suggested arming the *Talons* and Foster-Miller upgraded some of them with automatic weapons in 2005. After some extensive testing, three armed *Talons* (so-called Special Weapons Observation Reconnaissance Detection System or *SWORDS*) were fielded in Iraq in summer 2007 and patrolled the streets of Baghdad (Magnuson 2007). *SWORDS* can be equipped with an *M16* assault rifle, an *M249* machine gun, or a grenade launcher (BBC Online 2005a). These robots are tele-operated and incapable of firing their weapons without being controlled by an operator. However, *SWORDS* is a stable weapons platform and allows an operator, by using a remote control and high-resolution video camera, to shoot at a target with great accuracy and it can 'hit bulls eyes from as far as 2,000 meters away' (Jewell 2004). Up to now, *SWORDS* has apparently not fired a single shot in combat and there are still doubts about fielding this particular system in larger numbers (Sofge 2008c).

Foster-Miller is already marketing a bigger and more heavily armed successor system, which is called *MAARS*. In the meantime another EOD robot has been upgraded to a weapons platform. It has been reported that the manufacturer iRobot has added a 20-round shotgun to its *PackBot* (Marks 2006), but it has not yet been deployed. People in the industry believe that there is also a great market for robots in the police and domestic security areas (Shachtman 2007b). It might not be long before a major security contractor like Blackwater USA fields a potentially armed security robot in the streets of a major city.

Robotics and the Challenge of Urban Operations

The occupation of Iraq and the challenges faced by US and allied soldiers could be indicative for the future of war and in line with the Pentagon's expectation that urban operations will become more frequent and one of the main military challenges in the twenty-first century. While traditional warfare against conventional forces primarily fought on open terrain is possibly about to fade into history, unconventional and untraditional warfare against small non-state forces like insurgents and terrorists hiding in cities within a civilian population is on the rise. More than half of the world's current population of 6.7 billion lives in cities and about 4 percent in megacities with more than 10 million people (United Nations 2007, 9). Most of the 20 current megacities are located in conflict-prone developing countries, where also most urbanization occurs.

Many military analysts claim that 'urban operations are distinctive' and that 'urban environment is the most complex and challenging' of environments in which armed forces have to fight (Hills 2004, 9). A RAND study points out:

> The number of structures, firing positions, avenues of approach, enemy, noncombatants, friendly force units, key terrain, and obstacles per cubic kilometer, or the number of small-unit engagements, troop movements, and interactions with noncombatants per minute within that space are far greater in cities than in any other environment.' (Glenn 2000, 2)

Historically, urban operations tend to be drawn-out affairs with lots of house-to-house fighting and generally very high casualty numbers. According to Marine Corps experiments, casualty rates in urban operations can be expected to be very high, or about 46 percent (Hills 2004, 67). Obviously, the Pentagon is undertaking great efforts in exploring new ways of utilizing technology for urban operations that can minimize casualties. There is little doubt that robotics will play a key role in addressing the main tactical challenges connected to urban operations and in getting human soldiers out of the line of fire. One main function of military robots in urban settings will be reconnaissance. Small robots can see whatever satellites and airborne sensors cannot. They can look into buildings and underground facilities and acquire targets for human soldiers or other 'shooters'.

While military robots might yield the greatest benefit in urban operations, cities are also an environment that is in many other respects hardly suitable for robots. Letting robots explore streets and buildings by themselves is technically challenging. Allowing the use of armed robots in the close vicinity of innocent civilians is also at the very least morally questionable, if this means a greater risk to civilians. So it is difficult to say how useful military robots will eventually be in future urban combat. A lot will depend on the degree to which military robots can be built to operate safely and predictably and on the general willingness of states utilizing these systems to protect civilians.

Conclusion: 100 Years of Remote-control Weapons

Remote-controlled or 'robotic' weapons have been used in war ever since the First World War. Despite considerable resources spent on their development, they did not make much of a difference in the wars of the twentieth century. Most of the time military robots proved to be impractical, ineffective and overly expensive, which meant that they were (with the exception of the *V-1*) rarely used in battle. As a result, the use of robotic vehicles that was pioneered by the Germans and Japanese has been almost forgotten. However, the *possibility* of automated warfare seemed to reappear from time to time in various guises, but technology was, up to now, never capable of realizing any of the more ambitious visions of unmanned combat.

The main reason why the armed forces were so slow to adapt robots and other autonomous weapons was that they were not particularly effective compared with manned options. This problem can be seen most clearly in the robotic weapons of the Second World War era. Remote-controlled weapons were highly unreliable because their radio links often failed in combat, which made the weapons ineffective (Magnuson 2008b, 30–1). The other feasible solution was to 'pre-program' weapons by letting them descend on a target area through some timing mechanism. Such pre-programmed weapons were neither accurate enough to be used as precision weapons, nor powerful enough to become effective terror weapons. Many Allied bombers could carry several times more payload than both the *V-1* or the *V-2*. Using manned bombers therefore simply made more sense for the Americans and the British.

However, if a weapon such as the *V-1* or *V-2* had been much more precise and had been available earlier in the war, it could have easily affected the outcome of the war (Hutchinson 1997, 60). General Eisenhower believed that the *V-2* could have disrupted the preparations for the invasion of Normandy if it had been available six months earlier (Ropp 2000, 325). Germany and Japan both ran out of skilled pilots toward the end of the war, but still were able to retain considerable production capabilities despite strategic bombing. It was thus rational for the Axis powers to emphasize unmanned technologies. But without microchips or highly precise gyroscopes for inertial guidance, there was simply no chance of making unmanned aircraft and ground vehicles more than a very crude weapon – and a very expensive one. At that time in history unmanned systems could not revolutionize warfare. Instead, the revolutions that did happen were the nuclear and missile revolutions and they preoccupied strategic thinkers for most, if not all, of the Cold War.

The history of military robotics presents itself as a constant and very gradual improvement in the development of tele-operated and self-guiding weapons, which became better and better and which now form the basis for the recent breakthrough in military robotics. The possible advent of the autonomous military robot does not represent, from a technical point of view, any major discontinuity in warfare. It is simply the case that weapons became step by step slightly more autonomous over the last 100 years. First they were just remote-controlled; then they could be 'pre-programmed' to attack a particular area by themselves; later they developed the ability to identify some targets and pursue them; then they were able to pick individual targets; finally they might be allowed to launch themselves at targets they have picked themselves. Technologically there is absolutely nothing in the possible final step that can be seen to be in any way revolutionary. Weapons autonomy is a sliding scale and a tendency that has already been observed for a very long time.

Now the technology of robotics is maturing and computers are becoming faster and smarter, which promises a growing role for military robots. Michael Vickers and Robert Martinage claim that 'historically, the single greatest impediment to robotic development has been limited data-processing capability. Fortunately, computational power has increased by about six orders-of-magnitude over the last 35 years and the current technological forecast is for Moore's Law to hold for at least another decade' (Vickers and Martinage 2004, 30). All the pieces required for making AW work (sensors, guidance systems, machine intelligence) are available and it is just a matter of putting everything together (Reed 2005). Other than in decades before, it can be expected that robotic weapons could make a major difference in future wars to the point that they could again completely change the nature of warfare.

In order to understand the potential and pitfalls of military robotics, it is now essential to get a clearer idea of the general technological direction and the fundamental limitations of military robots. The next chapter argues that AW or, in other words, 'killer robots' are militarily desirable and that they could relatively soon become technically feasible, though they might always be somewhat unpredictable.

Chapter 2
Weapons Autonomy and Artificial Intelligence

The previous chapter showed that the idea, and in fact use, of machines for fighting and killing humans is very old. The automated killing machine of the land mine appeared in sixteenth-century Europe and has proved to be one of the most murderous inventions of mankind (Youngblood 2006, 6). Mines, though still causing a massive toll in human life (on average 24,000 a year), seem to somehow be different in nature from the 'killer robot' – an intelligent machine that does not simply sit and wait for a human to trigger it, but that can go out and actively search for human prey. What makes the killer robot so much scarier than mine warfare is its intelligence and perceived (or real) ability to make decisions over life and death. In other words, the killer robot does not simply kill (like a mine) – it can make the decision to kill (or not to kill), which elevates it ontologically and maybe even morally from the mere object to a subject capable of morally meaningful action. What is scary about the killer robot is not the fact that it would be more dangerous than mines, but rather its ability to make life and death decisions in place of a human. The concept of the lethal autonomous military robot is in some sense just the latest expression of a broader and quite disturbing trend in warfare, which is the general decline of human decision-making (Adams 2001).

At first this assessment seems surprising, as there are currently very few weapons systems that can be rightly termed autonomous in any meaningful sense. Up to now, wherever force is applied, humans have clearly remained in the decision-making loop. Nevertheless, the computer revolution of warfare has created unprecedented possibilities for automation. To some degree military networks and functions such as logistics are already quite automated and human decision-makers have become considerably dependent on analyses derived from computer models. Thomas K. Adams fears that the human in the loop could be removed gradually and step by step until everything is controlled by computers (Adams 2001). Will humans still be able to intervene effectively in automated systems? Will they even be able to understand them in principle?

The removal of humans from the battlefield and later from military decision-making at least on the tactical level will not happen overnight, but could be a drawn-out and gradual process, as described by Ravi Mohan:

> First, robots will engage in non lethal activities like mine clearing or I.E.D detection. (This is happening today.) Then you'll see them accompany human combat units as augmenters and enablers on real battle fields. (This is beginning to happen.) As robotics gets more and more sophisticated, they will take up potentially lethal but non combat operations like patrolling camp perimeters or

no fly areas, and open fire only when 'provoked'. (This is beginning to happen too.) The final stage will be when robotic weapons are an integral part of the battlefield, just like 'normal', human controlled machines are today and make autonomous or near autonomous combat decisions. (Mohan 2007)

Quite a few Pentagon officials and military robot designers have hinted that once the technology becomes reliable enough, military robots could be allowed to open fire without requiring human permission. Gordon Johnson from the Joint Forces Command research center in Suffolk, Virginia, has told the *New York Times* that: 'I have been asked what happens if the robot destroys a school bus rather than a tank parked nearby. We will not entrust a robot with that decision until we are confident they can make it' (Weiner 2005a), indicating that the Pentagon is not in principle opposed to the idea of AW. The roboticist Ronald Arkin from the Georgia Institute of Technology, a leading expert on the technology and ethics of military robots, also believes that 'the deployment of systems of ever increasing autonomy is inevitable' (Arkin 2007, 8). The eventual development and deployment of such weapons is certainly in line with larger historical trends in warfare.

This chapter looks into the limitations of artificial intelligence (AI) and the ability of computers or robots to become autonomous agents. Some of the technologies that could enable the development of autonomous military robots are discussed, as well as their inherent limitations.

The Push toward Autonomous Weapons

Both the Pentagon and the British Ministry of Defence (MoD) have repeatedly stressed that humans will remain in the decision-making loop wherever force is being used, and presumably this would never change. For example, the project manager of the US Robotic Systems Joint Project Office James Braden said in an interview, 'Any armed robot is always going to have a man in the loop saying "shoot" or "stop shoot"' (Nowak 2008b). But how credible are these affirmations in the light of the current robotics revolution of warfare?

Although it is possible to remote-control robotic weapons with a human watching and controlling every move of a robotic system, there are few technical obstacles and many good reasons to go even further and develop completely autonomous weapons. It can be assumed that many weapons that enter service in the next decade will allow a mixture of control methods, ranging from complete operator control to semi-autonomous to completely autonomous, and could be adjustable according to the situation (US Joint Forces Command 2003). As the technology advances, weapons are very likely to become increasingly autonomous to the point that the human in the loop will more and more come to be seen as the weakest link in the 'kill chain' (Featherstone 2007). It also seems obvious that at least some types of robotic weapons will have to be designed from the very beginning to function autonomously in order to be effective. While adjustable autonomy can easily disguise the true autonomy of weapons, some more revolutionary types of AW will need to function without any possibility of direct human control. Obvious examples are weapons that are extremely small, e.g. nanobots or micro electromechanical systems (MEMS), or weapons that need to respond in extremely short time frames, e.g. missile defense systems, or swarming robots that need to cooperate and coordinate themselves in real time.

There are currently two emerging schools of thought offering two different directions for the future development of military robotics. One school of thought views military robots as human extensions in the battlespace, or as force multipliers, and the other advocates autonomous robots as autonomous agents or a stand-alone independent capability without any necessity of having a human in the loop (Arkin and Moshkina 2007). The concept of robots as force multipliers is based on the idea that robots would work under the close supervision and in cooperation with human soldiers – so humans and robots would be fighting side by side, with robots taking over the somewhat more dangerous jobs. The concept of robots as stand-alone capability is based on the idea of strictly separating humans and robots, or jobs only humans can do and jobs only robots can do, allowing as much robot autonomy as is necessary or technically feasible. Another way of putting it is to distinguish between 'weapons that augment our soldiers and those that can become soldiers' (Bigelow 2007).

At the moment the 'robots as extension' school seems to prevail, as there is significant institutional resistance from staff and commanding officers to expand the role of unmanned systems. But the advantages of fully autonomous systems are only too obvious in the long term. It might even be the case that further technological progress will make it increasingly difficult for humans to effectively intervene in automated systems and to participate in warfare in any other way than giving the general strategic direction. It is even imaginable that intelligent machines will one day determine 'the real enemy' and decide on matters of strategy, as attacks might occur too fast for humans to respond and some novel means of waging war may disguise the originators of warlike actions such as in the case of strategic information warfare, WMD terrorism or economic warfare. These new ways of war have been termed by Chinese strategists 'unrestricted warfare' (Liang and Xiangsui 1999) and they will give nations subjected to such aggressions a hard time figuring out who the originator might be, or how to respond appropriately. Computerized analysis and assessment methods might become essential tools in international relations and matters of strategy.

Automating warfare, like automating economic production, offers many advantages. For example, it reduces the need to maintain large armed forces.

Reducing Manpower Requirements

The ultimate goal behind the introduction of robotic systems is to reduce manpower requirements for military operations. The main reason for this is that in the societies of the First World the military manpower pool has become smaller, as there are generally fewer suitable people in the age range of 18–30 who could be recruited for military service. The situation will only get worse in the coming decades (Schindlmayr 2002). In addition, fewer people are attracted to military service and fewer people in Western societies meet the physical fitness requirements (Coker 2002, 157). The other main reason to cut personnel is that defense budgets are bound to become smaller in the future. A greater reliance on robots will reduce personnel-related costs. The more functions that can be taken over by robots, the fewer human personnel are needed.

Reducing manpower requirements can be achieved in part by remote-controlled weapons and systems. At least fewer military personnel would have to deploy in theater, as thanks to satellite links, they could operate remote-controlled weapons even from their home country. Systems and platforms that are partially robotic could also reduce the number of crew members of ships, aircraft and tanks. For example, the new DDG-1000 *Zumwalt* (formerly DDX) destroyer will utilize lots of robotics – like an engine room completely controlled by robots – which allows cutting the crew from over 300 for a similar-sized ship to only 142. Future battle tanks only need a crew of two instead of four and similar reductions could be possible for many other types of platforms, such as artillery systems or submarines.

However, remote-controlled and partially roboticized systems have the obvious disadvantage that they still need humans somewhere to operate these systems. If one needs one or more human operators for every unmanned platform in the battlespace, as is currently the case with many already deployed robotic systems, then the savings in personnel would be small, if not zero (Shaker and Wise 1988, 64). At the moment, many types of unmanned systems require one to three human operators each, with more people needed for support on the ground. This creates the rather paradoxical situation that tele-operated unmanned systems could in some cases even increase manpower requirements (Keller 2005).

In order to avoid this trap, it would be highly likely that a single human operator would control several robotic systems. This would mean that the robots would need to be capable of operating largely autonomously with only few tasks, such as weapons release, requiring human intervention. But why stop at this point? If one operator could control a greater number of robots and every single robot required human confirmation for weapons release, then it would be relatively easy for an enemy to overload the system through a massive and fast attack.

Needing a human to confirm every single targeting suggestion of a robotic weapon is, in addition, not very economically efficient, especially if the human is a highly qualified and highly trained soldier, e.g. a fully trained jet pilot operating an unmanned combat aerial vehicle (UCAV). This was until recently the requirement for US Air Force (USAF) tele-operators of the *Predator* unmanned aerial vehicle (UAV). In order to meet an increasing demand for tele-operators, the requirements have been reduced and USAF officers, who are not fully trained pilots, are admitted to a new unmanned aircraft training course (Baldor 2008). As the numbers of armed forces personnel in most modern militaries are very likely to be significantly reduced over the next decades, the remaining human soldiers might be better used than having them spend endless hours in front of computer screens confirming targeting decisions already made by increasingly intelligent computers. It comes as no surprise that military pilots usually do not like the remote operator job (Page 2008g). The only alternative would be allowing less qualified military personnel or civilians operate military robots, which is also problematic. A less qualified operator might not be able to handle a complicated robotic system in some situations and a civilian technician would not be permitted to engage in 'hostile activities', such as pulling the trigger, as civilians cannot be lawful combatants (Stanley-Mitchell 2001, 279). Automating weapons further could thus sidestep the problem of having a growing number of military contractors in quasi-combatant roles – a tendency that has created lots of problems in Iraq. Well known is the example of the private military company (PMC) Blackwater USA, which was last year almost suspended from a Pentagon contract after some of its employees opened fire in a Sunni neighborhood in Baghdad, killing eight civilians (Mroue 2007).

The Pentagon also worries that remote-controlling military robots on the ground unnecessarily increases the dangers to soldiers and thus defeats the original idea behind military robots of taking humans out of the line of fire. The recently published *Unmanned Systems Roadmap* points out: 'Requiring a human in the loop generally necessitates having the operator in the local vicinity due to Line of Sight (LOS) constraints, and this close proximity potentially brings the human into the threat zone of which the robot was meant to keep him clear' (US DoD 2007, 43). Thus, it would be better to let robots operate on their own instead of having human soldiers constantly following them into action, who might be more occupied with operating the robots than with watching the enemy. In the worst case one could even end up needing additional soldiers for protecting the robot/ unmanned ground vehicle (UGV) tele-operators in the field.

On the other hand, autonomous systems would require no human operators and could be made much smaller than manned systems, or even tele-operated systems, thus also reducing the numbers of required maintenance technicians. In fact, many autonomous systems might be so cheap that they could be disposable and might therefore not require any maintenance personnel. This would allow cutting manpower requirements and the overall logistical footprint in theater even further. Theoretically, AW could allow a state to have very small and very inexpensive armed forces without compromising its military security or ability to project power.

Security of Data Links

The main problem with remote-controlling platforms and weapons is the dependency on data links, which transmit control and sensor data to a control station. Data links could use cables or could be wireless. Both possibilities have obvious disadvantages. If a cable is used for remote-controlling platforms, there is the disadvantage that the range of the platform would be limited to the length of the cable. This would normally be no more than a couple of miles. Cables could also get entangled on the ground or could be severed, which reduces their usefulness even further. This means that cable-controlled weapons would not be very useful in environments that are full of obstacles such as trees, rocks or buildings. So they would be hardly usable in jungle warfare or urban warfare.

If a wireless data link is used, there are limitations in terms of available bandwidth, especially if satellites are used for relaying control data. The available bandwidth capacities of military communication satellites are always very limited. This becomes an increasing problem with the number of remote-controlled platforms that have to operate at any one time in the battlespace (Boot 2006a, 26). It is possible to alleviate the problem by reducing the amount of data that needs to be transmitted, for example by partially automating the platform and only leave a few crucial functions to human operators, like weapons use (Richfield 2007). But normally a high-resolution video image would need to be transmitted for allowing the operator to make a decision whether or not to engage a target. However, '[p]assing imagery is still a bandwidth problem for everybody' (Pocock 2002). As a result, the transmission of high-resolution videos needed for supporting human targeting decisions is draining scarce military bandwidth capacities.

The problem is unlikely to go away because the laws of physics constrain the amount of frequencies and the transmission rates that are available for controlling unmanned systems. Thus 'bandwidth bottlenecks' would put clear limits on the number of unmanned systems that can operate at any one time in a particular area (Robinson 2007). Then the choice is between simply accepting these limitations, which is unlikely, or making military robots more autonomous so that there would be a lesser need for each system to transmit large amounts of data, which seems likely.

Wireless data links in particular also have the shortcoming that they do not work for some environments and that it would be relatively easy for an adversary to disrupt them by using radio jammers or electromagnetic pulse (EMP) weapons. For example, during the early stages of the Afghanistan conflict in 2001, remote-controlled robots were sent into buildings or caves, but communications with the robots could not always be maintained, which limited their usefulness (Magnuson 2008c). In the case that all important functions of a remote-controlled platform, such as weapons release, requires human input, any loss of the wireless connection to the platform, maybe through successful radio jamming, would make the platforms ineffective or, in other words, would result in a 'soft kill' of this platform. This might not be terribly difficult to engineer: even a technically competent individual could build a global positioning system (GPS) jammer with off-the-shelf components that has the power to knock out GPS-guided weapons (Brewin 2003). The program manager for the autonomous intelligent network and systems initiative at the US Office of Naval Research said in an interview: 'We were lucky in Afghanistan that they did not have technology to jam our GPS infrastructure. Without GPS, none of these platforms can navigate, and UAVs like *Predator* and *Global Hawk* would be rendered useless' (Lawlor 2003a). Signal jamming is even easier for wealthier and technologically more capable states. For example, Libya was reported to have jammed commercial satellite phones in Iraq for six months in 2005 (Shachtman 2007a). Jamming military satellites might be harder, but states like Russia and China might soon develop this capability. Both states already have anti-satellite (ASAT) weapons that could knock out Western communications satellites.[1] To counter the problem of radio jamming or otherwise severing data links, remote-controlled platforms could be equipped with an 'auto' mode to make them more survivable if communications are severed, which could include weapons use. In reality, it would mean that in a high-intensity conflict against a technologically sophisticated enemy, robotic weapons would be naturally in an 'auto' mode in order to avoid, or master, the problem of radio jamming from the beginning.

Another way of achieving the same effect of neutralizing remote-controlled platforms would be to attack control stations or command centers, which would become primary targets for an enemy. Control stations that are in theater could be easily identified and located because of the amount of radio traffic that passes through them. Even worse would be the case of a cyber-attack on the remote-controlled platforms. An adversary could try to electronically hijack the platforms and use them against their owners. Jason Borenstein argues that adversaries would have great incentives for doing so, as 'this could put very dangerous weapons, and whatever the power source is for the system, into the hands of an enemy' (Borenstein 2008, 10).

This is a serious danger and one that has already happened: a robot was electronically hijacked by an adversary. Steven Shaker and Alan Wise described a case where British soldiers used an explosive ordnance disposal (EOD) robot to disable a bomb in Northern Ireland and where the 'revolutionaries were able to override the EOD operator's radio control and have the robot turn on him. The operator barely escaped being blown up by his own robot' (Shaker and Wise 1988, 169). It is imaginable that a hacker could take over a whole robot army and cause havoc. Although the control signals for a military robot would be protected with a very high grade of encryption, no encryption would, in principle, be unbreakable once the age of quantum computing starts (Garfinkel 2004). Obviously, an AW or unmanned system that does not need to exchange much data with control stations would be much harder to hijack, which makes weapons autonomy a highly desirable feature, especially from a long term perspective.

Eliminating the Human Factor

The term 'human factor' summarizes all of the shortcomings of human beings compared with machines. This includes a whole range of psychological and physiological aspects that limit human effectiveness and that would be desirable

---

1   Russia is known to have had ASAT weapons since the 1970s and China tested an ASAT weapon in January 2007, proving its capability of destroying satellites in low earth orbit.

to overcome or to eliminate by transferring certain functions to machines and by increasing their overall autonomy.

Human fallibility   Humans do make mistakes and their level of performance usually drops over time. Especially tasks that require a high degree of concentration cannot be sustained by a human for very long. Highly repetitive work, or work that does not offer any change, such as watching a CCTV video screen, will cause boredom, will lower attention and will increase the number of mistakes. It has been pointed out that 'a human's attention to detail on guard duty drops dramatically in the first 30 minutes' (Porknoy 1987). Humans are simply not particularly good at tasks that require sustained high accuracy or sustained attention, which is often needed for the operation or supervision of machines. Machines, on the other hand, can carry out any task without variation in performance. The memory of computers is much more reliable than human memory and computers tend to be faster in finding and retrieving information. Humans also make mistakes because of their psychology, which makes them occasionally irrational and sometimes results in bad judgment. Especially in the heat and stress of battle humans are prone to making stupid mistakes because it is very hard for humans to control their emotions in extreme situations. Computers and robots are certainly not infallible, but they do not make certain kinds of mistakes that humans make and they tend to be more predictable in their performance – at least whenever computers deal with 'well-defined problems' in which predetermined responses can be matched exactly to predefined situations. However, in less defined situations computers and robots could perform much less predictably.

Lower response times   Military strategists claim that 'the essence of success in future war will certainly be to make everything happen you want to happen in a very short period of time – instantly if possible' (Warden III 1995, 17). Automated systems are far more capable of prevailing under such conditions, as they can produce instant effects and respond far quicker to suddenly appearing threats than humans. Undoubtedly, decision cycles are getting smaller and may soon transgress the human ability for making timely decisions. The time necessary for planning and executing an air strike was about three days during the 1991 Gulf War, which was shortened to about one hour during Operation Iraqi Freedom in 2003. In 2005, with the use of armed *Predator* drones continuously operating in the Gulf region '[t]he whole thing, from legal decision to command to execution, took five minutes' (Shachtman 2005). In the future it might be necessary to make the decision for attacking a target within a fraction of a second. The roboticist Kevin Warwick has argued that a transistor can change its response a million times faster than a neuron in a human brain (Warwick 1997, 138). In terms of response speed, machines will always vastly outperform human beings. This human shortcoming is increasingly becoming obvious in aerial warfare where pilots have to react in time frames of split seconds to take evasive action or to open fire in order to survive in air combat. It takes a human at least 0.3 seconds to respond to any stimulus and twice as long to make a choice of several possible responses (Kosinski 2006). Computers are far less limited and could make a decision in a millionth of a second or even less time.

Information explosion   Machines are able to process a much greater amount of data and also more complex data much more quickly than a human can. Modern warfare has become so overly complex that military commands are practically drowning in the information that is available to them. The amount of information needed for making good decisions is constantly growing, as the factors influencing the success of a military action have become more numerous and complex. Van Creveld claims that during the Vietnam War US military decision-makers were completely overwhelmed by the information flowing in every day: 'The intelligence component of MACV ... alone received three million pages of enemy documents per month' (Van Creveld 1985, 246). Obviously only a fraction of the information was valuable and even less received attention and resulted in any kind of action. With the great proliferation of sensors on the battlefield, the masses of data they produce and the ever growing complexity of military technology, the task of command is getting ever more difficult. Computers are needed for analyzing vast amounts of information and are already used for advising military commanders. In the end, it could be a fairly small step for computers to switch from an advisory to an executive function (Adams 2001).

Fatigue   Human operators who remotely control robotic platforms would inevitably suffer from fatigue after some time. It might be possible to stretch mission times for human crews to 72 hours or more by using drugs or other performance enhancers (Coker 2004, 108), but it is unlikely that humans will be able to match the endurance of machines. Some UAVs can be in the air for more than 24 hours, which is much longer than human fighter pilots can do (without drugs). Future UAVs could spend weeks, if not months, airborne. It is also likely that UCAVs could be sent on intercontinental bombing missions or could patrol the airspace for extended periods of time. Remote operators get exhausted after spending many hours in front of computer terminals and working in shifts may cause operators to suffer even more from fatigue than operators of manned platforms, as a recent US Air Force study has unveiled (Tvaryanas et al. 2006). Shift work also always means that the next tele-operator to take over will have an incomplete picture of whatever happened before. From this point of view it would make sense to make unmanned platforms operate autonomously instead of tele-operating them, which is in any case a job for which humans are not particularly well suited.

Communication with machines   In addition, machines interface much better with other machines than humans with machines and it is already apparent that some unmanned platforms perform significantly better without human operators (Blackmore 2005, 149). Network-centric warfare places a premium on constant communication and exchange of information of all units with each other. Human soldiers do already interact a lot with machines, but this will even increase in the future. Machines are much faster in collecting, processing, transferring and acting upon information. A verbal or typed command simply takes much longer than a command generated by a computer. When larger numbers of unmanned systems are deployed in battlespace, these systems would need to very quickly coordinate each other, for example to avoid several unmanned systems attacking the same target while ignoring others. Target selection routines that automatically assign targets to robotic systems would be much faster and more effective than having human tele-operators work out which robot attacks which target. However, one possibility to improve the performance of human tele-operators that is being explored by the Defense Advanced Projects Agency (DARPA) is to make humans more machine-friendly by creating a neural man–machine interface. Humans could control machines (e.g. take evasive action or fire a weapon) by the power of thought. But such methods are still quite crude compared with the way machines can exchange information with each other.

Conclusion   Chances are that automation could eliminate some human errors and make the operation of such systems safer. Here the case of the *USS Vincennes* is instructive. Equipped with the semi-automated *Aegis* air defense system, it accidentally downed an Iranian airliner in 1988 while it was operating in the Persian Gulf during the so-called tanker war episode of the Iran–Iraq War. There were clearly many complex factors that contributed to the accident – a year before the *USS Stark* was almost sunk through an air attack in the Gulf; the *USS Vincennes* was at that time involved in a surface engagement with Iranian patrol boats; and the commander was under stress to make a decision about engaging a potential Iranian *F-14* descending into an attack position. However, a US Navy investigation concluded that a human radar operator, who confused a nearby friendly *F-14* with the Iranian airliner, made the decisive mistake that led to the tragedy (Rochlin 1997, 163). The lesson learned was that the *Aegis* system was simply too complex for the human operators and required an expert user (C.H. Gray 1997, 66). It might therefore be safer to automate a system completely than to allow too much human intervention. Another case that seems to confirm this conclusion is the catastrophe of Chernobyl in 1986. The experts who were summoned from Moscow to deal with a reactor irregularity only made things much worse when they decided to override the safety mechanisms and to manually steer the reactor to get it back under control (Dörner 1996, 28–36). Dietrich Dörner, who has analyzed the psychological factors in this and similar accidents, writes that humans are simply not good at understanding and managing dynamic systems, especially those that are more complex (Dörner 1996).

More-autonomous weapons are, from a military point of view, highly desirable, as they could potentially be much more efficient and effective than less autonomous ones. However, this does not automatically mean that intelligent AWs are technically feasible or practical. So it is necessary to look at the problem of autonomy and artificial intelligence closer in order to get a better idea of the prospects for such weapons and their future potential.

Robot Autonomy

The term 'autonomy' is like the term 'robot' – very ambiguous. It can be understood in a political, philosophical, or in a purely technical sense. The word autonomy comes from the Greek words 'auto' (self) and 'nomos' (law) and means self-rule or self-governing. So the political meaning of autonomy is quite obvious: the ability of a political community to govern itself. In a philosophical sense autonomy generally describes the ability of an agent to determine their own actions, which means that there is an inherent ethical dimension of autonomy. In Kantian ethics autonomy is the precondition necessary for making an agent a moral agent. Moral autonomy is for Kant based on reason, which is the ability of an agent to limit their own actions according to self-given laws. Any agent that is rational, meaning they can deliberate about actions and consequences and act on their own judgment, is an autonomous and thus also a moral agent. Many ethicists have already pointed out that there are at least no philosophical reasons why robots could not become moral agents in a Kantian sense (Versenyi 1974). This kind of moral robot autonomy would lie further in the future and has little to do with robot autonomy in the technical sense or the term autonomy as it is used and understood by roboticists.

In a technical context autonomy of a machine just means its capability for unsupervised operation. An autonomous machine is simply a machine capable of carrying out a certain function on its own without the need of a human operator. The machine usually has to rely on a set of instructions that is in some form given to the machine, for example through software. Machine autonomy is, unlike in the philosophical sense, not a question of to be or not to be, but rather a matter of degree on a sliding scale. Lesser need for human intervention and supervision means greater autonomy. This means machine autonomy in a technical sense only implies that the human operator becomes unnecessary and allows no conclusions whatsoever about the moral, or even political, autonomy of machines. As the discourse on autonomous robots gets seized more and more by philosophers coming from the angle of ethics, the confusion about 'autonomous weapons' in the public debate increases. Here the focus will be on the technical meaning of machine autonomy.

There are now three general types or degrees of machine autonomy: pre-programmed autonomy, supervised autonomy and complete autonomy.

Pre-programmed autonomy In this case a machine carries out a particular function by following instructions that have been inserted into the machine by a designer or user. Normally, a pre-programmed machine is computer-controlled and it does its work with very little variation. This means that such machines have no or little capacity to vary from the original instructions or from pre-programmed movements (G. Chapman 1987). A typical example of a pre-programmed machine is an industrial robot that is used for welding, spraying or the assembly of cars. With respect to weapons, pre-programmed autonomy would apply to quite different classes of weapons such as mines, smart bombs and cruise missiles. In addition, there is also the special case of weapons with *structured control*, which are capable of responding to a greater range of stimuli with different behaviors. The instructions given to these weapons can be much more complex than in the case of other pre-programmed weapons and are generally hierarchically organized in 'if-this-then-that' algorithms that govern the behavior of such machines (Lerner 2006a). An example of such a weapon with structured control is the *Phalanx* close-in weapons system, which is a computer-controlled gun installed on almost all classes of US warships. *Phalanx* can, once activated, autonomously select and engage targets within the narrow parameters of its programming.

Limited or supervised autonomy   Supervised autonomy means that a machine, usually a robot, is capable of carrying out most of its functions autonomously without having to rely exclusively on pre-programmed behaviors. In other words, the possible variance in behaviors is far greater than in the case of pre-programmed autonomy, which allows the robot to find its own way and to do many other things without the need of continuous human intervention. More complex functions such as targeting and weapons release would normally still have to be controlled by a human operator, who is cognitively more capable of making such decisions. Robots with limited autonomy are also less capable of dealing well with situations not foreseen by their programmers and therefore need some human supervision. Exceptional circumstances or situations are simply flagged to a human operator, who then decides how to proceed. Supervised autonomy represents the current state of the art in military robotics and a growing number of military robotic systems fall into this category. The goal for many roboticists, however, is to build completely autonomous systems, where humans no longer have to closely watch the performance of robots.

Complete autonomy   Robots with complete autonomy only exist as experimental robots and are built entirely for research purposes. Completely autonomous robots are able to operate by themselves without the need for any human input. They are often able to learn by themselves and to modify their behavior accordingly. At the moment such robots are simply not intelligent enough to be useful for humans. The quite unpredictable and therefore uncontrollable behavior of robots with cognitive abilities makes them potentially dangerous and therefore unsafe for military purposes. However, the long-term goal of DARPA is indeed the development of self-learning truly autonomous robots that can be used as robot soldiers on the battlefield (Melymuka 2002). This is a very ambitious goal considering the current state of AI research and DARPA's own estimation for the realization of truly autonomous robots with human-like reasoning is that they will not arrive before 2030 (Ichbiah 2005, 507). Table 2.1 gives an overview of degrees of technical autonomy.

Conclusion   Weapons, or more generally autonomous systems, can have very different degrees of autonomy. In addition to the classification developed above,

Table 2.1   Autonomy types

Tele-operation		Continuous remote control
Pre-programmed autonomy		Autonomous operation within narrow parameters
	Structured control	Autonomous operation with a range of pre-programmed behaviors
Supervised autonomy		Autonomous operation most of the time
	Tele-operation with exception handling	Operator is informed when problems occur
	Directed autonomy	Operator intervenes at decision points
Complete autonomy		Operator only gives objectives, while the robotic system can find solutions and handle many problems by itself

which more generally applies to robotic systems, it can be said that weapons autonomy is affected by four main factors: 1) the trigger mechanism; 2) target selection; 3) mobility of the weapon; and 4) the navigational abilities of the weapon. To determine the degree of autonomy of a weapon one needs to ask: is the weapon triggered by an operator or by itself? Are the targets chosen by an operator or by the weapon itself? Is the weapon stationary or mobile? If it is mobile, does the weapon need external input for finding its target, or can it find its target by itself?

For example, a mine can usually trigger itself, but it falls short of all the other characteristics of autonomy. It neither chooses its targets, nor is it mobile, nor can it navigate. A cruise missile, on the other hand, is not self-triggered and does not usually choose its target, but it can move towards its target and find its target by itself. Finally, a weapon (a hypothetical one for now) that can trigger itself, that can choose its targets by itself, that is self-propelled and that can navigate by itself, would exhibit the highest degree of autonomy, no matter whether the weapon would be clever enough to reflect on the purposefulness or ethicality of its actions. In other words, weapons that exhibit a very high degree of technical autonomy can be fairly stupid. Whether or not anybody would want to use such weapons is a completely different matter.

In the future a fifth and sixth factor for describing weapons autonomy might also become important: self-repair/self-healing and self-replication. Current weapons are already optimized for keeping the amount of maintenance and repair activities required for their operation as low as possible. Some weapons such as modern tanks and aircraft have a self-diagnosis function that helps maintenance technicians to quickly locate the source of errors and technical problems. A bit further in the future are weapons that could service and repair themselves in the field. This might be achieved with nanobots inhabiting these weapons like bacteria and repairing them when required, or by specially engineered materials. For example, the US Air Force is trying to develop skin-like air frames that can self-heal damage caused by heat and stress (Buxbaum 2008).

Table 2.2   Weapons autonomy matrix

Weapon	Land mine	Cruise missile	Anti-ship missile	Phalanx CIWS	Brilliant submunitions	Future nano-tech weapons
Self-triggered?	yes	–	–	yes	–	?
Self-targeting?	–	–	yes	yes	yes	?
Self-propelled?	–	yes	yes	–	yes	yes
Self-guiding?	–	yes	yes	–	yes	yes
Self-repairing?	–	–	–	–	–	?
Self-replicating?	–	–	–	–	–	?

Nanotechnology might not only enable self-healing weapons, but also self-replicating ones. In fact, a weapon that could do all the things mentioned above *and* self-replicate might be the ultimate doomsday weapon. Cyberpunk author Philip K. Dick described such autonomous self-replicating weapons that have been let loose after a war between the UN and the Soviet Union in his short story 'The Second Variety' (Dick 1986b). In Dick's story the development of autonomous and self-replicating 'claws', which can hunt down and ambush Soviet forces, is an act of desperation by the UN. After six years all Soviet forces are destroyed, but the robot 'claws' evolve out of control and eventually destroy all of humanity. While this is just a science fiction story, self-replicating (nano-)robots could be in the reach of science within 10–20 years. When it comes to molecular-scale weapons one could think of biological weapons like smallpox, which already exist and which can also self-replicate out of control. So there is really nothing in the laws of physics or biology that could make self-replicating weapons impossible. Table 2.2 shows a weapons autonomy matrix for current and future weapons systems.

Artificial Intelligence

Autonomous platforms would have to utilize artificial intelligence (AI) to control their behavior and to allow them to operate successfully on their own. Without AI autonomous systems would remain rather primitive weapons of relative little military utility. The smarter an AW, the more complex tasks it can carry out, thus the more useful it will be militarily. For this reason the development of artificial intelligence has been a priority for DARPA ever since the launch of the 1983 Strategic Computing Initiative (SCI). Without AI the pursuit of military robotics could turn out to be a dead end – at least with respect to the development of autonomous platforms. The answer to the question whether or not it will be possible to make machines sufficiently clever to carry out many tasks on their own will very much decide the future of military robotics.

There is certainly reason for skepticism. AI has been pursued for many decades with rather limited success, despite the high hopes researchers had in the 1970s and

1980s. Even more surprising is that it is still hard to say what machine intelligence actually is and how it compares with human intelligence. For a discussion of the future of military robotics it is essential to have at least a very basic look at the discipline of AI and its application in robotics. This will allow a better understanding of the shortcomings of current 'intelligent' machines and also the prospects for overcoming them.

What is AI?

The field of artificial intelligence is already quite established in computer science, but there is still a lot of disagreement about the definition and the direction of AI. Up to now the field of AI lacks a unifying theory that could connect the great variety of sub-disciplines that have developed over its history of roughly 50 years. In terms of research goals, it can be divided into 'weak AI' and 'strong AI', whereas the former is aiming at solving narrow problems, while the latter would be the aim of creating a universally intelligent machine, or a machine that can match and possibly exceed human intelligence. In addition, there is the so-called 'nouvelle AI' approach, which was developed by Rodney Brooks from MIT and which aims to build simple robots of the intelligence level of insects and then gradually develop robots of greater complexity from there.

The discipline of AI was officially founded by John McCarthy at the British Dartmouth Summer Conference in 1956, where McCarthy coined the term (S. Williams 2002, 14). At the conference McCarthy, Claude Shannon, Nathaniel Rochester and Marvin Minsky proposed a research agenda for the development of AI, which aimed at using computers to simulate the human brain, thus already implicitly comparing mechanical with biological systems. So it can be said that AI aims to technically reproduce or mimic some human intellectual and cognitive abilities and allow machines to do more complex work. Marvin Minsky, who is a leader in AI research, defines AI in the following way: 'Artificial Intelligence is the science of making machines do things that would require intelligence if done by men' (Minsky 1968, V).

One of the first problems AI experts tried to tackle was to teach computers to play chess. The chess problem was ideal because it is generally acknowledged that it requires intelligence, it is based on simple rules that can be taught to a computer and it is immensely complex thanks to the almost infinite number of possible chess positions. For a long time the chess problem was indicative of the slow rate of success in AI research and for the discipline's exaggerated optimism of what AI could do in the near future. For example, it was predicted that computers could beat a Grand Master within 10 years (Campbell 1997, 93). However, it took almost 40 years for this to happen when *Deep Blue* eventually defeated world chess champion Gary Kasparov in 1997. The days are now definitely gone when humans could seriously compete with computers in the chess domain. This could mean that the strongest games of chess will probably from now on be played by chess programs against each other and no longer by world-class human players.

Opinions diverge how important the success of AI in the chess field is. Some see in the computer's success nothing but an expression of superior capabilities in computation, while others believe there has been a qualitative shift in the way computers play chess that makes them such particularly tough opponents (Dennet 2007). AI pioneer John McCarthy even regrets his discipline's strong interest in solving the chess problem, as it distracted from solving more fundamental problems, such as understanding the mechanisms and elements that make up human intelligence and on which AI research should focus (J. McCarthy 2007). This includes the human ability to understand natural language, to recognize patterns, to apply knowledge and to learn. If it was possible to bring together all of these abilities in one computer program, then it would be theoretically possible to have a computer of human-like intelligence, potentially able to quickly outperform humans in all areas of intelligence.

Computer scientist and science fiction author Vernor Vinge believes that such an 'ultraintelligent machine will be built and that it will be the last invention that man need make' (Vinge 1993). It could simply invent anything else and therefore tremendously speed up the development of new technology. Vinge coined the term 'singularity' to describe the process of AI-triggered exponentially accelerating technological progress. Many AI researchers believe that the development of strong AI, or 'artilects' (artificial intellects) as 'artificial brain-builder' Hugo de Garis calls them (De Garis 2005), could be a truly earth-shaking event of potentially cosmic significance. Strong AI has been the Holy Grail in AI research: highly desirable, but still unobtainable. How, or whether at all, strong AI could be reached, is still very much disputed. Some prominent researchers in the field of AI believe that the development of strong AI will happen some time in the twenty-first century and maybe as soon as around 2029 (Briggs 2008).

Top-down AI

The approach that was prevalent in AI research in the earlier decades of AI (before the 1990s) was the so-called top-down approach. The proponents of this approach thought that human-like intelligence could be reproduced within a very long and complex computer program that is based on simple rules. Relevant knowledge could be fed in a structured way into a computer. Then the computer would be given rules how to apply this knowledge, which was believed to be similar to the way the human brain works. The knowledge would be represented in the computer system as descriptions or symbols. For solving a problem a top-down AI computer system would try to match its symbolic representation of the world (or better the segment of the world) to the input it got. This approach has many disadvantages, which have become particularly obvious in robotics.

Shakey Shakey is an early experimental robot that was developed by the Stanford Research Institute in the mid-1960s. It looks like a big box on wheels. The robot had some TV sensors on top and could respond to commands given to it in typed natural language. When given the command to move an object, Shakey could identify the object, move towards it and push it. However, it did this incredibly slowly because of the way it worked. The robot had an internal symbolic representation of its (small) world, which it compared to the sensor data. This approach required an operating environment for the robot that had very little complexity and therefore consisted of blank walls and larger geometrical objects placed in a small room (Moravec 1999, 26). Once the robot moved or manipulated the world, the symbolic representation had to be updated according to the changes. So every move or change resulted in a long pause in which the robot processed the changes. Obviously, the more detailed or exact the internal symbolic representation of the robot, the greater the amount of necessary calculations and the slower the robot. The fundamental difficulty of robots to operate in a changing environment or an environment changed by the robot is called the 'frame problem of AI'. Any robot that has an internal symbolic representation of its world will occasionally succumb to the frame problem and simply get stuck whenever it manipulates the real world and it then has to figure out what has changed and what has not. The frame problem was essentially the reason why DARPA's 1980s autonomous land vehicle project turned out to be failure: off-road the vehicle moved even slower than most people can walk (Pollack 1989).

Expert systems   In the 1970s the first so-called expert systems were developed, which were based on large databases with expert knowledge arranged in a logical structure that made it easy to retrieve relevant pieces of knowledge in the form of advice. Expert systems ask a user questions in a logical sequence and use a database with expert knowledge (or statistical data) and decision trees for coming up with an answer or solution (Georges 2003, 35). They became commercially viable and very successful in the 1980s and they were believed by some AI experts to be a possible approach for creating human-like common sense. However, expert systems tend to be by design very narrow. They can only solve a very narrow set of problems for which they were originally programmed. This means that they are completely useless for any other kind of problem.

Cyc   Nevertheless, some people in AI believed that expert systems still had some greater potential. For example, AI researcher and entrepreneur Douglas Lenat started a project called *Cyc* (for encyclopedia) in 1984, which aimed at feeding a computer with all basic common knowledge so that it could understand a general conversation and be able to answer general questions. The main problem that had to be tackled was to bring common sense knowledge, such as 'snow is white' or 'if it rains you get wet', into a logical and coherent structure and to feed about a million such facts and rules into a computer. After more than 20 years *Cyc* is still a far cry away from its original goals. Despite enormous efforts its ontology and knowledge base remains vastly incomplete. Most people working in AI consider expert systems to be impractical for achieving strong AI. Of course, expert systems have proven to be useful for assisting human decision-makers and they will continue to be used for many such applications. However, there is little danger that they could ever become clever enough to replace the human expert, as they lack the common sense and the intuition of a human. In the military domain, some weapons such as the aforementioned *Phalanx* gun system can be described as some sort of expert system.

Bottom-up AI

In the late 1980s there was an evolutionary turn in AI research, which explicitly opposed the top-down approach. Like biological systems, which evolve in the direction from the simple to the more complex, the complexity and structure of machine systems should be built up from the bottom rather than be imposed on the system from the top. The paradigm of evolution was applied to computer systems and to robots for generating new and innovative solutions to the classical AI problems. Some researchers like Rodney Brooks from the MIT AI Lab emphasized the need for embodiment of AI systems that allowed them to learn and gain experience in the physical reality, while others used computer simulations to simulate life – a discipline called 'Artificial Life' or 'A-life'. The methods used for making computers learn and solve problems by themselves without depending on a rigid externally provided knowledge base and structure are usually discussed under the headings of *neural networks*, *evolutionary* or *genetic algorithms* and *autonomous agent systems* and have one thing in common: they give up the idea of completely controlling machine learning (as in top-down AI) and allow the computer or robot to learn by itself. These methods are briefly described below to give an idea of how bottom-up AI works. The methods are sometimes combined, for example one could use genetic algorithms with neural networks, and there are lots of variations in these methods, as they are themselves evolving in the process of research.

Neural networks   Neural networks is one of the oldest methods used by AI researchers for modeling the human brain. The general idea is that the brain consists of a large number of neurons that are connected to each other and that can be used to store information and to solve problems. So every neuron can pass on instructions or information by changing the state of other neurons to which it is connected. Neural networks can process information in a parallel and non-sequential fashion and are therefore able to process a great amount of data much faster than sequential computing, which approaches problems step by step. In addition, neural networks can learn from experience by 'memorizing' successful solutions. Neural networks have been successfully applied to a great number of AI problems, for example statistical analysis, speech recognition, image analysis and data processing (e.g. data mining). Some AI researchers use neural networks as an approach for building an artificial brain. One of the more prominent is Hugo de Garis, who suggests that the human brain has about 10 billion neurons, but that computers will soon exceed that number of neurons and are generally far less limited with respect to the number of neurons they could incorporate. Computers could have 'capacities trillions of trillions of times above human levels' by the end of the twenty-first century (De Garis 2007).

Genetic algorithms   Genetic algorithms are currently used for search engines and for solving optimization problems. There are many varieties of genetic algorithms, but they generally share the feature that they select candidate solutions according to their evolutionary fitness and create successive generations of solutions by using the genetic operators of recombination and mutation. This method also allows evolutionary programming in which pieces of software code can be combined according to evolutionary principles to produce new software code that is better adapted (Kelly 1995, 375–7). Genetic algorithms generally look for approximate solutions and not for the perfect solution, which has the advantage that they do not have to go through every single possibility for solving a particular problem. This means the problem-solving process is terminated as soon as a solution is found that satisfies the minimum criteria, or when a predetermined number of successive generations have been reached. The main advantage of genetic algorithms is that they can solve problems where the number of elements and possibilities is very large, which makes them ideal for code-breaking and planning tasks. Genetic algorithms are sometimes used for the development of learning robots that would be able to adapt to changing circumstances and to modify their behavior accordingly. In particular, they can be used for robot navigation. A genetic algorithm could help the robot to plan a route or develop a plan for achieving an objective that is given to it.

Autonomous agents   One of the latest methods in AI is the so-called autonomous agent approach. A software agent or 'bot' acts on behalf of a user. For example, it collects or manipulates information for the user in a computer system or network. Multi-agent systems contain many software agents or bots that can interact in some way that allows them to collaborate or compete with each other. The agents could be able to learn from continued interaction and could develop strategies. A possibility for designing multi-agent systems that has been explored is predator–prey systems, another is swarm systems. Predator–prey systems have two populations of agents, a predator and a prey population, which compete with each other and which create the dynamics for the whole system. Predator–prey dynamics can be described in nonlinear differential equations (Lotka equations) for modeling. Generally, predator–prey systems can be used for creating purposeful and cooperative behavior. Small numbers of predators have to cooperate in order to catch fast-moving prey. Predators and prey can co-evolve and improve their survival strategies, so the predators will learn how to find and attack prey, while the prey will find ways of evading or escaping predators. Similar are swarm systems, which also rely on collaborating agents that allow the whole to carry out a collective task. The interesting thing is that swarming agents do not need to communicate much for achieving highly coordinated collective behavior, as can be seen in an ant colony. Two developers of multi-agent systems from the University of Texas at Austin claim that:

Instead of searching the entire space of solutions, coevolution allows identifying a set of simpler subtasks, and optimizing each team member separately and in parallel for one such subtask. In the end, each agent knows what to expect from the other agents, and explicit communication is not necessary. (Yong and Miikkulainen 2001, 1)

Multi-agents systems could be used for controlling the behavior of one complex robot or the behavior of a population of simple robots that could collaborate to achieve a particular task.

Nouvelle AI   Rodney Brooks can be seen as the founding father of this new approach to AI. In particular, he has promoted the idea that before roboticists aim to develop high-tech robots that can reproduce many human abilities, they should first develop very simple life-like robots and then build slightly more complex ones and so on. The emphasis is to build a simple insect-like robot that can operate autonomously in the real world first and then proceed from there. Such a simple robot does not need to have any symbolic representation of its world, but can instead use real-time sensor data for guiding its immediate actions. This speeds up the response of the robot to its environment and sidesteps the frame problem (Copeland 2000). Only basic behaviors are programmed into the robot, such as moving its legs and avoiding obstacles, but the hope is that more complex behaviors emerge through largely uncontrolled learning processes.

Evolutionary robotics   Brooks built a small six-legged robot called *Ghengis* at the MIT AI Lab in 1988, which had a very simple programming for controlling its behavior. In essence it worked like an 'augmented finite-state machine' or like a more sophisticated thermostat or a slot machine. Certain internal conditions trigger certain behaviors like moving a particular leg. *Ghengis* had infrared (IR) sensors that allowed it to move over all kinds of terrain and to walk towards any perceived IR activity (Brooks 2002, 44–50). Brooks codified his general approach in a set of simple rules:

1. Do simple things first.
2. Learn to do them flawlessly.
3. Add new layers of activity over the results of the simple tasks.
4. Don't change the simple things.
5. Make the new layer work as flawlessly as the simple
6. Repeat, ad infinitum (quoted from Kelly 1995, 53).

Roboticist Kevin Warwick from the University of Reading has used a similar approach for developing a number of relatively simple robots with the goal of letting them interact with each other. One of his research projects was called *Seven Dwarfs* and was based on the development of a larger number of small autonomous wheeled robots that could move around. They could learn how to avoid obstacles and successive generations of the *Seven Dwarfs* would be smarter than earlier ones. A later generation even incorporated the possibility of communication between the robots so that they were aware of each other. Warwick wrote that 'the behaviours obtained from these robots have been eye-opening and in many cases very unexpected, particularly where parallels with human or animal behaviour can be observed' (Warwick 1997, 171). Thus very simple robots are able to develop fairly complex behaviors over time, which cannot be predicted.

Hans Moravec from the Carnegie Mellon University suggested that artificial emotions could be embedded in the programming of the robot as a general guidance for its behavior (Moravec 1988, 70; Moravec 1999, 115–23). A program could simulate pain when the energy supply is low so that it will start looking for a power source, or happiness could be simulated to reward and reinforce successful problem-solving strategies. Emotions like fear might improve the robot's ability for self-preservation and therefore its survivability, while the emotion of anger might allow it to mobilize additional energy and speed in critical situations. So artificial emotions could help robots to learn and evolve in terms of behavior with the hope to make them one day truly intelligent.

This evolutionary approach to AI and robotics obviously has its advantages and disadvantages. The main advantage is that elegant solutions could be found to very difficult problems, such as for pattern recognition, search engines and optimization. Because bottom-up AI is so powerful, AI developers and robot designers therefore more and more embrace the design mantra 'cheap, fast, and out of control' (Brooks and Flynn 1989). The big drawback is that computer systems or robots applying such methods like genetic algorithms or genetic programming can come up with unpredictable solutions or behaviors that may be effective and may work for the robot, but that may sometimes be unwanted. This inherent unpredictability of such systems can create dynamics that are extremely difficult for humans to control, or even to comprehend.

Military Applications of AI

AI can be applied to many different kinds of military systems and tasks and indeed AI is already incorporated in many military computer systems and robots. In the future, the number of military AI applications will undoubtedly grow, as powerful and cheap microchips can be built into practically any kind of weapon or piece of military equipment. One could even easily foresee a future in which any weapon used by the armed forces, including small weapons, is smart or self-guiding and incorporates some AI.

Military Decision-support Systems

The development of a battle management system was part of the original 1983 Strategic Computing Initiative. It is essentially a planning and decision-support tool that helps a military commander to cope with the growing amount of information and its complexity. A battle-management system can track friendly and enemy forces and helps to develop military plans and implement them. Battle-management systems also have a wargaming function that can serve as a decision aid. They can game battles in advance and this allows a commander to see what kind of effects certain decisions might have – as well as in relation to the enemy's behavior.

In the future genetic algorithms will generally be used in military computer systems for planning and other decision-support functions. For example, there is the FOX Genetic Algorithm (FOX-GA), which was developed under a US Army Research Laboratory contract. FOX-GA is able to assist human commanders in military decision-making by generating and evaluating a very large number of possible courses of action (COAs). According to a study by the Canadian Defense Research and Development Agency, 'this system can evaluate up to 3000 friendly COAs per minute while manually, the process requires 10–15 minutes to wargame one friendly COA against one enemy COA' (Boukhtouta et al. 2002, 8). Out of a great number of possibilities a smaller list of different courses of action that meet the minimum criteria will be presented to the commander, who can then choose whatever option the commander thinks is best. Alternatively, the commander can select a few options for further development. In this case, the few selected courses of action could be analyzed in greater detail and depth.

DARPA also pursues other battle management software, which aims at significantly reducing the number of required military staff officers in a military headquarters and which might someday allow largely automating military decision-making at the tactical level. In June 2008 DARPA awarded a contract to BAE Systems to develop *Deep Green*, an intelligent software program that can automate many staff functions and act as a decision aid to human commanders. *Deep Green* can help commanders visualize tactical situations and can predict likely possible futures, which are represented in graphs. Commanders can play through unlimited 'what if' scenarios and they can develop battle plans that increase their own options and reduce the risks. *Deep Green* will consist of four functional components: 1) a commander's associate that can convert a commander's battle sketches into courses of action; 2) *Blitzkrieg*, which games through a commander's decision and produces likely battle outcomes; 3) *Crystal Ball*, which generates and maps possible futures, including important decision points; and 4) automated course of action generation, which can produce machine-generated courses of action, although DARPA acknowledges that military leaders generally do not like it – so it would be mainly used to augment human decision-making with some machine-generated courses of action (*Defense Industry Daily* 2008).

The main intention behind a system like *Deep Green* is not to replace the human military commander with a machine, but to enable commanders to master the enormous complexity of modern war. 'By focusing on creating options ahead of the real operation rather than repairing the plan, *Deep Green* will allow commanders to be proactive instead of reactive in dealing with the enemy' (*Defense*

Industry Daily 2008). *Deep Green* will not only speed up decision-making and implementation (in order to get inside the enemy's decision cycle), but will also allow commanders to consider a greater number of possibilities and help them to avoid making certain kinds of mistakes.

The Behavioral Control of Unmanned Vehicles

The navigation of UGVs used to be an immensely difficult problem because of the higher degree of complexity of the environment in which a UGV has to operate compared with UAVs. Unmanned aerial systems can easily navigate with the help of GPS as they do not have to avoid obstacles. Military UGVs, on the other hand, must be able to traverse through unknown terrain and be able to identify an obstacle and to plan an alternative route. This means the UGV must be able to recognize various kinds of obstacles, such as a tree or cliff, and find a way around these obstacles. At the same time, the UGV should know that it can drive through a bush, but it cannot drive through a wall. Furthermore, the UGV should know when a hill or ditch is too steep and would result in the vehicle to roll over (Lerner 2006a).

A combination of various sensors such as video sensors and laser/radar (laser detection and ranging (LADAR)) sensors can certainly help, but without some common sense knowledge of the operating environment the UGV will always have serious problems with respect to making the right decisions about choosing its route thorough difficult terrain. Even more challenging for a UGV is the problem of responding appropriately to enemy fire or other enemy activities and to know when it has to seek cover, or when it should return fire. Proactively looking for targets and engaging them before they can open fire would require an unmanned system to generally recognize targets and to understand what a legitimate target is and what is not. Such an ability of discrimination is still beyond what is technically feasible today. In any case, UGVs would be much slower in terms of moving on the battlefield under operational conditions than human soldiers and this is unlikely to change soon.

Automated Target Recognition

A key technology for making weapons more autonomous is the capability of automated target recognition (ATR), which would allow a robot or robotic weapon to independently identify an object as a target and to make a decision whether or not to engage this target. Obviously, ATR can also help to reduce the danger of fratricide and can allow the precision engagement of individual targets. ATR is based on a computer analysis of the signatures and movements of an object in the battlespace. This could be the automated analysis of a radar signature, or the analysis of a video image, or an analysis of any other property of the object that has been picked up by a sensor. The ATR system would simply compare the sensor data with any target data in its target database, taking into account that different angles of attack produce different signatures. So if the ATR system could match a radar signature of a target with that of a *MiG-29* contained in its database, the computer could conclude that this is an enemy aircraft and could respond accordingly. Of course, the computer would have to know in advance what particular types of platforms can be expected in the area of operations and which type is used by which side (Rhea 2000).

There are now various computer analysis methods possible for matching targets to available target data. This includes mathematical algorithms, neural nets or autonomous agents systems. For increasing the reliability of ATR, several different sensors could be used in combination. The analysis of the data derived from different sensors could be compared with each other.

ATR is not a trivial task and even the systems in use today still have substantial problems to distinguish, for example, a Russian *T-62* tank from an American *M60* tank when seen from different angles (*Armada International* 1998). Weather and visibility conditions are also important, as well as enemy counter-measures, which could seriously impede the accurate identification of targets. Of course, one could ask the question whether a human soldier would always do better, which is certainly not the case.[2]

In general, it can be said that it is much easier to identify a large object like a tank or aircraft than a small object or a person. However, it might be possible in the future that software that analyzes a digital video stream could automatically identify and track a particular person that walks past a video camera. The London Borough of Newham introduced such a system in 2002, but it seems to have failed to automatically recognize any criminal known to be living in this area (Meek 2002).

DARPA has recently funded a technically less ambitious project called *DigitalTripwire*, which is described as a 'small automated human detection system'. It would allow placing a small video camera for weeks or even months on the battlefield that would be automatically monitored by software, which could alarm human personnel in specified cases (US DARPA 2007a). The aim is to classify objects into broad categories rather than look for specific individuals. A similar project has been launched by the US Office of Naval Research, which aims to spot dangerous individuals in crowds by searching for indications of physiological stress. This could enable military/security personnel, or maybe even a robot, to determine who might be a suicide bomber or assassin and take appropriate actions (Marks 2006).

Even in the long run it would always be very difficult for any ATR system to divide humans, which it could some day certainly distinguish reliably from other objects, into combatants and civilians. Identifying whether or not a human holds a gun or any other object might also be extremely difficult for a computer, especially if the humans concerned are not cooperative and employ deception.

---

2   In April 1994 two American *F-15*s accidentally shot down an American Blackhawk helicopter in the No-Fly-Zone over Iraq. The *F-15* pilots visually identified the helicopters, but believed them to be Iraqi because the shape of the Blackhawk helicopter looked from a particular angle similar to a *Mi-24 Hind*.

Self-coordination of Robotic Systems

Military strategists rediscovered in the 1990s swarming as an effective tactic in warfare (Arquilla and Ronfeldt 2000). It is based on the biological concept of swarms of animals such as bees, fish or birds, which move in large groups in a highly coordinated manner. This allows these animals to work toward the same goals and to survive attacks from predators. Military swarming is a tactic that is based on the idea that an enemy is attacked by many autonomous units simultaneously from many directions. These units then suddenly disperse, regroup and attack again, possibly in many waves, an action which is called 'pulsing on a target'.

Although swarming as a military tactic has been used by nomads and other irregular fighters throughout the history of warfare, it is now becoming more interesting for regular forces because of the development of network-centric warfare. In the future, small robots could be deployed in swarms and attack a larger enemy target in many waves until it is destroyed. Each component of the robot swarm could be relatively simple or dumb, e.g. it might only carry a simple 'swarm algorithm' that tells the individual swarm component where to be and what to do relative to the swarm as a whole. However, the swarm as a whole might be able to develop quite complex and intelligent behaviors. Swarming robots could be very hard to defeat, which could make them a highly effective weapon. The US military tested a swarm of 120 small robots equipped with swarm intelligence in 2003 in the context of a DARPA project (Knight 2003). Some swarm-based weapons are already under development, which is discussed in Chapter 3.

Conclusion: The Dilemma of Intelligent Weapons

This chapter has shown that growing weapons autonomy is in many respects militarily highly desirable and a great improvement over tele-operated systems. The arguments put forward by the proponents of autonomous systems are all old and have been repeated endless times: decision cycles are getting shorter, machines are faster, they make fewer mistakes and are overall more efficient, and so on. Most of it sounds quite reminiscent of the debate on AW that took place in the 1980s. At that time, people in computing like Gary Chapman indicated that any AWs that were conceived in the 1980s posed substantial engineering problems. It was obvious to them that the software controlling such weapons would have to be overly complex, would be prone to have bugs and that they would behave unpredictably in situations not foreseen by their programmers (Belin and Chapman 1987). It would have been irresponsible to deploy any half-baked largely unintelligent AW. Indeed, it did not happen. SCI projects like the autonomous land vehicle and the Strategic Defense Initiative (SDI) were shelved because they turned out to be technologically too ambitious at the time.

However, technology has changed so tremendously as to make the 1980s debate look vastly outdated. AI and AW are no longer hypothetical. They have become very real and they will be with us relatively soon. They will also be very different in many respects from what was envisioned in previous decades. AI is no longer limited to a top-down approach, meaning that the software architecture is neatly laid out and designed by software engineers and can be represented in structural diagrams. Nowadays, AI software has become much more life-like. Neural networks and genetic algorithms have the ability to evolve by themselves and to build up complexity by themselves. A programmer using these new programming techniques usually just defines a 'fitness function' and this allows the program to search for solutions by itself and even to learn by itself.

As software becomes ever more complex, the control of the programmer over the machine learning process is more and more reduced. A programmer can influence the direction of the search of a program for a solution, but the programmer cannot control the result that the program will eventually find. Of course, it is important to see for what purpose the program is developed and whether or not there are links to the physical reality. If a search engine does not produce the optimal results I want, it is unfortunate but something anybody could live with. But if the software controls a robot and the robot comes up with unanticipated and undesired solutions that result in unwanted behaviors, it could be a serious problem.

This bottom-up approach to AI applied to robotics could lead to the creation of machines that can develop behaviors we did not anticipate and that we might not even fully understand. The more complex and intelligent these machines become, the harder it will be to control their behavior. This is not an immediate problem considering the relative simplicity of current robot software, but it could become a major problem in the future.

This dilemma of creating intelligent AW was brilliantly analyzed by Algis Budrys in his short story 'First to Serve', which he wrote in 1954. Budrys's portrayal of future technology is a bit misleading, but it is still highly accurate considering the fact that the story was written more than 50 years ago. In the story the Pentagon wants to build a robot soldier that is smarter and tougher than a human soldier. A Pentagon research laboratory actually manages to create such an ideal robot soldier. The dilemma is that the robot mimics human beings too perfectly, even to the degree that it shows individuality and self-awareness. This turns out to be an undesirable feature because a robot that is smarter than its human military commanders might eventually reject stupid orders from a less intelligent, less competent human being. Making the robot more like an automaton than a human, however, will only make it slow, stupid and cumbersome. In other words, it would lose its military value, as it would no longer possess the autonomy and ingenuity to do its job well. In the latter case the robot would have to be given orders like:

> Go out on patrol and report back. If I'm not here, report to so-and-so. If there's nobody here, do this. If that doesn't work, try that. If such-and-such happens, proceed as follows. But don't confuse such-and-such with that or this.

This is obviously not a very good solution as the robot designer points out himself:

> Can you imagine fighting a war on that basis? And what about that reorientation problem? How long would all those robots sit there before they could all be serviced – and how many man-hours and how much material would it take to do the job? Frankly, I couldn't think of a more cumbersome way to run a war if I tried …

In the first case the soldier robots would be simply too perfect for humans:

> Or, we can build all our robots like streamlined Pimmy's when all his circuits are operating, without our test cutoffs. Only, then, we'd have artificial human beings. Human beings who don't wear out, that a hand-gun won't stop, and who don't need food or water as long as their power piles have a pebble-sized hunk of plutonium to chew on. (Budrys 1989)

So the long term choice is between creating a perfect robot soldier, which would be likely to get out of control at some point, or creating a stupid automaton, which is not particularly useful without constant human supervision. In the story it turns out that the self-aware prototype robot kills an officer in a fight. The Pentagon subsequently decides to shelve the project until somebody can figure out how to create a 'zombie' or 'slave' -like robot.

It remains to be seen what military organizations are going to do: push ahead with the technology to create the perfect robot soldier or build the perfect automaton without any brains to speak of. Both possibilities will create their own legal and moral dilemmas. The legal and ethical issues raised by 'robot soldiers' and more generally AW are discussed in more detail in Chapters 4 and 5.

Chapter 3
The Robotics Revolution of Warfare

This chapter discusses the military robotics revolution in the context of 'official' visions of future warfare. It is argued that all branches of warfare (aerial, land and naval) will be transformed by the increasing proliferation of unmanned systems. Military robots will initially take over all of the 'dangerous, dull and dirty' tasks and will operate under close human supervision. But someday – maybe as soon as 10–15 years – robots will be able to operate autonomously and could largely replace human soldiers in the battlespace. With machines becoming smarter and more capable, there is a lesser need for humans going into action, or even of humans being in continuous control of unmanned systems. Increasingly advanced AI will enable robots to operate more autonomously and they will develop many 'humanlike capabilities', which will enable them to develop effective strategies and purposeful behavior (Hambling 2006b). Computers may never become universally intelligent, but they could easily be able to outsmart humans in many domains that are relevant for warfare.

Machines will not only dominate the familiar macroscopic space, but will soon also conquer the microscopic space. Thanks to increasingly autonomous robotic systems warfare could expand in directions and spaces far beyond imagination. Nanotechnology will enable the development of 'invisible machines' that can unnoticeably invade other countries or even our bodies (T. McCarthy 2001). They will be able to collect intelligence or could even attack mechanical, electronic or biological systems with extreme precision. It is very likely that robots of all varieties and sizes could relatively soon outnumber humans on future battlefields.

Automated war is definitely possible, but it does not mean that all future wars will be completely automated, or that they should be automated. The only argument that is made in here is that automation seems to be the direction in which warfare is currently moving. In a world where machines can make decisions in almost no time and where targets hundreds, if not thousands, of miles away can be destroyed in a fraction of a second with deadly precision, there seems to be simply no place for humans to fight in traditional or archaic ways. Any attempt to do so might one day be seen as deserving the label 'Quixotic'. Modern-day warriors could find themselves similarly obsolete as the medieval knights after the proliferation of gunpowder weapons in sixteenth-century Europe. Automation may eventually make war impossible – at least war as a human endeavor fought by humans. Nowhere is the imminent disappearance of humans in the battlespace more obvious than in the aerospace domain.

The Transformation of Aerospace Power

Aerial warfare is the newest branch of warfare, as it is only about 100 years old. It is also the branch of warfare that has undergone the most rapid and fundamental changes in its short history. Unmanned systems have been part of its history practically from the early days onward. Today, the robotics revolution could eventually make aerial warfare without pilots a real possibility. The days where human combat pilots like modern knights take to the skies and 'dogfight' with other pilots are clearly numbered for many reasons. First of all, it can be said that air defense systems are becoming ever more capable and will soon be able to track stealth aircraft (Sweetman 2007). Such a development will make it increasingly difficult for manned aircraft to survive and will in any case require unmanned systems for the suppression of air defense systems. These could also become much harder to defeat once they consist of large distributed sensor networks with a high degree of resilience. Secondly, modern technology also makes it possible to build aircraft that can fly at hypersonic speeds (faster than Mach 5) and which can endure g-forces far beyond what a human pilot would be capable of (Brzezinski 2003). The maximum acceleration that a human can endure for a short time is 9g, or nine times the body weight. A smaller unmanned aircraft can be built to endure up to 20g (Friedman and Friedman 1996, 298). It is quite doubtful that a human pilot could even control an aircraft at hypersonic speed, as everything would be happening far too fast and the slightest pilot error could result in a crash. Once warfare transgresses earth and reaches into space, the number of humans who could fight there is likely to be close to zero.

The Vision

In 1990 the US Air Force (USAF) published its first service vision with the title 'Global Reach, Global Power', which was quickly updated one year later to address the geopolitical changes triggered by the end of the Cold War (US DoD 1990). The Air Force vision was again updated in 2000 and published under the slightly changed title 'Global Vigilance, Reach and Power' (US DoD 2000b). Both visions underline the element of change and the need to become 'lighter and leaner' and at the same time 'more lethal' (US DoD 2000b, 5). There is also a noticeable broadening of the Air Force mission, which now includes unspecified new threats (US DoD 2000b, 6). While the Air Force visions only generally outline the future direction of the service, the 'US Air Force Transformation Flight Plan' from 2003 contains a very detailed framework for transforming the Air Force's capabilities from an 'industrial age force to an information age force' that can deal with new military challenges such as asymmetric warfare (US DoD 2006b).

The new vision of the USAF is to be able to conduct global strikes and to produce 'exact effects' in the whole spectrum of warfare. It includes such key phrases as agility, mobility, network-centric and effects-based operations, information superiority, sustainability and endurance. All of this shall contribute to the Air Force's 'ability to find, fix, assess, track, target and engage anything of military significance, anywhere' (US DoD 2000b). The service vision emphasizes the expeditionary character of the Air Force and also the growing importance of outer space. The Air Force underlines its intention of taking advantage of revolutionary technology and aims at developing the right mix of capabilities, including manned, unmanned and space systems. It is expected that the US will be less able to rely on forward bases in the future. This increases the importance of long-distance operations. In essence, the Air Force is seeking the capability to strike at targets worldwide from the continental United States. Furthermore, the Air Force aims to improve its airlift capability for providing the US Army with the mobility to deploy quickly in theater.

Although the USAF vision and roadmap documents do not spell it out, it is quite obvious that 'unmanned air systems' (so the new official term) will play a key role in providing many of the capabilities that the Air Force currently seeks. A look at the planned future capabilities makes it clear where it is going. These include an 'Advanced Standoff Cruise Missile', an 'Air Expeditionary Force Weapon', a 'Common Aero Vehicle', an 'Extended Range Strike Aircraft', a 'Hypersonic Standoff Weapon', a 'Hypervelocity Missile', a 'Long Range Cruise Missile', a 'New Long Range Platform' and a 'Robust Autonomous Attack Missile' (US DoD 2003, C7–C8). The 'Air Force Roadmap 2006–2025' states:

> Some future missions will benefit from having a human presence, but for many missions, the unmanned aircraft will provide far superior capabilities. Future RPAs [remotely piloted aircraft] may be able to provide close air support (CAS) in threat environments that will be unsurvivable for AC-130 gunships. (US DoD 2006b, 109)

So it is likely that the USAF will hold onto its new manned fighter planes (and maybe develop a new manned bomber (B-X) planned for 2018) until they will all be phased out in the 2030s and 2040s, which is about the time when the technology for truly autonomous systems could be available. Aerial warfare is already changing through the growing use of unmanned systems in the context of operations in Iraq and Afghanistan.

Tactical Unmanned Air Systems

The USAF wants to be able to continuously monitor the battlespace and to rapidly find, track and engage targets. This requires systems with very high endurance that can operate in the battlespace for extended periods of time. For this purpose, the USAF is already using a great variety of UAVs like *Predator* or *Global Hawk*. The 'US Air Force UAV Strategic Vision' points out that these systems have 15–30 hours of endurance, which would be 'considered to be "persistent" today, are but the first step in a path that may lead to increases in endurance by orders of magnitude' (US DoD 2005a, 6). The vision further explains:

Persistence is enabled by a number of technologies. Fuel-efficient engines and airframes can be designed without regard to human factors limitations; the space and weight normally allocated to on-board aircrew and life support systems can now be made available for more payload and/or fuel, or they can be traded in order to design a smaller vehicle. Autonomous in-flight refueling, potentially with unmanned tankers, and advanced power sources will allow for increased endurance. Combined, these technologies could lead to systems, such as lighter-than-air and near-space vehicles, with endurance measured in weeks, months, or even years. (US DoD 2005a, 6–7)

In order to further extend the time they can loiter over a target area, future military UAVs could be aerostats, solar-powered gliders, or even nuclear-powered gliders. In effect, they could become cheap alternatives to earth observation and communication satellites that can be routinely used on a tactical level. For example, the US military has already deployed *Tactical Aerostats* (airships anchored to the ground) in Iraq. DARPA has funded a solar-powered UAV called *Helios* that completed a test of 40 hours of autonomous flight in 2003 (Blackmore 2005, 160), while the USAF has already funded at least two feasibility studies for a nuclear-powered version of *Global Hawk*. These aerostats and gliders could remain in the air and provide real-time intelligence for months at a time without much need of maintenance or refueling. Although they would be quite vulnerable to enemy fire, they have the advantage over satellites that they can be easily moved to areas of interest, that they can continuously remain over the target and that they offer a much higher resolution than spy satellites, as they fly at lower altitudes. These persistent UAVs would not only carry various sensor payloads, but would also be able to function as communication relay nodes for wireless networks. Furthermore, UAVs may be used in the role of tanker aircraft such as the *KC-10* and *KC-135* (Bone and Bolkcom 2003, 16).

The trend in terms of UAVs is definitely going in the direction of building smaller and stealthier systems because bigger UAVs are not very survivable in a high threat environment (Abatti 2005, 2, 7). As a result, smaller and cheaper UAVs could prove to be more efficient, more survivable and could provide flexible aerial reconnaissance on a tactical level. These small aerial vehicles, or micro aerial vehicles (MAVs), are roughly the size of a model aircraft and some of them have already been fielded by the US forces, such as the *Raven* (or *RQ-11A*) (Featherstone 2007, 43). *Raven* weighs just 4.2lbs, can stay in the air for 80 minutes to transmit video imagery and costs only $35,000 each. Nine thousand of these modified model planes have been delivered or are on order by the US forces (US Navy and Marine Corps 2008). Obviously, MAVs would be overall more fuel-efficient and cheaper in terms of unit price and operation than big UAVs or aerostats. They can also be easily carried by soldiers in backpacks (like *Raven*) and they might become cheap enough to be disposable.

The next step is to make small UAVs autonomous and to arm them so that they are able to search for targets by themselves, which turns them into 'hunter-killers'.

The 'Transformation Flight Plan' states that in order to increase the number of targets it can strike with precision, the Air Force wants 'to develop miniature munitions that can loiter on their own to detect and destroy timecritical targets as they emerge' (US DoD 2003, 64). Lockheed Martin currently develops such a system, which is called the *Low Cost Autonomous Attack System* (LOCAAS). LOCAAS could be launched from a fighter jet like the *F/A-22* and could be equipped with various types of warheads. LOCAAS can loiter for half an hour over an area of 33 sq. miles (or 80 sq. km) and attack targets of opportunity. Its laser radar system (LADAR) was originally designed to autonomously identify and attack targets, but a human operator will, at least for the time being, make the final decision to attack a target (Braybrook and Biass 2004, 43). LOCAAS is not the only autonomous loitering munition-carrier under development internationally. There is, for example, the Israeli *Harpy*, the British *White Hawk* and the German *Tactical Advanced Recce Strike System* (TARES), which are similar (*Defense Update* 2007).

Brilliant munitions could be packed in loitering munition carriers or they could be deployed in large swarms of drones that deliver these munitions close to their target. Boeing currently develops small swarming drones called *Dominator* weighing just 100lbs. and carrying three brilliant armor-piercing submunitions each. More than 600 *Dominators* could theoretically fit into a *C-17 Globemaster* and be released hundreds of miles away from their intended targets. The USAF is still too traditionally minded and is not yet buying into the concept of swarming drones as a replacement of manned bombers. The British, too, have for some time considered the option of using transport aircraft as launching platforms for cruise missiles as a future replacement for its aging *Tornado GR4* fighter/bombers (the so-called FOAS concept), but then decided in the end to pursue UCAVs instead. States with a smaller defense budget might consider more seriously autonomous swarms of 'intelligent' drones as a viable and cheap alternative to bombers. It could be just a matter of time until someone will go for it (Hambling 2006a).

The US and some eight or nine other states are currently working on UCAVs, which could be used for a whole range of missions including the suppression of air defense and strike missions. In the future, they could provide combat air support to ground forces or even be used in an air superiority role. Unlike UAVs, which can only be equipped with a few smart munitions for some limited missions, the term UCAV implies that an unmanned aircraft is from the beginning designed to carry out the functions of a manned combat aircraft. The term also originally only referred to the Boeing *X-45*, but has now been extended to include all dedicated unmanned combat aircraft.

In principle, there are two ways of going about designing a UCAV (McDaid and Oliver 1997, 148). The first is to take a manned aircraft and install some remote-control equipment inside it, or design a manned aircraft and simply leave out the cockpit. This approach would even allow converting existing manned aircraft into UCAVs or using existing 'proven' designs for building a UCAV. The second approach is to design the UCAV as a reusable cruise missile. This would allow making the UCAV considerably smaller and therefore much more survivable and cheaper than a traditional aircraft design. Cost savings could be as much as 60–90 percent compared to a manned aircraft (McDaid and Oliver 1997, 148). The downside is that a modified cruise missile will not be able to carry anything like the bomb load of an *F-15E* or *F-16E* (about eight tons). However, the gained advantage is fuel efficiency. Considering the fact that the reduction of fuel consumption is desirable for numerous reasons, this will be an influential factor for relying primarily on unmanned aircraft. For example, the *Predator* only requires a hundredth of the fuel needed for operating an *F-16* (Thomson 2008).

UAVs that have been converted to weapons platforms by combining them with guided missiles and laser-guided bombs – like the *Predator*, which was modified to carry two *Hellfire* missiles – are strictly speaking not UCAVs. In contrast, the *MQ-9 Reaper*, which is based on the *Predator*, was designed to be primarily an unmanned combat aircraft. It is bigger, much faster and more powerful than the original *Predator*. It can cruise at 300mph for 14 hours and it can carry up 3,800lbs. (1.7 tons) of weapons, or up to 14 *Hellfire* missiles or a smaller load of laser-guided bombs or JDAMs (Joint Direct Attack Munition), which is more than 10 times the weapons load of the *Predator A* (General Atomics). The *Reaper* can be operated by two pilots from a ground control station who 'fly' the drone.

The *Predator/Reaper* program has been a great success and other air forces are trying to develop a similar capability. In 2007 the British MoD procured three *Reaper* drones from the US and already has two UCAVs under development (*Taranis* and *Mantis*). The US Army has recently introduced a more autonomous version of the *Predator/Reaper* called *Sky Warrior*, which has operated in Afghanistan since October 2007. The USAF formed its first *Reaper* fighter wing in August 2008, which will phase out the *F-16* and transition to a drone-only unit. The drone pilots would be able to operate the aircraft from a facility near Las Vegas in the US while maintenance crews would still have to deploy in theater.

Before the *Predator*'s unexpected rise to glory the USAF had a big UCAV program, designated *X-45*, between 1998 and 2006, which was merged with another UCAV program and which was temporarily known as J-UCAS (joint unmanned combat air system) in 2005. The Air Force wanted a low-cost medium-range subsonic unmanned strike platform with a range of more than 300 miles capable of in-flight refueling, which could be stored in a container for up to 10 years. The UCAV was supposed to have a primary search and destroy mission hunting enemy air defenses and other mobile targets of opportunity by loitering over the target area for some time (30 minutes to two hours) (Tirpak 2002). The contractors Boeing and Northrop Grumman built several prototypes (*X-45A to D* and *X-47A to B*) and the first one flew in 2002. In 2006, the USAF decided not to continue the program, probably in part because the *Reaper* already offered some of the capability that was sought in the *X-45* and in part because it was probably technologically not revolutionary enough. However, when canceling the *X-45* the Air Force announced some unspecified 'next generation long range strike' program (Axe 2006).

Global Strike

The USAF aims to develop the capability of striking globally from the American continent without any need of forward bases or the forward deployment of troops. DARPA and the USAF have a whole range of research and development (R&D) programs that could turn this vision into reality within a decade. Some of the revolutionary aircraft will be hypersonic and some will be optimized for long endurance, which means that the aircraft are very likely to be unmanned.

Information about these officially secret projects is scarce, but a few of them have been at least publicly announced. For example, a new type of UCAV is called *Switchblade* and is currently developed by DARPA and Northrop Grumman. It has a quite revolutionary design in so far as it would be able to shift its shape in mid-flight. *Switchblade* has a so-called 'oblique flying wing' design, which means that it can change its aerodynamic configuration by swiveling its wing around 60 degrees in flight to reach supersonic speeds (Shachtman 2006). It is designed for long endurance surveillance, strike and hunter-killer missions and is expected to have an intercontinental range of 5,000 miles. At the moment, *Switchblade* is little more than a design study, but a prototype could fly as early as 2010 with the aircraft becoming operational by 2020 (G. Warwick 2005).

Since 1997/98 DARPA has had a research program called 'Force Application from the Continental United States', or the FALCON program. The program is still classified and a good deal of information that can be found on it amounts to little more than speculation. One part of it is the *hypersonic cruise vehicle* (HCV), which is designed to be a reusable cruise missile that can rapidly strike anywhere in the world and which would be also able to transport small satellites into orbit. According to *Aviation Week*, the 'global-reach hypersonic cruise vehicle (HCV) [will be] capable of delivering a 12,000-lb. payload at a distance of 9,000 naut. mi. from the continental U.S. in less than 2 hr' (Norris 2007). Maximum speed will be in excess of Mach 4. HCV could be also used as a bunker-busting munition that can destroy its target through kinetic energy caused by the impact at hypersonic speeds. A prototype for an expendable HCV designated *HTV-2* is going to be tested in 2008 and 2009 and is expected to reach Mach 20+. Another program, called *HTV-3X Blackswift*, is the size of a fighter jet and will be able to reach Mach 6. Apparently *Blackswift* is intended to be a replacement for the already retired *SR-71 Blackbird*. DARPA describes the program as a:

> flight test program [that] will develop a reusable, air-breathing hypersonic testbed to demonstrate a runway take-off, Mach 6+ cruise for at least 60 seconds, lateral maneuver, aileron roll, and a runway landing. It is envisioned that flying this reusable hypersonic testbed in a relevant, flight environment will permit the future development of enhanced-capability reusable hypersonic cruise vehicles for intelligence, surveillance, reconnaissance, strike or other national need missions. (US DARPA 2008)

The program specification says nothing about whether the ultimate aim is the development of a manned or an unmanned aircraft, but considering the envisioned capabilities – which would be difficult for a human pilot to meet – it will most likely be unmanned.

The other more secret part of the FALCON program, the *common aero vehicle* (CAV), is designed to be an 'experimental manoeuvrable re-entry vehicle carrying a variety of payloads through a suborbital trajectory, and re-entering and dispersing the payload in the atmosphere' (Norris and Warwick 1999), which could deliver munitions to any point on the earth within hours. The CAV might be launched with a rocket, or might be air launched, and would be able to leave the atmosphere and re-enter it. It will be able to carry out a whole range of roles: the hypersonic delivery of nuclear weapons and conventional munitions, the transport of satellites, and maybe even of troops to far away places in no time (Page 2008h). A prototype is under development with the designation *X-41*. The CAV could carry a payload of 1,000lbs. and could reach any point in the world in two hours. According to the *Washington Post* a first generation CAV could be carried to the upper layer of the atmosphere (100,000ft.) by a space plane and could be ready by 2010 (Pincus 2005). The CAV could come in a manned and an unmanned version depending on the role for which it is used. According to Pentagon plans it should be operational by 2025 (Tuttle 2003). Once states have the capability of transporting satellites and weapons cheaply into and through space, it will only be a matter of time before outer space becomes a battlefield of future wars.

Directed Energy and Space Warfare

Many science fiction stories, ever since H. G. Wells's *War of the Worlds* and Buck Rogers, have it that the weapons used in space and in the future are ray guns. However, ray guns, or directed energy weapons (DEWs) like lasers and microwave weapons, are no longer science fiction but a reality and they will increasingly influence the evolution of aerospace power. The aerospace engineer Gary Lai even claims that 'their development will significantly change warfare forever' (Lai 2003). The US military has already built several prototypes of DEWs, which could be placed on airborne, or even spaceborne, platforms. Some of them could be fielded even before 2010. This includes the *airborne laser* (ABL), the *advanced tactical laser* (ATL) and the *active denial system* (ADS). Laser weapons in particular are likely to be placed on robotic platforms, or to be designed from the beginning as AW. Lasers can have an effective lethal range of several hundred miles (as in the case of the ABL) and a human would simply be incapable of aiming with the same precision or engaging targets that move at very high speeds. DEWs are also likely to be placed on larger moving platforms, such as aircraft or warships, which makes precise aiming, or 'laser beam control' as it is called, quite difficult. Over large distances a fire control computer would have to calculate the tilt of the laser beam caused by atmospheric conditions and adjust the laser gun accordingly to achieve the required accuracy for hitting a target. Doug Beason vividly describes an ABL missile interception scenario set in the near future, which illustrates the technological challenge:

> Simultaneously the target acquisition computer churns through millions of possible engagement scenarios, performing a real-time parametric optimization of firing angles and altitudes, all being updated from ABL altitude, attitude, and velocity, as well as outside temperature, air density, humidity, and other data relayed back from the sensors. (Beason 2005, 151)

Even at shorter distances, the use of laser weapons on the battlefield would increase the speed of engagement to such an extent that humans would not be able to respond quickly enough to threats that suddenly appear. Thomas K. Adams argues that:

> With DEWs, active countermeasures (dodging, throwing chaff, deploying decoys, returning fire) become enormously more difficult and in many cases impossible. It is hard to see many roles for humans in this kind of lightning duel. Human perceptions and motor coordination skills are simply not capable of intervening usefully. Defense then relies on instantaneous, automated responses and passive measures, of which the best are probably speed and size. (Adams 2001)

It is more than probable that the deployment of DEWs will influence and encourage the development of increasingly autonomous types of weapons. One application that has been proposed by analysts from the Lexington Institute is to arm UCAVs with DEW. 'A microwave-armed UCAV could be the ultimate SEAD weapon, able to fly over known sites or along penetration corridors as a precursor to the ingress of manned aircraft or cruise missiles' (Thompson and Goure 2003, 27). Furthermore, UCAVs equipped with high-powered lasers could be used in a bomber role and engage ground targets with high precision and even stealthily, as they would provide no identifiable signatures of an attack (Thompson and Goure 2003, 21). One day, lasers might be placed in space for destroying not only ballistic missiles in flight, but also targets on the surface of the earth (P. Rogers 2001).

The ambition of the USAF ever since the 1960s has been to turn outer space into the ultimate 'high ground' from which wars could be conducted and won. Air Force General Thomas White claimed the 'people who control space will control the world' (quoted in B. Chapman 2008, 17). Apart from the use of space for communications, reconnaissance, weapons guidance and weather monitoring, space is increasingly seen as a future battlefield. This battlefield will not be inhabited by human fighters, but by a myriad of unmanned spacecraft, some of which could be armed and capable of disabling ballistic missiles or satellites in space. In the 'Vision for 2020' the US Space Command argues that 'during the early portion of the 21st century, space power will also evolve into a separate and equal medium of warfare. Likewise, space forces will emerge to protect military and commercial national interests and investment in the space medium due to their increasing importance'

(US DoD 1997, 4). Like navies that protected trade routes, nations would develop space warfare capabilities for protecting their space assets.

In 1996 General Joseph Ashy said, 'It's politically sensitive, but it's going to happen. Some people don't want to hear this, and it sure isn't in vogue, but – absolutely – we're going to fight in space. We're going to fight from space and we're going to fight into space. That's why the U.S. has development programs in directed energy and hit-to-kill mechanisms' (Scott 1996, 51).

Despite this evident American desire to fight in space, there are up to now no space-based weapons known to be in existence that can strike targets in orbit or on earth, although anti-satellite (ASAT) weapons have been under development for some time. Space warfare remains up to now more of a vision than a fact. When it arrives (probably many years after 2020), space will, in any case, be no place for human warriors, but for superfast autonomous space weapons that can offer the required endurance, precision, speed and deadly efficiency.

The Transformation of Landpower

Land warfare is the oldest branch of warfare and also the most human-centric one. Traditionalists like Admiral J. C. Wiley argue that 'the ultimate determinant in war is the man on the scene with the gun. The man is the final power in war. He is in control' (Wiley 1967, 72). This conventional wisdom, which is still true for the current reality of war, is possibly about to change forever. Ground robots are already used in significant numbers for explosive ordnance removal and they are increasingly getting armed with machine guns, grenade launchers and Tasers. The autonomous robot soldier may still be in the more distant future, but there are few technological reasons that could prevent its eventual development. The 'man on the scene with the gun' could be replaced by the autonomous robot on the scene with a gun that could take over (under human supervision) most, if not all, of the functions of infantry soldiers.

Initially, robot soldiers could be introduced into small infantry units and operate as part of a team keeping soldiers out of danger and providing some additional impressive firepower (Sofge 2008b). But once soldiers have to confront military robots of an adversary, the battlefield might become far too lethal for humans and all the fighting will have to be taken over by robots. John Pike believes 'by the end of the century there will be virtually no humans on the battlefield ... Robots do what you tell them and they don't have to be trained' (*Arizona Star* 2007). Of course, robots are also fearless, are more easily replaceable and never get tired or distracted. In short, the advantages of robot soldiers are too great to ignore.

The Vision

The US Army has probably the most radical vision of transformation of all US service branches and aims to change its divisional structure, which it has had since the Second World War, to a modular structure organized in smaller, rapidly deployable self-sufficient combined arms brigade combat teams. Its current 10 large and heavy divisions comprising 15,000–20,000 soldiers each will be split into 42 brigades of about 3,500 soldiers (Sloan 2008, 25). The US Army is currently undergoing the most expensive and fundamental modernization in its history. According to the 'U.S. Army Posture Statement' the *Future Combat Systems* (FCS) program would be the core of the modernization effort:

> … and will provide our Soldiers an unparalleled understanding of their operational environment, increased precision and lethality, and enhanced survivability. These improved capabilities cannot be achieved by upgrading current vehicles and systems. FCS will use a combination of new manned and unmanned air and ground vehicles, connected by robust networks, to allow Soldiers to operate more effectively in the complex threat environments of the 21st century. (US DoD 2008, 5)

The US Army wants to field altogether 15 new brigade combat teams with the first one to be ready by 2015. Each brigade will consist of 2,245 soldiers equipped with 14 different FCSs, including eight classes of manned ground vehicles and up to six classes of unmanned systems, or altogether 151 robots (Weiner 2005a). All the vehicles are lightweight and optimized for the easy and quick transport into theater. The brigade would be fully digitized, meaning that soldiers and combat systems form a network (or system of systems) that makes available tactical information to any part of the network in near real time. The overall costs of the *FCS* program are currently estimated to be in excess of $300 billion (DiMascio 2006).

Several prototypes have been built so far, but the program is still evolving and it is probably too soon to predict the look and the final capabilities of the *FCS* as they will be fielded some time after 2012. The robots would be an integral part of the *FCS* concept and they would be partially tele-operated and partially capable of autonomous operation under human supervision. Some of them will be armed and might be able to fire their weapons autonomously. This includes not only armed unmanned vehicles, but also autonomous or tele-operated mortars and unattended sensors and missile launchers (AUSA 2007, 12–13).

Apart from the *FCS* the US Army is investing in a great range of robotic programs that will be used for automating logistics and some other non-combat functions. Some robot sentries for guarding bases and checking inventories have already been deployed in the US and elsewhere.

Sentry Robots

Since the 1980s some commercial sentry robots have been developed and some have already been marketed to potential military and civilian buyers. Quite well known is the *programmable robot with logical enemy response*, or *PROWLER*, which was 'the first outdoor robotic sentry/surveillance system' (Everett 1998). It was designed by the now-defunct Robot Defense Systems (RDS) in Colorado. *PROWLER* was a two ton sentry robot vehicle that could be armed with various weapons like machine guns or grenade launchers and could be programmed to fire at will (M. Rogers 1984). A security specialist at RDS claimed in a *Newsweek* interview in 1984 that robot sentries would be inevitable, simply because they would come much cheaper in the long run than armed security guards (M. Rogers 1984). Another obvious advantage of robot sentries is that they never get bored and that they will therefore perform their duties much more reliably than human guards.

Sentry robots could take over some police functions or could be employed by commercial security companies. Many of them will be stationary sensors that can respond to an intruder. However, some of them will be mobile and able to patrol a larger area autonomously. For example, General Dynamics has developed an armed sentry robot called *mobile detection assessment response system*, or *MDARS*, which has already successfully completed testing at Hawthorne Army Depot, Nevada (Osborn 2007). The US Army has recently awarded General Dynamics a $40 million contract to supply 24 more of the four-wheeled and semi-autonomous guard vehicles. The vehicles can patrol a military facility, can check inventories and gates, spot intruders over 300 yards and operate 16 hours without refuelling (Shachtman 2008b). *MDARS* could be armed with non-lethal weapons (controlled by a human operator) that can attack intruders over a range of 30 yards.

Another good example is the *Guardium* robotic vehicle developed by Israeli Aerospace Industries (IAI). It is capable of autonomous operation on- and off-road and will carry weapons that would be controlled by human operators from a command center. *Guardium* can reach a speed of 50 mph and can carry a payload of 660lbs. including sophisticated sensor equipment for the detection of intrusion. It would be well suited for patrolling a security perimeter, sensitive sites and infrastructure and for the suppression of 'suspicious elements' that come close to it. A *Guardium* security vehicle costs about $600,000 per unit and the control station comes at several million dollars (Farrell 2008). Israel is also deploying stationary sentry robots armed with 50-caliber machine guns along its 37-mile-long border with Gaza. There will be a 1-mile broad, potentially automated, 'kill zone' in which individuals and vehicles can be engaged with computer-controlled machine guns and missiles. Although there would be a man in the loop for the time being, the Israeli Defense Forces (IDF) might allow autonomous operation at a later point (Arkin 2007, 5).

Quite similar is Korea's Samsung Techwin *SGR-A1* stationary sentry robot, which might soon guard the border to North Korea and other important national sites and infrastructure (BBC 2005b). It will be equipped with lethal and non-lethal weapons and can be controlled by an operator or operate autonomously. *SGR-A1* will be able to detect intruders with infrared sensors over a distance of 2.5 miles. Once intruders come close enough (circa 500 yards), the sentry robot can sound an alarm or even open fire. It is expected that South Korea is going to buy 1,000 *Techwins* at a cost of $200,000 each, but there are still technical problems that need to be ironed out. Some mobile sentry robots are also under development.

South Korea's armed forces are pushing hard for the rapid deployment of military robots because they fear that recruitment shortfalls could weaken the country's ability to counter an attack by the North. North Korea still has more than 1 million men under arms (*The Star* 2006).

Unmanned Land Combat

The *FCS* will enable the US Army to conduct unmanned ground operations. It will altogether include three classes of UGVs that can be used for forward reconnaissance and even ground combat. Lockheed Martin is developing the backbone of all the UGVs in the *FCS* program: the *multifunction utility/logistics and equipment* (or *MULE*), which is the size of a *HUMVEE* and which could be ready by 2014. The *MULE* will come in three variants: the transport, counter-mine and assault versions (ARV) – all of them capable of semi-autonomous operation (US Army 2008). The *MULE-ARV* is a light, wheeled, unmanned tank weighing about 9.3 tons and it could carry 30mm guns and *Hellfire* missiles. *MULE* will in principle have the ability to identify, track and engage a target, but a human will remain in the loop for making the final decision over weapons use. Military robotics expert Erik Sofge explains it in the following way: 'If a target is detected, the machine will calculate its own firing solutions and wait for a remote human operator to pull the trigger' (Sofge 2008b). The US Army plans to procure at least 1,700 *MULEs* in different versions (Sofge 2008a).

Further in the future the Pentagon wants to build robots on legs because legged robots could cope with much more difficult terrain than vehicles on wheels or tracks. Wheeled vehicles only allow access to 30 percent of the earth's land surface, while tracked vehicles allow access to up to 50 percent (Shaker and Wise 1988, 73). In other words, legged robots could conquer the other half of the land surface, which has been off limits for military land vehicles so far. Most likely such legged military robots would not resemble the *Imperial Walkers* from *Star Wars*, but would rather look like oversized insects or bugs, as they would have to keep their silhouette low for stealthiness. A lot of progress has already been made in building legged robots. The experimental small robot *Big Dog* can move on four legs, can negotiate difficult terrain and can even keep upright if it is kicked during movement. *Big Dog* could follow soldiers into combat and carry their gear and additional ammunition. *Big Dog* is still remote-controlled, but a fully autonomous version could be fielded by 2014 (Lerner 2006b). Still further in the future are tank-size, legged autonomous robots that could carry an impressive amount of firepower. Apparently, there are already plans for an autonomous legged hunter-killer robot, which could be heavily armed and be developed by 2032 (Lopez-Calderon 2006). That walking robots are no longer science fiction is also proven by the heavy machine company John Deere, which has recently developed a prototype of a van-size legged robot for logging, which is called *Timberjack Walking Machine*. *Timberjack* has an operator inside, who controls the six-legged machine with a simple joystick (Lippert 2008).

Supersoldiers and Robot Soldiers

A recent Hollywood blockbuster was *Iron Man*, which showed off arms producer Tony Stark confronting his enemies in a futuristic exoskeleton that turned him into a technologically enabled superman. *Iron Man* carried tank-defeating missiles and could outfly fighter jets. Nothing less than that seems to be the ambition of the US Army, which aims at turning its soldiers into invincible 'one-man tanks' or 'F-16 on legs' (Ames 2003). For this purpose the Army has funded several programs that view the individual soldier as an advanced weapons system. The first program that stated this goal was the now officially cancelled *Land Warrior* system (Scully 2007), which featured a helmet-mounted display with tactical Internet, digital communications, night vision, GPS and a thermal-imaging and video scope on the weapon that allowed soldiers to defeat enemy camouflage and to shoot around corners (Cerasini 2003, 37–8). The current program is called *Future Force Warrior* and will include improved versions of all of the above and, apart from that, a new powerful *Metal Storm* weapon[1] and a powered exoskeleton for which Robert Heinlein's 1959 novel *Starship Troopers* provided the inspiration (M. Williams 2006a).

The Army 'Iron Men' or cyborg soldiers could be a first step toward the eventual development of autonomous robot soldiers. Powered exoskeletons for human soldiers would provide at least some of the advantages of robots: more protection, superior strength, greater firepower and improved mobility. The Army's *Future Force Warrior* would essentially be a robot that has a human inside.

The US Marine Corps has a similar research program for robotic exoskeletons that could equip humans with superhuman strength. It is called *Marine Exoskeletal Augmentation Program* (MEPAC) and would allow soldiers to move heavy equipment much faster. Raytheon Sarcos has already demonstrated a fully functional prototype of a gas-powered robotic exoskeleton that could be fielded in a few years from now – not as a 'combat suit' but rather as a 'power suit', as featured in *Aliens*, which can be used for loading big cannon shells or for lifting other heavy equipment. Few other applications are currently possible, as the suit still requires a power cord (Page 2008c).

However, the disadvantages of such 'human inside' cyborg warriors would be numerous, too. Most importantly, human cyborgs with robotic exoskeletons would be enormously expensive, thus limiting the numbers of soldiers that can be equipped with them. Some US soldiers in Iraq already carry gear worth $100,000 each and this includes no fancy exoskeletons, jetpacks or nano-armor. As soldier equipment gets ever more sophisticated, it is no surprise that the US Army's

---

1   A *Metal Storm* weapon has the projectiles stacked one after the other inside the barrel instead of loading them from a magazine. A computer chip controls the triggering of each round and this achieves a rate of fire of up to 1 million rounds per minute. *Metal Storm* weapons are believed to be perfect for military robots, as the weapons never jam, have no recoil and can be easily computer-controlled (compare Gourley 2001).

Assistant Secretary of Acquisition, General Yakovac, said: 'I believe eventually we are heading to the "million-dollar" man' (NDM 2005). How big an army could one field at such inflationary cost? Secondly, it would be unavoidable to significantly and maybe permanently modify the bodies of cyborg soldiers to make them more effective (Singer 2008), which will create serious ethical dilemmas. For example, will cyborg soldiers ever be allowed to quit once millions of dollars have been invested into their body upgrades?[2] Finally, there would be ethical questions over whether permanent body improvements, genetic or otherwise, should be permitted at all in liberal societies committed to the idea of equality and equal chances.

Creating robot soldiers from the beginning would simply sidestep the problems connected to cyborg warriors and it might be more effective and cheaper in the long run as well. Defense expert John Arquilla likened the attempt of making the individual soldier invincible to the 'armored knight of the middle ages' (quoted in M. Williams 2006a). Cyborg soldiers could turn out to be a niche technology rather than the mainstream of future warfare. More revolutionary in terms of warfare could be the combination of AI, robotics and nanotechnology, which could lead to the development of weapons that are powerful beyond imagination.

A declared goal of Pentagon planners is the development of a *Terminator*-like humanoid military robot, which could fight in human environments such as cities and inside buildings. A study by the Alpha analysis group of the US Joint Forces Command, which was created in 2002 to guide the US armed forces' 'transformation', explored the role of military robots. The title of the study was 'Unmanned Effects: Taking the Human Out of the Loop' and it predicted that the *tactical autonomous combatant* (TAC), or the humanoid military robot, could be a reality as soon as 2025.[3] The aim is (at least officially) not to completely replace human soldiers, but to equip them with new capabilities at the tactical level. The leader of the Alpha group, Gordon Johnson, argued in an interview that TACs would only be deployed if they fulfilled three conditions: 1) they would only be used in combat if their performance matched the performance of humans; 2) they would have to demonstrate that they would protect human life; 3) they would need to be cost-effective (Lawlor 2003b). DARPA has recently suggested a research project to build autonomous robots that can work as team members of a human-led small infantry unit. The robots could be directed (presumably by voice) to kick in doors of urban dwellings and enter them before human soldiers do (Turse 2008a, 246).

---

2   Tim Blackmore points at the case of a special operations soldier who got a computerized prosthetic leg that enabled him to go back into battle. Blackmore asks: 'What if the soldier wishes to leave the field with such a sophisticated, expensive limb? Will the soldier be asked to trade in the limb for a more standard steel prosthetic ... What if the soldier can't have the limb unless he works (for the army) to pay it off?' (Blackmore 2005, 198).

3   This study is not in the public domain, but a summary of it was published on the US Joint Forces Command website and is now archived (after having been withdrawn from the web) under: <http://web.archive.org/web/20021022172516/http://www.jfcom.mil/about/fact_alpha.htm> accessed 25 May 2008

The Marine Corps is already planning for an unmanned future and anticipates that at some point the human inside its MEPAC might become unnecessary. The robotic exoskeletons would then become, according to the program specification, a 'fully sensing and interactive endoskeletal entity that has outgrown its practical need for unmitigated Marine contact, and can act constructively on its own' (Shachtman 2007c).

Other armed forces are also interested in fielding robot soldiers for urban warfare. In 2007, Singapore also announced its goal to build a military robot that can fight in urban environments like a human soldier. Singapore's Defense Science and Technology agency offered $650,000 to anybody who could develop a robot soldier for urban combat and aims to deploy such a system as soon as possible. One particular challenge is that the robot would have to navigate without GPS inside buildings so that it could autonomously explore the upper floors of a building (*New Scientist* 2007a).

At the moment there are still considerable obstacles to building humanoid robot soldiers. The biggest problem is probably finding a suitable power source for such robots: 'Lithium-ion batteries won't do it' (Benford and Malartre 2007, 156). The small size of humanoid robots would effectively prevent them running on fuel like a vehicle or using a nuclear reactor like a nuclear submarine. For being effective on future battlefields, TACs would need to be able to operate for one day without the need to recharge their power source. Honda's humanoid walking robot *Asimo* only manages to operate for about one hour before it needs to recharge its batteries (Honda 2005). In addition, it is still very difficult to equip such robots with enough intelligence to operate effectively, even when under general human direction, but this problem might be solvable in a time frame of 10–20 years. In the meantime, 'humanoids' might be tele-operated and used for very limited and specific roles. For example, an American company, Vecna Technologies, has announced that it wants to build a humanoid robot that can be used for extracting wounded soldiers from the battlefield without putting other soldiers or medics at risk. The so-called *Bear* robot would use a combination of legs and tracks and would be able to step over obstacles and carry a soldier (Simms 2008).

Land warfare is probably the most challenging task for military robots because of the immense complexity of the environment and the required versatility of robots, which might have to operate within civilian populations with lots of humans around who shall not be harmed. Up to now, it is not quite clear whether autonomous military robots would ever be capable of operating under such conditions without endangering non-combatants. Even the president of General Dynamics Robotics Systems, Scott Myers, admitted in an interview with *USA Today* that 'we're a long way from being there' (Komarow 2006). However, if the task was to fight a fast, high-intensity war in which necessity dictates having little regard for civilian casualties, robots would be most likely to perform much better than humans in the long run. They would be fearless, would shoot faster and more precisely and they could fight 24 hours a day, seven days a week without suffering from fatigue.

The Transformation of Seapower

The future of naval warfare will be characterized by two phenomena: the disappearance of large capital ships and a broadening of the mission for navies. The navies around the world are getting smaller and smaller and in the future fewer countries will be able to support a 'blue water' navy. The number of US warships has dropped from 600 at the end of the Cold War to currently 285, and the number of Royal Navy ships dropped from 160 in 1990 to 82 in 2007. Secondly, the mission has broadened because large naval battles have become extremely unlikely. Instead navies will engage much more in littoral combat. Their mission has already expanded to include activities such as fighting piracy, terrorism and smuggling, transporting troops and attacking targets on land – activities which will continue to grow in importance.

In addition, the classical navy mission of being able to fight other navies and to project power overseas is becoming ever more difficult because of technological development that favors the defense and makes surface fleets increasingly vulnerable. Even during most of the Cold War, surface fleets were threatened by anti-ship missiles of ever greater sophistication. The response to the threat has been adding additional layers of protection to capital ships and in particular to aircraft carriers. US carrier groups are heavily protected by a whole array of ships that accompany them, including a nuclear submarine, several frigates and one *Aegis* cruiser (Libicki 1994, Ch. 1). Analysts fear that soon it could be futile to protect capital ships once hypersonic cruise missiles are available to potential enemies (Friedman and Friedman 1996, 180–204). As a result of spaceborne surveillance and terrestrial sensor networks, fleets can no longer hide in the vastness of the oceans, but can be tracked and engaged from increasingly long range. Large capital ships and aircraft carriers would no longer be able to survive in such an environment.

It is not clear what will eventually replace current warships, but future warships are likely to be much smaller, stealthier and longer range. In the long run, submarines might be the only type of large warship that still makes sense because they are so difficult to track (Keegan 1988, 317–19). New technologies could enable submarines to dive deeper and could even enable military bases on the seabed (Zhongchang et al. 1998). Some analysts suggest using simpler and cheaper ships that would effectively be 'trucks' for deployment of a range of unmanned systems. One idea that was temporarily pursued in the 1990s was the so-called *Arsenal Ship* concept. The *Arsenal Ship* would have been a large but stealthy warship that carried 500 vertically launched cruise missiles and that could be operated by a very small crew of no more than 50 sailors (Leonard et al. 1999, 127–9). The military analyst Christopher Cavas has taken this general idea further by proposing thinking of ships and submarines as 'mother ships' that can 'send off swarms of unmanned things' (Cavas 2004). They could launch UAVs and UCAVs for reconnaissance and strike missions, small unmanned surface vehicles (USVs) for littoral combat missions or unmanned underwater vehicles (UUVs) for mine-clearing or anti-submarine warfare. The ships carrying the swarms of unmanned and robotic systems could be converted container ships and could have very small crews or no crews at all. It is unlikely that a fully roboticized navy could be possible, as the oceans are a challenging environment to operate in, but there are few technological reasons why navies should not increasingly rely on unmanned systems for most of their missions, including monitoring the coastal regions and for littoral warfare.

The Vision

The US Navy produced a vision paper in 1992 entitled 'Forward ... From the Sea', which noted the shift 'away from having to deal with a global maritime threat and toward projecting power and influence across the seas in response to regional challenges' (US DoD 1992, 1). The vision emphasized the Navy's mission to protect the sea lanes, to project power and to cooperate with other navies. Naval forces would provide a peacetime presence in crisis regions, would be able to quickly respond to crises and could play a key role in fighting regional conflicts. The Navy would allow a 'Maritime Prepositioning Force', which would not be dependent on forward land bases and which would enable the Navy to launch attacks from the sea through its carrier battle groups. Furthermore, the Navy vision pointed at the Navy's ability to dominate the littoral battlespace and to deploy and support ground forces in the littoral areas. The report closes with the Navy's intention to expand its littoral warfare capabilities.

Although a lot of the ideas about network-centric warfare originated from the US Navy, the Navy is paradoxically not very willing to accept many of the implications of the Revolution in Military Affairs (RMA). Most of its current procurement programs are very traditionally minded and primarily aimed at improving existing designs and systems rather than replacing them with newer and more revolutionary systems. For example, the Navy is still investing heavily in aircraft carriers and has ordered two new *CVN-21* supercarriers, which can only marginally provide more firepower than current *Nimitz* class carriers with 25 percent of increased sortie generation (US Navy 2008). Another example is the new *Virginia* class submarine, which will simply replace the nuclear *Los Angeles* class attack submarines. Somewhat less traditional are the now partially cancelled *DDG-1000 Zumwalt* destroyer and the *littoral combat ship* (LCS). The *LCS* is less traditional because of its modular design, which allows it to be equipped with a variety of mission-specific packages. However, all of these Navy procurement programs are already vastly over budget. The *CVN-21* was originally expected to cost $8 billion each and now is estimated at $9.6 billion each; the cost for a *Virginia* class submarine has gone up 35 percent to a projected $2.6 billion each; the cost for the *DDG-1000* has shot up from $2.8 billion to $3.8 billion; and the projected cost for the basic module of the *LCS* has been adjusted from $200 million each to $300 million each (US Congress 2006, 15–21). In effect, it would require some unlikely miracles, as Admiral Cebrowski said in a speech, for the

Navy to realize its goals (Fuentes 2005). The *DDG-1000* destroyer has already been partially cancelled and more cuts could follow. Instead, Cebrowski suggests building a much larger fleet of smaller and inexpensive vessels, many of which could be unmanned (Shah 2005).

The US Navy has been very reluctant to incorporate robotic systems, though the new ships it has ordered will have a high degree of automation that allows significantly smaller crews to sail them. However, completely robotic systems are still too novel a concept for the Navy and have met considerable resistance. The best example is the *X-47* UCAS, which still has a very uncertain future. The Navy is skeptical that unmanned aircraft could be able to master 'the challenging carrier environment', in particular carrier landings and mid-air refueling, both of which would be crucial for most missions for naval aircraft (Butler 2007). The transformation to a navy consisting of a large fleet of smaller, primarily unmanned systems could take many decades.

Littoral and Surface Warfare

The US Navy and some other navies are interested in deploying USVs because they are cheap and have a lot of endurance. They could be used for patrolling coasts and harbors to fight smuggling and piracy. They might also prove useful in littoral warfare, for example backing up amphibious landings or for attacking coastal defenses. The only USV that is already operational worldwide is the Israeli/British/American *Protector*, which has been in use with the Singapore Navy since 2005 (*Defense Update* 2006). *Protector* is a very fast and stealthy unmanned speed boat and is equipped with sophisticated sensor systems for ocean surveillance and targeting. In addition, it carries a machine gun, which can be remotely controlled. The system is now being aggressively marketed to the US Coast Guard and the US Navy by BAE Systems and Lockheed Martin.

Underwater Warfare

UUVs were first developed in the 1970s, mainly for the purpose of oceanographic mapping. In recent years the interest of national navies in UUVs has grown substantially. There are currently hundreds of different UUV types under development worldwide, but many technical problems are not yet solved (Tiron 2002). Unmanned operations in the deep sea present the particular challenge that radio signals for controlling UUVs do not travel well in water (Bongard and Sayers 2002, 304). As a result, navies normally use cables to control UUVs from manned platforms, which allows them to carry out missions such as providing communications and reconnaissance. However, an autonomous design would be much more preferable or would even be the only viable solution for some missions. Autonomous military UUVs would be primarily used for mine-hunting or mine-laying and future versions could even find and disable sea mines buried in the seabed. Apparently, the US Navy already successfully used *Remus* UUVs for the clearance of mines in the Iraqi port of Um Qasr in 2003. According to defense analyst James Carafano, '*Remus* robots searched nearly a square-mile area and removed a number of mines in 16 hours. Divers would have needed 21 days to complete the same mission' (Carafano 2007). UUVs could also be used for anti-submarine warfare, reconnaissance, mine counter-measures and for special operations. They are usually designed to fit into a torpedo tube and could loiter in an assigned area of the ocean and track and follow contacts. Potentially, UUVs could in the future carry weapons and could hunt and kill enemy submarines by themselves.

Naval Aviation

The range of carrier-based aircraft has only marginally improved since the Second World War and is about 200–450 nautical miles without aerial refueling. A study by the Center for Strategic and Budgetary Assessments asks rhetorically: 'Will an operational strike system with limited tactical reach and persistence – one optimized for pulsed strikes against land targets at ranges out to about 450–475 nm – be able to tackle future operational challenges and threats that are likely to appear over the long term? The answer is: probably not' (Ehrhard and Work 2007, 26). For improving the range and endurance of carrier aircraft there are two main possibilities: the first option is to replace the carrier aircraft with a cruise missile that can autonomously destroy pre-set targets over large distances (the *Arsenal Ship* concept); the second option is to carrier-base UCAVs that could strike targets at a range of 1,500 nautical miles without aerial refueling (Ehrhard and Work 2007, 2).

   Since 2000, the US Navy has invested in one UCAV program, designated *X-47 Pegasus* and managed by Boeing and Northrop Grumman. While the former Air Force program of Joint Unmanned Combat Air System (*J-UCAS/X-45*) has been cancelled, the *X-47* UCAS-D program is still alive and on track for a possible deployment of carrier-based UCAVs by 2020. The naval UCAV would have five times the endurance of manned carrier-based aircraft and would have much greater range, which allows carriers to attack over greater distances and stay out of the range of enemy fire. UCAVs would also be stealthier, more survivable and could take over more dangerous missions. The UCAV could carry a great variety of smart weapons, including air-to-air missiles. Currently, the *X-47* would be less capable than the *F-18E/F* and *F-35N* in terms of speed and payload, but this could be compensated through its better endurance and the employment of greater numbers. However, combat roles for unmanned aircraft could still be too bitter a pill to swallow for the admirals in the US Navy (Page 2007c).

   Overall, there could be a robotics revolution in the area of naval warfare in the making, but paradoxically it may not originate from the US. Smaller navies might be under bigger financial pressure to incorporate unmanned systems in order to compensate for the lack of expensive large capital ships. Unmanned naval systems could prove to be highly effective for coastal defense and as area denial weapons locating targets and laying mines. Finally, the realm of the deep sea would be an environment, like outer space, which would be far better suited for robots than for humans.

The final section of this chapter deals with robots conquering the microscopic space. The nanotechnology revolution of warfare may be even more far-reaching than all of the robotic systems described above.

The Nanotechnology Revolution of Warfare

The revolution in military robotics and AI goes hand in hand and will in part be enabled by the nanotechnology revolution, which some observers believe will have a tremendous impact on all areas of society in the next few decades. It can be said that there is a moderate vision and a radical vision of nanotechnology. The former offers a more complex picture, while the latter appears to have more in common with science fiction, rather than with reality. The radical visionaries of nanotechnology affirm that paradise would be possible, but that nanotechnology could also create dangers that are simply unprecedented in their scale and potential consequences. Of course, nanotechnology will also affect warfare and will enable all kinds of 'cool new weapons' (Gubrud 1997). However, the most dangerous weapons of all could be molecular-size programmable machines capable of self-replication, or 'nanobots' or 'nanites'. Nobody knows for sure whether or not such machines would be possible, but nobody can completely rule it out either.

The Nanotechnology Vision

Richard Feynman is usually credited to be the visionary who laid the foundations of nanotechnology. He delivered a lecture to the American Physical Society in 1959 with the title 'There Is Plenty of Room at the Bottom' in which he proposed building very small machines and storing large amounts of information in very small spaces. He offered $1,000 to the first person to develop a motor no bigger than 1/64 of one inch and another $1,000 for the first person to shrink a page with text to 1/25,000 of its size (Berube 2006, 51). His most famous scholar was Eric Drexler, who coined the term 'nanotechnology' and who formulated an elaborated vision of nanotechnology in his influential book *Engines of Creation* (Drexler 1987). In his book, Drexler claimed that molecular machines could be able to assemble practically everything imaginable in a very short time, provided there is enough raw material, energy and construction plan. 'Machines able to grasp and position individual atoms will be able to build almost anything by bonding the right atoms together in the right pattern' (Drexler 1987, 58). The assemblers would resemble factories of a cellular scale with assembler arms that mechanically move atoms. Of course, a molecular assembler would be able to build copies of itself and the number of assemblers could grow at an exponential rate, which would enormously speed up construction processes. Similar to von Neumann machines, the molecular assemblers would have to consist of several assembler arms, a 'tape' of instructions and a simple computer (Drexler 1987, 57). 'Armies' of molecular assemblers could even construct very large objects like skyscrapers very quickly. In effect, the vision and promise of nanotechnology as formulated by Drexler was that of creating a new age of abundance, where humble raw materials could be used for creating flawless things in unlimited quantities. Furthermore, nanotechnology would enable nanobots that repair our bodies from the inside, strong AI and computers that can store our minds, cheap space travel and much more.

But Drexler also warned that a nanotech future would not only be the key to paradise, it could also result in our doom. Those fantastic self-replicating and assembling nanobots could replicate out of control and consume our world. Drexler describes it in the following words:

> Tough, omnivorous 'bacteria' could out-compete real bacteria: they could spread like blowing pollen, replicate swiftly, and reduce the biosphere to dust in a matter of days. Dangerous replicators could easily be too tough, small, and rapidly spreading to stop – at least if we made no preparation. (Drexler 1987, 172)

Up to now, the threat of runaway nanobots remains hypothetical. The current reality of nanotechnology is somewhat different.

The Current Reality of Nanotechnology

After two decades of research, nanotechnology is now at an advanced stage of development with growing economic significance. An early industry study called 'Big Money in Thinking Small: Nanotechnology What Investors Need to Know' assessed the economic impact of nanotechnology as quite substantial and cited several similar reports.

> *In Realis* predicted $100 billion by 2005, $800 billion by 2010, and up to $2 trillion by 2015. *Evolution Capital* estimated that yearly nano sales are currently $20–$50 billion, and growth will be $150 billion in 2005 and $1 trillion by 2010. The NNI estimated that 2001 sales were $30 million, and that 2015 sales will reach $1 trillion – a 110 percent compound annual growth rate. (Mauboussin and Bartholdson 2003, 14)

Of course, one needs to be very careful with these frequently quoted trillion-dollar figures, as they tend to be based on calculations that do not distinguish between the value of finished products and the value of their actual nanotechnology (NT) components (Keim 2007). Anyhow, many countries have by now recognized the importance of staying ahead in the nanotechnology field and have launched national funding schemes. It has been estimated that at least 30 states have nationally funded research projects in the area of nanotechnology and spent $3 billion on it in 2003 alone. The biggest government-funded research effort is the American National Nanotechnology Initiative (NNI), which was officially launched in 2001. It covers the establishment of research centers, the funding of particular research programs and investment in nanotech start-ups. NNI funding totaled $697 million in 2002 and reached $1.4 billion in 2007 with a further increase planned for 2009 (US Executive Office of the President 2008). Outside the US, Japan, Germany, the UK and South Korea have substantial national funding programs for nanotechnology, with growing revenues generated by companies through nanotechnology applications (Nanowerk 2007).

Nanoscience and nanotechnology comprise a great variety of disciplines and applications and cover several industries. Closely associated to nanotechnology are the disciplines of physics, chemistry, molecular biology, engineering and electronics. Main applications range from new, extremely hard materials (carbon nanotubes) to detergents, cosmetics, new microprocessors and much more.

Military Applications

Nanotechnology could revolutionize several sectors of military relevance, including computing, sensors, materials, robotics and medicine, within the next decades (Altmann 2006, 61–79). There is already a growing awareness on the part of military organizations about the potential of nanotechnology, which is indicated by the growing military funding for nanotechnology-related research. The US DoD undoubtedly leads the way. It founded the Institute for Soldier Nanotechnologies at MIT in 2002 and Pentagon funding of nanotechnology research went up to $450 million in 2007 (US Executive Office of the President 2008). The British military has also expressed its desire to utilize nanotechnology for the development of better weapons and equipment. Numerous British government reports have already stressed the growing importance of military nanotechnology. For example, the Development, Concepts and Doctrine Centre of the British MoD claims that:

> Nanotechnology *will* result in more-capable systems and artefacts that are smaller, lighter, cheaper and less energy hungry. Out to 2020, its application is *likely* to be predominantly in electronics and materials, including bacteria resistant agents, stain resistant materials and nanocomposite materials. After 2020, nanodevices are *likely*, such as nanobots. (UK MoD 2006, 59)

Another, earlier MoD study pointed out that possible military uses of nanotechnology could include cryptography, precision weapons, stealth and counter-stealth, network-centric warfare (NCW), miniature batteries, decision aids, self-repairing military equipment, new medical treatments, new miniature sensors and new weapons of mass destruction (WMD) (UK MoD 2001).

The biggest near-term benefit that the military could gain through nano-technology is the miniaturization of weapons systems and sensors, as well as the development of ever more powerful computers that can be used for controlling

AW and mini/micro-systems. In particular, nanotechnology could enable the development of super-fast quantum computers that would be by many orders of magnitude faster than current computers (Dunne 2006). Nanotechnological approaches to computing may enable biological-based computer systems (biochips) that could be far better in cognitive tasks than today's computers, which mainly excel in numerical computation. It also means that computers will shrink so much in size that very powerful computers could be incorporated into small machines or even in textiles, allowing 'wearable computers'.

Something that has been on the military's wish list for a while are small sensors that can detect the presence of chemical or biological agents. A nanodot with a string of DNA attached to it could precisely determine the presence of one particular toxin. A great number of such nanosensors could be integrated into a small computer chip that reduces a lab to the size of a fingernail. Such WMD-detector chips could be built into the uniform of soldiers and could highlight a WMD threat in a soldier's helmet display (Ratner and Ratner 2004, 39–43). Nanosensors could be used for detecting many other physical changes such as heat, electrical or magnetic forces or pressure. In theory, nanosensors could be made mobile by putting them on a micro-robot. Such microscopic-scale robots could be able to fly by using a small rotor, possibly guided by a GPS signal. DARPA has recently even proposed funding a chemical shape-shifting robot that could squeeze itself through small openings in buildings, such as under doors. Although the 'ChemBot' idea sounds a bit like the T-1000 in *Terminator 2*, it would rather be based on an imitation of soft creatures such as snails (K. C. Jones 2007).

Nanoparticles could be engineered as networked sensors and distributed widely on the battlefield. Kristofer Pister from the University of California has introduced the concept of 'smart dust', which would be micro electromechanical systems the size of a grain of sand. Smart dust micro-robots could be powered by micro power sources and could be used as intelligent sensor networks. Every single 'smart dust' micromachine would only possess a rudimentary capability, but deployed in larger numbers (maybe in millions) they could form an intelligent sensor network that could survey a large area and that could detect and identify objects by their signature. Such a smart dust network could be highly resilient, as a large proportion of the smart dust network would need to be destroyed in order to degrade it (Hambling 2005, 329).

Nanotechnology may not allow making macro-scale objects completely invisible, but it can result in the development of chameleon-like camouflage. 'By changing the colour(s) and texture to that of the background, the person/object would merge with it' (Altmann 2006, 82). At least from a distance, such chameleon camouflage could make soldiers or vehicles near invisible. Furthermore, nanotechnology could enable the development of very light and extremely hard materials that can be used as armor for soldiers and platforms, which could significantly improve their survivability on future battlefields. Soldiers could also carry biosensors monitoring their medical condition and microneedles worked into their combat suits could inject drugs for greater performance. It might even be possible to enhance body tissue like muscles to make soldiers stronger or to implant computer chips into the brain as a neural interface (Altmann 2006, 88–91).

Nano-wars

Although hardly any nanotechnology-based military systems have been deployed so far, there are already several military thinkers who have tried to envision a nanotech war. One of the first analysts, who developed a theoretical framework of a war with small machines, was Martin Libicki from the National Defense University. He developed the concept of 'Fire Ant Warfare' in his influential paper 'The Mesh and the Net/Speculations on Armed Conflict in an Age of Free Silicon' (Libicki 1994). His argument is that the current revolution of warfare would undergo three stages. The first one he calls 'Pop Up Warfare', which was the kind of war conducted by the US in Operation Desert Storm: large platforms employing stealth and long-range precision-guided munitions (PGMs). The second stage he calls 'The Mesh', which will be enabled by large numbers of sensors distributed on the battlefield. The sensors will locate and quickly destroy the enemy whenever they go out in the open. The final stage would be 'Fire Ant Warfare', which is the logical conclusion to The Mesh. Sensors become ever smaller and ever numerous, which means that ever smaller objects will be detected and tracked by it. As a result, large platforms are no longer survivable and wars will be fought by smaller and smaller robotic systems. The 'battlefield [would be] dominated by scads of sensors, emitters, and microprojectiles', which could be hidden in terrain and could remain operational for a very long duration waiting for an enemy to pass by (Libicki 1994).

Other analysts like Steven Metz have picked up Libicki's vision and have pointed out that technology could make Fire Ant Warfare possible relatively soon. In 1996 Sandia National Labs had already developed a *micro autonomous robotic vehicle* (MARV) the size of a cubic inch with all necessary mobility, computing power and energy supply for operating autonomously. Since then ever smaller machines have been built. For example, the New York University professor Nadrian Seeman has even built a nano-size walking robot made from DNA fragments (Ichbiah 2005, 498).

Analysts from the National Defense University suggested weaponizing biological nanobots:

> In unconventional terms, bionanobots might be designed that, when ingested from the air by humans, would assay DNA codes and self destruct in those persons whose codes had been programmed. Nanobots could attack certain kinds of metals, lubricants, or rubber, destroying conventional weaponry by literally consuming it. (Petersen and Egan 2002)

Such lethal nanobots might not arrive very soon, but weaponized mini-robots of a size of less than 1/2 inch are much closer to reality. While it could be possible to remote-control a single mini/micro-robot used for a particular reconnaissance or assassination mission, mini/micro-robots deployed in swarms of thousands would have to be able to operate largely autonomously because individual control by a human operator would be technically unfeasible (Dudenhoeffer and Jones 2000, 973). Human control over swarms of mini/micro-robots could only be retained on a higher strategic level.

The implication of such invisible armies of mini/micro-machines that can track everything and everybody and which might be able to attack biological or mechanical systems will be that the role of humans would be inevitably largely reduced. War would expand into the microscopic space with invisible machines taking over the sensing and killing. The long-term perspectives for nanotech wars are frightening, especially if assemblers and molecular manufacturing would be possible and practical (Gubrud 1997).

Nanotechnology could revolutionize fabrication and shrink factories so much in size that they would no longer be detectable by traditional means. They could produce anything and destroying them would only result in the rapid creation of new ones (T. McCarthy 2001). Nanotechnology could also make it possible to build extensive underground facilities for civil defense that could allow a nuclear weapons state to survive a nuclear war with relative ease (Gubrud 1997). Autonomous nanobots could construct such underground bunkers in a way that it would not be noticeable from the air or space. Whole underground cities could be created in complete secrecy. As such defenses would be relatively inexpensive, states might even compete to create them, reminiscent of the 'mine shaft gap' in *Dr. Strangelove* with the similarly precarious outcome of making a nuclear war more likely.

Military intervention overseas could become technically easy, as it would only be necessary to transport some small nano-factories abroad, which could then in place simply produce tanks and any other equipment needed within hours. Spare parts and any additional equipment could arrive by 'fax machine'. Permanent stocks of military equipment or permanent overseas bases could become unnecessary (Toffler and Toffler 1995, 221–4). If nano-factories could produce AW, then it would not even be necessary to deploy many human soldiers, if at all, which would further reduce the logistical footprint. This means in a nanotech war no side could ever win through attrition or fancy tactics, only by overwhelming the other side in an instant and most devastating surprise attack (Gubrud 1997).

Traditional deterrents could become irrelevant once whole new armies could be created in days (Hambling 2005, 368–9). It would be useless to attack the enemy's forces in the field or his production capacity. As a result:

> Military planners will seek a target that is large enough to find and hit, and that cannot be easily replaced. The natural choice, given the circumstances, will be civilian populations ... So, too, will the future targeting of civilians be a choice of desperation, made by planners desperate for something they can find and destroy. (T. McCarthy 2001)

Mass murder on a global scale could be the possible, or even the most likely, result of a future nanotech war.

Conclusion: Traditionalists versus Revolutionaries

This chapter has shown that military robots have a lot of potential and that current US service visions at least implicitly acknowledge the importance of unmanned systems for the planned transformation of the armed forces. However, there is also a lot of institutional resistance by the traditionalists in the armed forces to the idea of military robots in combat roles. Twenty years ago Steven Shaker and Alan Wise pointed out that 'the resistance of factory workers to the entry of industrial robots could be minor compared to the unwillingness of some of the military has towards accepting combat robotics ... Their resistance is likely to be fiercer to what has occurred in the factories' (Shaker and Wise 1988, 170).

It is certainly true that the US armed forces, which are in the lead in terms of utilizing robotics, have an ambivalent, if not contradictory position towards military robots. On the one hand, the number of research projects in the area of military robotics seems to grow constantly, with more and more systems actually entering service. On the other hand, the US armed forces spend most of their procurement budget on very traditional items. The US Air Force spends most of its budget on manned aircraft such as the *F/A-22* and *F-35* fighter and strike aircraft; the Navy prioritizes two new supercarriers and the *Virginia* class submarine; and the Marines still invest heavily in the *V-22 Osprey* tilt-rotor aircraft. Only the Army is less traditional with its *FCS* and its large robot component. In terms of money, military robotics is still minuscule. Out of an overall procurement budget of $84 billion in 2007, only $2.7 billion or 3.2 percent were spent on unmanned systems (US DoD 2007).

The director of the Pentagon's study group Alpha, Russ Richards, acknowledges that 'the greatest hurdle is likely to be overcoming military culture ... Just getting present-day decision makers to allow robots to perform some functions that are currently being performed by humans will be difficult.' And he adds: 'It will be difficult to overcome the resistance to replacing human pilots, soldiers, sailors, and Marines with robots. Or, to allow machines to make decisions. The case will have to be made based on the imperatives' (Piquepaille 2003).

Bureaucratic infighting about the future of unmanned systems now seems to be in full swing. While the USAF aims for the control of all UAVs, it has also been very reluctant expanding the numbers of armed UAVs such as the *Predators*. The Air Force has also been most committed to the idea that only full pilots should be allowed to operate UAVs (Page 2007d). Recently Secretary of Defense Robert Gates had to relieve two Air Force generals of their duties, in part because they refused to expand drone operations (Page 2008f).

In the long term the armed forces will not be able to resist political, economic and operational pressures to increase the numbers and roles for unmanned systems once they become more capable. The US Congress mandated in 2001 that one-third of all combat aircraft shall be unmanned by 2010 and that one-third of all ground vehicles shall be unmanned by 2015 (US Congress 2001). It could take some time before military robots outnumber manned platforms, but it is likely to happen within the next two decades. In the long run the political, economic and operational pressures will be too great and the most modern armed forces around the world will utilize growing numbers of robotic systems of increasing autonomy. However, concerns about the legality of AW could potentially stop this development, or at least put some constraints on the use of robotic weapons. Chapter 4 therefore looks at the legal aspects of weapons automation.

Chapter 4

The Legality of Autonomous Weapons

This chapter discusses the legality of AW according to international law and the question of their compatibility with generally accepted principles and customs of war. The issue of legality of autonomous military robots is hotly debated and some people such as David Isenberg, a military analyst and independent writer, and Gary Chapman, a computer scientist and former head of the public interest organization Computer Professionals for Social Responsibility, claim that they are, or would be, illegal (Isenberg 2007; G. Chapman 1987, 95–100). This is rather difficult to prove and would be even more difficult to determine what it means. Should states be prevented from developing or deploying autonomous robotic weapons? Is this already an arms control issue? Should they be punished through sanctions? What degree of autonomy in robots would still be permissible? International law is simply not quite clear, as the terms 'robot' or 'autonomous weapon' do not appear in relevant international treaties. So the critics of AW have to argue on the basis of generally accepted fundamental principles and customs of warfare.

Obviously, international law can be broken and it is often difficult to make somebody responsible for breaches of international law. At the moment there are only very few and limited mechanisms in place for dealing with crimes of aggression and war crimes. For example, international/national tribunals have been set up in the past to put war criminals on trial after a war or conflict (e.g. concerning the human rights violations in Yugoslavia and Rwanda) (Brown 2001, 246). There is also the UN International Court of Justice (ICJ) in The Hague, which claims to have a global jurisdiction and which deals more with states. More recently, an International Criminal Court (ICC) was established (also in The Hague) in 2002 through the Rome Statute of 1998, which is mainly concerned with bringing to justice individuals who have committed war crimes or crimes against humanity.

Even these limited instruments of international justice are not universally accepted (e.g. the US does not accept the compulsory powers of the ICJ and is not a member state of the ICC). Any state that decides to violate an international treaty will normally get away with it. Nevertheless, international norms are usually not broken without consequence, even if it is only a loss of prestige that the nation violating these norms will suffer. In the long term it is beneficial for states to adhere to international norms and treaties, as they can then expect other states to do the same (Morris and McCoubrey 2006, 50). In other words, international law, including the law of armed conflict, is based on a universal consensus on its underlying moral principles and an agreement that serious violations of these norms should be punished by the international community represented by the

UN or any other legitimate authority. Without that consensus and the general willingness of states to comply with these accepted moral principles, international law would only remain a dead letter.

Throughout the history of international law the consensus on which military practices should be outlawed and which weapons should be prohibited has changed, while the underlying moral principles defined in the philosophical tradition of Just War Theory have remained largely the same (Kaszuba 1997, 28–9). This has to do to some extent with technology and to some extent with general changes of attitudes toward war in society. For example, the area bombing of cities, which was aimed at destroying the economic capabilities of an enemy but which was very likely to harm civilians, was an accepted military practice in the Second World War and was not punished as a war crime after the war. Technically speaking, it wasn't because 'during the Second World War there was no agreement, treaty, convention or any other instrument governing the protection of the civilian population or civilian property' (Guisández-Gómez 1998). As technology changed allowing more discriminate bombing and society changed in the sense of having less tolerance for collateral damage, area bombing would now be seen as an indiscriminate military practice and therefore an illegal one. Also, some weapons that were once prohibited like feathered arrows, catapults, balloons firing projectiles, helicopters or submarines were banned because they were once deemed to be inhumane weapons, or weapons that gave one party an unfair advantage. Today the use of none of them would amount to a war crime (May 2007, 72). To determine whether or not AW would fit readily into the moral framework of war as it is contained in the law of armed conflict is not easy. It would be even harder to predict whether they would have to be outlawed indefinitely, or whether international norms could accommodate them in the future. Experience has shown that prohibitions of weapons are often lifted once they proliferate more widely. In addition, there are no clear rules why particular weapons are banned. Instead the law of armed conflict and its underlying moral principles offer only some guidance as to whether a particular weapon or class of weapons may or may not comply with it. Whether or not this is, in fact, the case will have to be determined by the international community as a whole and by the legal experts informing political decision-makers.

Autonomous Weapons and the Law of Armed Conflict

The law of armed conflict makes up the so-called *jus in bello*, which deals with the issue of allowed and prohibited practices in war. It consists of numerous conventions of war and international treaties that regulate the conduct of the belligerents in war. The *jus in bello* aims to restrain war as much as possible in order to reduce the damage and suffering caused by war. There are two main legal sources for the *jus in bello*: the Hague Conventions (1899/1907) and the Geneva Conventions (1864/1929/1949). While the Hague Conventions are more concerned with the rights of combatants and prohibited military practices, the Geneva Conventions focus more on the rights and protection of non-combatants. In addition, there are many other relevant international laws and treaties that restrict particular military practices or weapons (e.g. the Convention on Certain Conventional Weapons or the Chemical and Biological Weapons Conventions). Furthermore, there are also geographical restraints for the conduct of war such as the prohibition to place nuclear weapons in space or on the seabed and the demilitarization of the Arctic regions. The *jus in bello* is based on four fundamental principles: the principle of necessity, the principle of proportionality, the principle of discrimination (or distinction) and the principle of humaneness. These principles are not very clear-cut and are sometimes in conflict with each other.

Military Necessity

The principle of military necessity dictates that military force should only be used against the enemy to the extent as is necessary for winning the war. Although a soldier 'has allowed himself to be made into a dangerous man' and by this virtue of being a combatant has implicitly agreed to be killed at any time, Michael Walzer, who is a prominent scholar of the Just War tradition, affirms 'no one can be killed for trivial purposes' (Walzer 2000, 145, 156). Any military operation/action has to pass the condition that it is necessary for winning the war and is not carried out of frivolity. At the same time, any measure or operation, however grave in its moral consequences, can be justified by the principle of necessity, if it would be crucial for winning a war and if the other principles of the *jus in bello* are observed as much as possible. Technology can largely affect the calculation of military necessity, as is shown in Michael Walzer's example of submarine warfare during the two World Wars.

German submarines during the First World War were ordered to sink enemy vessels on sight, despite the fact that the submarines were unable to assist many survivors – many of whom could be civilians. In practice, not even limited help was provided to survivors. The rationale for this was that the risks for the submarine crews helping survivors could be great, as submarines are generally very vulnerable when surfaced. German military commanders therefore pleaded to necessity, as 'the only alternative ... was not to use submarines at all, or to use them ineffectively' (Walzer 2000, 147). The military practice of submarines sinking ships without making any effort to help the survivors of sunk ships was continued in the Second World War. After the war Admiral Dönitz was not charged for this violation of accepted principles of war at the Nuremberg Trial (Walzer 2000, 148). So the new technology created pressures to relax some other customs of war, such as the obligation to help the wounded and the shipwrecked codified in the Geneva Convention.

What can be learned from this example with respect to the use of AW? Once AW are widely introduced, it becomes a matter of military necessity to use them, as they could prove to be far superior to any other type of weapon. Conducting war with human soldiers might become militarily ineffective, which would further increase pressures to automate warfare even more. Theoretically, this could result in wars exclusively waged by machines, while humans might stand back and watch. From a certain point of view automated wars could be seen as a humanizing tendency, as the lives of human soldiers no longer need to be put at risk. If the main or even only targets of AWs were other AWs, then the rule of necessity can be relaxed, as machines killing other machines is hardly a problem for human ethics. Thus the bar for using force could be lowered, if the intended targets were machines. On the other hand, weapons automation could turn out to be a slippery slope.

Many legal and ethical restraints of war could suddenly become ineffective with potentially disastrous consequences. As pointed out earlier, such automated wars would be most likely extremely fast and extremely destructive. Humans would just become collateral damage in a contest of automated war machines. So it might be necessary to restrict, or maybe even prohibit, AW from the beginning in order to prevent a dynamics that will lead to the complete automation of war that is justified by the principle of necessity.

Proportionality

International law rules that the use of force and the means employed should always be proportionate to the military objective in order to protect civilians. The principle is established in the Geneva Convention and it prohibits 'an attack which may be expected to cause incidental loss of civilian life, injury to civilians, damage to civilian objects, or a combination thereof, which would be excessive in relation to the concrete and direct military advantage anticipated' (Geneva Convention (1977) Protocol I, Art. 51, Para. 5b.). Put crudely, it would be completely disproportionate and therefore illegal to carpet bomb a city to destroy a military unit deployed in it.

Like the principle of necessity, the principle of proportionality also protects enemy combatants from excessive and unnecessary use of force. This means that soldiers would have to make some utilitarian calculation any time they use force where they weigh military advantage that could be gained by an action against the humanitarian consequences. In reality, such a rational calculation would often be very difficult, as soldiers would usually not know how great the real military advantage relative to winning the war would be in order to justify the use of force, or even how much overall damage could be caused by choosing a particular course of action.

It can be argued that an AW could potentially use force more proportionately than human soldiers. A computerized weapon could more quickly and precisely calculate blast and other weapon effects that cause collateral damage, while such calculations would be 'far too complex for the warfighter to make in real time. AW could perform hundreds of these same calculations in real time, increasing the lethality of the engagement while simultaneously reducing the probability of collateral damage' (Guetlein 2005, 5).

Would the deployment of AW most likely result in the disproportionate use of force? This would largely depend on how much firepower an AW actually controls and how many of them are used at a time. If an autonomous robot controls a nuclear weapon, the collateral damage could be enormous. However, if the robot used a highly precise microprojectile or a weak focused laser beam, the damage done, even in the case of missing the intended target or choosing a wrong target, would be comparatively small. This would suggest keeping the amount of firepower that an AW (or a swarm of AWs) would be able to control relatively low as to avoid the weapon causing highly disproportionate damage in case of malfunctioning. In addition, as robots would have no right of self-defense, they would not be entitled to the same aggressiveness and use of firepower as human troops in combat situations.

Much more challenging than developing an AW that uses force proportionately could be developing one that could also reliably discriminate between combatants and non-combatants.

Discrimination

Discrimination has always been the principle of the law of armed conflict that has been most respected by belligerents in war because it is the least ambiguous principle. The Geneva Convention calls for the clear division of all people and targets into two main categories: soldiers/combatants and civilians/non-combatants, or targets and non-targets (J. Johnson 1999, 37). The purpose is to restrain war and to protect civilians as well as soldiers under certain circumstances (e.g. when they are surrendering). The reasoning for the principle of discrimination is that combatants are participating in the wrongdoing of the enemy nation, which morally justifies making them targets, while enemy nationals not participating in the wrongdoing are innocent and it would be immoral to target them (Regan 1996, 87). The Geneva Convention established the principle of discrimination in numerous general provisions on the protection of non-combatants and civilian property. An additional protocol from 1977 says clearly that:

> In order to ensure respect for and protection of the civilian population and civilian objects, the Parties to the conflict shall at all times distinguish between the civilian population and combatants and between civilian objects and military objectives and accordingly shall direct their operations only against military objectives. (Geneva Convention (1977) Protocol I Additional to the Geneva Conventions, Art. 48)

To deliberately target civilians or civilian objects is also prohibited, according to the Hague Convention of 1907 (The Hague Convention (1907), Art. 23).

In practice, the principle of discrimination means that the *aiming point* for the use of military force must be a military target. However, some collateral damage caused by an attack on a military target is permissible, as long as the principles of proportionality and discrimination are adhered to (Green 1993, 147, 151). If a military target is struck by a bomb and the bomb also kills a nearby civilian, it would not be a war crime as long as the civilian was not the intended target. At the same time, it would be prohibited to knowingly attack a military target that is not distanced enough from civilian structures as to keep the risk to civilians low.[1] On the other hand, there is also the moral obligation on the part of every belligerent not to place military objects directly next to civilian objects.

Although the principle of discrimination is very straightforward in its simple classification of legitimate and illegitimate targets, there are many problems with it. Some of the problems started with the development of weapons of mass destruction (WMD) and the rise of aerial warfare. Interpreted strictly, it would automatically outlaw any weapons that are inherently indiscriminate, such as WMD and in particular nuclear weapons – an interpretation that has been rejected by many states, including the United States and the United Kingdom (May 2007, 169). Similarly, the use of strategic bombing by the Allies and Axis powers during the Second World War was not considered to be a war crime, despite the fact that mainly civilians suffered from it. Massive bombing was also carried out during the 1991 Gulf War, during the 1999 Kosovo air campaign and the 2003 Iraq War. Although the aiming points for these later air campaigns were carefully selected military targets and the bombs were also much more precise than their Second World War counterparts, the substantial amount of collateral damage and civilian losses in these air campaigns is undeniable. It would probably be nearly impossible to conduct a truly discriminate air campaign against an enemy nation with zero civilian casualties. This might suggest that bombing could be considered as an illegal military practice and that bombers are illegal weapons – something few people actually claim.

Nevertheless, public expectations about 'surgical strikes' have become unrealistically high, which becomes an increasing problem for the conduct of military operations in general. The military lawyer Charles Dunlop even speaks of 'lawfare' – a concept that was first formulated in the book *Unrestricted Warfare* written by Chinese officers in 1999 (Liang and Xiangsui 1999, 55–6). Dunlop considers this tendency of exploiting real or alleged violations of the law of armed conflict to be a 'means of confronting American military power' (Dunlop 2007). In other words, the use of any military force is obstructed or discredited by the abuse of the law of armed conflict, which was always intended to restrain war, not to make it in principle impossible.

The other problem with the principle of discrimination is that it is very hard to observe in an irregular conflict, where the enemy blends in with the civilian population. This makes it particularly difficult for soldiers to distinguish between combatants and non-combatants. They often have to operate within civilian-occupied urban areas and are sometimes forced to fight the enemy even while

---

1   Protocol III, Art. 3 of the Geneva Convention refers specifically to the use of incendiary ammunitions, but Peter Rowe has suggested making it a general provision that attacks on military objects located in concentrations of civilians should be prohibited. Peter Rowe, 'Kosovo 1999: The Air Campaign – Have the Provisions of the Additional Protocol I Withstood the Test?', *International Review of the Red Cross* 837 (31 March 2000) 147–64.

innocent civilians are nearby. Enemy combatants might deliberately misuse protected civilian objects such as churches/mosques or hospitals as sanctuaries. This can sometimes result in indiscriminate tactics, such as the use of heavy firepower within a city. A good example of this dilemma created by irregular warfare is the battle of Fallujah in 2004, where US forces attacked the not completely evacuated city with massive firepower in order to drive the insurgents out (West 2005). In effect, the principle of discrimination could hardly be observed.

How would AW go together with the principle of discrimination? This depends first and foremost on their technical sophistication. It can be said that precision ammunition like the GPS-guided Joint Direct Attack Munitions (JDAMs) are generally praised as a moral progress toward humanizing warfare, as they are more discriminate, allow better targeting and minimize overall collateral damage. However, although JDAMs fall within only 43ft. of their target, they still destroy anything and kill anybody in a circle of 82–115ft. (Conetta 1995, 6). That is still not precise enough as to call smart bombs 'discriminate'. AW could be, in the long term at least, a military and moral improvement over smart bombs because they are likely to be more, rather than less, discriminate. Instead of targeting a geographical area where the enemy is believed to be at a given moment, which is difficult in modern warfare where enemy forces are highly mobile, AW could search for and target individual military objects, or even individual people, with pinpoint accuracy and with little collateral damage. In other words, AWs do not necessarily violate the principle of discrimination and might improve on current indiscriminate military practices.

Humaneness and Outlawed Weapons

The principle of humaneness summarizes in some sense all other principles of the law of armed conflict and is the essence of Just War Theory. War should not cause more suffering than is absolutely necessary for deciding the war – even among those that have agreed to fight it. This general aim to limit the damage and suffering in war has sometimes resulted in efforts to ban particular weapons or military practices that were seen to violate the principles of Just War. For example, the crossbow was allegedly banned by Pope Innocent II in 1139 at the Second Lateran Council in Rome. It was deemed to be such a dangerous (or effective) weapon that it should be used only against pagans. The crossbow was also a weapon that was considered to be incompatible with the code of chivalry 'as it allowed a man to strike without the risk of being struck' (Green 1993, 122). It was dishonorable for a knight to fight without risk and this principle of chivalry has survived in the prohibition of perfidy (use of false emblems, uniforms, flags or misuse of the white flag) (Geneva Convention (1949) Protocol I, Art. 37, 39) and the prohibition of massacre (not to allow the enemy to surrender) (Geneva Convention (1949) Protocol I, Art. 40).

However, the first modern attempt of creating an international treaty for banning a particular class of weapons was the St. Petersburg *Declaration Renouncing the*

Use, in Time of War, of Explosive Projectiles Under 400 Grammes of Weight of 1868 (Green 1993, 127). The rationale for this ban was that small explosives would injure rather than kill and would therefore 'uselessly aggravate the sufferings of disabled men, or render their death inevitable' (Schindler and Toman 1988, 102). This concern of weapons causing 'superfluous injury or unnecessary suffering' was later incorporated in the Geneva Convention, which again outlawed such weapons (Geneva Convention (1949) Protocol I, Art. 35, Para. 2).

A range of other weapons have been banned through international treaties for similar reasons. This includes asphyxiating gases, biological weapons and other poisons, expanding bullets (so-called dum-dum), air-delivered incendiary weapons, anti-personnel mines, fragmentary weapons with plastic shrapnel and blinding lasers. The Rome Statute that established the International Criminal Court of Justice in 1998 affirmed the ban of the following types of weapons: 'poison or poisoned weapons' (XVIII); 'asphyxiating, poisonous or other gases, and all analogous liquids, materials or devices' (XIX); 'bullets which expand or flatten easily in the human body' (XX); 'employing weapons, projectiles and material and methods of warfare which are of a nature to cause superfluous injury or unnecessary suffering or which are inherently indiscriminate in violation of the international law of armed conflict, provided that such weapons, projectiles and material and methods of warfare are the subject of a comprehensive prohibition' (Rome Statute of the International Criminal Court (1998)).

The Ottawa Treaty of 1997 established an international ban of anti-personnel land mines and prohibits the use, stockpiling, production and transfer of such weapons and was ratified by 149 countries by 2006 (Youngblood 2006, 168). The treaty was the result of a public outrage concerning the fact that civilians in war zones or former war zones are killed and maimed by the tens of thousands every year. In some sense it was a victory of the principle of humaneness that resulted in an enforceable international norm. However, two observations shall be made: first, anti-personnel land mines are an obsolete weapon with little military value for most states, thus it is easy for them to ban land mines; secondly, it is a ban of anti-personnel mines and not of mines in general. More sophisticated anti-tank mines, remotely triggered mines, or sea mines are not outlawed because they are considered to be more discriminate. So the Ottawa Treaty is in no way a comprehensive ban of all automated or autonomous weapons, or even an indication that most states would favor such a ban.

Apart from the issues of humaneness and discrimination, there is also a general concern for the environment incorporated in the law of armed conflict. The Geneva Convention states that 'it is prohibited to employ methods or means of warfare which are intended, or may be expected, to cause widespread, long-term and severe damage to the natural environment' (Geneva Convention (1949) Protocol I, Art. 35, Para 3). In 1969 the Edinburgh Institute therefore concluded that:

> Existing international law prohibits the use of all weapons which, by their nature, affect indiscriminately both military objectives and non-military objects,

or both armed forces and civilian populations. In particular, it prohibits the use of weapons the destructive effect of which is so great that it cannot be limited to specific military objectives or is otherwise uncontrollable (self-generating weapons), as well as of 'blind' weapons. (Edinburgh Institute 1969)

This Edinburgh interpretation of international law would seem to include nuclear weapons, but in reality the nuclear powers do not consider nuclear weapons to be in principle illegal weapons. The same exception could apply to AW.

However, states have the duty under Article 36 of Additional Protocol I of the Geneva Convention that they must assess the legality issue of a weapon beforehand: 'In the study, development, acquisition or adoption of a new weapon a High Contracting Party is under the obligation to determine whether its employment would, in some or all circumstances, be prohibited' under the Protocol or other international law (Geneva Convention Additional Protocol I (1977), Part III, Art. 36). In the case of AW states must assess whether any particular autonomous weapons system would comply with international law before actually deploying it. The question is: are AW already covered by the prohibitions of weapons and practices under international law and how would existing international law affect their use?

First of all, it would be difficult to argue that AW could be inherently inhumane or would cause 'unnecessary suffering', as 'autonomous' refers to the control method of the weapon rather than the weapon itself. It might be the case that an AW could be poisoned (e.g. a poisoned microrobot or poisoned microprojectile) or would be deliberately designed for maximizing injuries (e.g. flechette or shrapnel weapons), in which case the weapon would clearly be illegal (Hague Conventions (1899/1907), Art. 23(a) and Rome Statute of the International Criminal Court (1998)).

Otherwise, an AW would only be illegal if it was inherently indiscriminate, or if it would cause long-lasting damage to the environment, or if it was otherwise uncontrollable. This would imply that any AW that cannot reliably discriminate between legitimate and illegitimate targets is illegal, unless it is deployed in a manner in which the danger to civilians would be negligible. It would also already be illegal to release a weapon into the environment that could have a long-lasting negative impact. For example, large numbers of nanoparticles or other micromachines deployed as sensors or weapons on enemy territory could become a long-term environmental or health hazard for the population (Shelley 2006, 77–80) and would in this case be illegal. Finally, any self-foraging and self-replicating machines could be considered uncontrollable weapons and would therefore also already be forbidden under the conventions of international law.

Points of Concern

There is no clear answer to the question of whether or not AW would be generally illegal under existing international law. However, some critics have pointed at some main problems connected to these weapons. These concerns are discussed below and include the question whether they would be indiscriminate weapons, the issue of 'targeted killing' and the issue of robot war crimes and legal accountability.

Indiscriminate Weapons?

Many concerned scientists have made the argument that AW would be inherently indiscriminate and therefore illegal according to international law. For example, Gary Chapman believes that AW could not possibly distinguish between an enemy combatant, who is a legitimate target, and a surrendering enemy combatant, who has become a non-combatant and would therefore be an illegitimate target (Belin and Chapman 1987, 96–7).

The key matter of dispute seems to be generally the reliability with which armed autonomous robots would be able to choose and attack legitimate targets. It is not clear what degree of reliability, or better which failure rate, would be acceptable for robots. In the case of cluster bombs, a reliability rate of anything less than 99 percent of bomblets exploding in the blast is not considered good enough. Therefore the US Congress recently passed a moratorium on the export of cluster munitions (Lumpe 2007). Better than 99 percent reliability would be a very high bar for AW. The US Congress and the Pentagon apparently believe that technology will eventually solve all the problems of making AW discriminate weapons and the connected legal issues, as military robotics projects receive generous funding. At the same time, there is the serious risk that it might not happen. It could be illusionary to expect a military robot to choose legitimate targets with near 100 percent reliability. So what are the real odds for a technical solution?

Critics have pointed at three main deficiencies of autonomous military robots that would potentially indefinitely prevent them from becoming discriminate weapons. The first argument is that machine perception is not good enough for a robot to fully comprehend its environment. Secondly, there is the so-called 'frame problem' that the understanding of a robot of its external environment would always have to be incomplete and would lead to somewhat faulty behavior. Finally, there is the argument that the control software would have to be very complex and would therefore be more brittle and more likely to contain bugs, making military robots indefinitely unsafe.

Weak machine perception   Over the last few decades a major problem for robots has been making sense of their environment by using their various sensors. As computers have become more powerful, there has been a tendency in robotics to simply equip robots with a high-resolution video camera and a powerful image processor for analyzing the video images. Although there has been a lot of progress in image processing, a computer system still has a big problem distinguishing a shadow from a real obstacle (Lerner 2006a). Of course, a robot can also use other kinds of sensors such as laser and radar sensors for identifying obstacles, but it is still very difficult for robots to operate in unknown and complex terrain. Roboticist Daniel Wilson has pointed out that a robot could be easily 'misled by sudden changes in lighting, shadows, and atmospheric conditions' (Wilson 2005, 57). Even bigger is the problem of distinguishing between legitimate and illegitimate targets, especially in the chaos of combat and the presence of enemy counter-measures. Distinguishing between a harmless civilian and an armed insurgent could be beyond anything machine perception could possibly do. In any case, it would be easy for terrorists or insurgents to trick these robots by concealing weapons or by exploiting their sensual and behavioral limitations (Sharkey 2007a). Noel Sharkey can already see 'a little girl being zapped because she points her ice cream at a robot to share' (Sharkey 2007a).

The frame problem   The so-called frame problem of AI deals with the fundamental issue of how a given situation is represented in a robot that interacts with its environment. In its narrow form the frame problem is about how the properties of an object change (or do not change) as a result of an action by a robot without having to write endless formulae that describe the effects or lack of effects caused by a certain action. For example, moving an object would change its position, but not its color, while painting an object would not change the position, but the color (Stanford Encyclopedia of Philosophy 2004). The problem becomes even bigger in more complex environments and in conditions where the problems the robot has to solve are also more complex. Daniel Dennet has described such a complex problem in a thought experiment that features a robot (R1) that has to get its batteries from a room with a time bomb. The batteries are on a wagon and the robot manages to pull the wagon with the batteries out of the room, but unfortunately the time bomb is also on the wagon and explodes. 'R1 knew that the bomb was on the wagon in the room, but didn't realize that pulling the wagon would bring the bomb out along with the battery. Poor R1 had missed that obvious implication of its planned act' (Dennet 1987). The robot designers go back to the drawing board and redesign the robot so that it can understand the implications of actions. The robot goes back in again, but it gets stuck in analyzing all possible solutions and implications, as it is unable to understand what are relevant and irrelevant implications – until the bomb explodes. It still seems unlikely that AI could ever find a short cut for 'instinctively' finding which elements of a situation or which implications of an action would be relevant and require attention and which ones are not relevant and can be ignored. This means the robot has either to go through all possibilities, which might take an infinite amount of time, or it might have to be programmed to ignore most of them with the consequence that it is likely to miss an important detail. For example, an AW would not only have to recognize the difference between a tank and a school bus, but would also need to be able to judge when launching a weapon would endanger nearby civilians. Noel Sharkey said in his keynote speech at the Royal United Services Conference that 'most soldiers would not for example blow up a school full of children if there is a sniper on its roof, but who knows what a robot would do' (Fleming 2008). As a result, military robots would be either too slow to make them militarily useful, or would be prone to use force indiscriminately and disproportionately, as they would often miss important details or incorrectly interpret situations.

Weak software   The so-called 'software crisis' has been discussed in computer science for over 30 years. The issue is that software should be reliable, safe and trustworthy, but in reality it usually isn't because the software gets ever more complex and companies are under pressure to develop new software at a fast pace (Shore 1987). In the 1960s AI expert Marvin Minsky observed:

> When a program grows in power by an evolution of partially understood patches and fixes, the programmer begins to lose track of internal details, loses his ability to predict what will happen, begins to hope instead of know, and watches the results as though the program were an individual whose range of behavior is uncertainty ... [Programs] will be developed and modified by several programmers, each [acting] independently ... The program will grow in effectiveness, but no one of the programmers will understand it all. (Of course, this won't always be successful – the interactions might make it get worse, and no one might be able to fix it again!). (Quoted in H. Lin 1987, 143)

More recently, virtual reality pioneer Jaron Lanier has voiced his concerns in *Wired* that today's software is fatally lagging behind the available hardware in terms of quality (2000). Software got bloated in the process of growing hardware resources, but it has not gotten qualitatively better than it was decades ago. This means that Moore's Law does not make software any better or computers considerably smarter, as claimed by people like the inventor and entrepreneur Ray Kurzweil. Lanier writes:

> The larger a piece of computer software gets, the more it is likely to be dominated by some form of legacy code, and the more brutal becomes the overhead of addressing the endless examples of subtle incompatibility that inevitably arise between chunks of software originally created in different contexts. (Lanier 2000)

Lanier thinks that the problem only gets worse through better hardware as it 'motivates an ever-faster turnaround of software revisions'. Using automated programming tools will not get rid of these problems, as 'many of these are systemic and might arise even if non-human agents were writing the code'. In the end, this would be only to our advantage: 'The very features of computers which drive us crazy today, and keep so many of us gainfully employed, are the best insurance our species has for long term survival as we explore the far reaches of technological possibility' (Lanier 2000). If Lanier is right, the software controlling autonomous military robots would likely suffer from brittleness and numerous undiscovered bugs. Under such conditions autonomous military robots or even commercial service robots could never get off the ground as discriminate weapons or safe tools.

Targeted Killing

Technology already makes it possible to identify and kill particular individuals over long distances. Without doubt, robotics will further increase military capabilities for conducting extremely precise pinpoint attacks. Although such precision strikes seem to be a morally better solution 'than to target the enemy's conscripts and killing them in their thousands' (Peters 1996), it also raises the legal and ethical dilemma of assassination. According to Bruce Berkowitz from RAND, 'The problem today is that modern weapons are so accurate and modern intelligence and communications systems are so sophisticated that it often seems impossible *not* to target a particular person' (Berkowitz 2003, 120). The temptation for assassinating the members of a terrorist cell or the leaders of an enemy military or government will become ever greater through better technology and more precise weapons. In fact, robotic weapons have already been used for many targeted killings of al-Qaeda operatives in the Middle East and Asia. According to the *New Statesman*, the armed *Predator* drone was used for at least 80 targeted killings in Iraq, Afghanistan, Yemen and Pakistan, also killing numerous civilians in the process (Graham 2006). An article in *Mother Jones* estimates the overall number of al-Qaeda operatives killed by focused air strikes in Iraq as high as 200 (Case 2008).

Not too far into the future, individuals could be targeted by AW that could find and kill known terrorists, maybe by tracking their mobile phones or through facial recognition. For example, the *Predators* have been recently equipped with a tracking device that can locate and target known terrorists through their mobile phones (Page 2008b). The promise of new robotic assassination devices might be so tempting for military and intelligence organizations that 'the art of war may quickly become the art of political assassination or summary execution' (Kaag 2008). Using assassination as a means of waging war could even become a distinctive new mode of conflict, as a military analyst speculates:

> Assassination, destruction of individual sites, and counter-intelligence missions will be far more common. When flying robots weighing less than a gram act as spies collecting accurate, digital, and up-to-date information are feasible – as they will be soon – then organizations won't need a full fledged network of human spies to gather data. Those same robots in slightly different configurations could easily kill a selected individual or group, perhaps by putting strychnine in their coffee or cyanide in their corn flakes. (Mandel 2004, 60)

It may soon be possible to send autonomous hunter-killer mini-robots to search for and kill a particular person using facial recognition or any other biometric system. Some of the technologies and efforts in developing high-tech assassination tools were described in Chapter 3.

The concept of warfare by assassination seems slightly reminiscent of the CIA's Phoenix Program (and the similar North Vietnamese assassination program) (1967–71), where South Vietnamese police and US Special Forces were used to neutralize the 'Vietcong infrastructure' and admittedly killed more than 20,000 Vietcong (the real number was probably much higher) (Ranelagh 1986, 436–41). While political cadres of the Vietcong at least often had the option to resist 'neutralization', assassination by robot is completely asymmetric and would appear to be even less morally justified than the Phoenix Program.

While few people would feel particularly sorry for a killed dangerous terrorist, simply murdering them through the use of high-tech weapons is probably not always legal according to international law and would depend on the exact circumstances in each case (Schmitz-Elvenich 2008, 257). However, any policy based on simply eliminating dangerous individuals, in contrast to apprehending them and putting them on trial, would hardly be acceptable to the general public in a democracy (Berkowitz 2003, 129). Not only might the wrong people be targeted, it also undermines the principle of the rule of law.

With respect to the possible illegality of targeted killings there are two different cases that need to be considered: first the person that is individually targeted is a lawful enemy combatant in wartime; secondly, the person targeted is a criminal according to international law. In the first case international law is not quite clear. International law expert Leslie Green writes that assassination of specific individuals of the enemy forces in contrast to targeting enemy personnel in general 'would be contrary to customary law', but it would not be specifically forbidden in the Hague Regulations (Green 1993, 137). On this matter the Lieber Code of 1863, which is considered to be the precursor of the Geneva Convention, states:

> The law of war does not allow proclaiming either an individual belonging to the hostile army, or a citizen, or a subject of the hostile government an outlaw, who may be slain without trial by any captor, any more than the modern law of peace allows such international outlawry. The sternest retaliation should follow the murder committed in consequence of such proclamation, made by whatever authority. Civilized nations look with horror upon offers of rewards for the assassination of enemies as relapses into barbarism. (Lieber Code (1863) Art. 148, Section IX (Assassination)).

This means that targeted killing in war is at the very least a morally questionable practice within the moral and legal framework of war.

The second case of killing international criminals in neutral countries is generally outlawed according to international law, especially if it was done covertly and without consent of the government of the neutral country. Unlike soldiers in wartime, who may be killed naked taking a bath (Walzer 2000, 142), terrorists (if they are not 'illegal combatants' in an international conflict) are civilians in peacetime and would need to be dealt with using conventional law enforcement methods. If they resist arrest or pose an *immediate* threat to others, the principle of necessity allows that they may be killed. Killing them abroad without giving them the opportunity of being arrested and receiving a fair trial would fall itself under the definition of international terrorism.[2]

---

2   UN Resolution 1556 (2004) defines terrorism as 'criminal acts, including against civilians, committed with the intent to cause death or serious bodily injury, or taking of

The use of AWs that are programmed to kill particular individuals could be a problem for international law and should be clearly outlawed, even if such highly targeted attacks could reduce the risk to innocent civilians. In any case, the general debate on the morality of extra-judicial kidnappings and targeted killings of terror suspects is already decided: it is both illegal and immoral and this policy will therefore most likely be discontinued with the end of the presidency of George W. Bush in 2009. However, assassinations with novel devices such as lethal mini/ micro-robots or new types of nano-engineered biological weapons could be carried out covertly and with very little risk of exposure. It could be extremely difficult to effectively prohibit and prevent such high-tech assassinations. As a result, some governments might think that they could get away more easily with assassinating people for political reasons and might do so more often.

Robot War Crimes and Legal Accountability

An issue that has been raised by the ethicist Robert Sparrow and the military analyst David Isenberg is that AW could potentially interrupt the clear chain of military command that is required by international law. Article 1 of the Hague Convention requires any combatant 'to be commanded by a person responsible for his subordinates' (Hague Convention (1907), Art. 1). It would be difficult to say this about an autonomous military robot, which may be commanded by a superior officer, but which would be both capable of autonomous behavior and incapable of assuming full responsibility for its actions. Isenberg therefore claims that 'international Law of Armed Conflict dictates that unmanned systems cannot fire their weapons without a human operator in the loop' (Isenberg 2007). But this matter is far from being obvious and AWs are very likely to be deployed relatively soon, which could be done in the light of a different interpretation of international law. This means military organizations will have to find a solution to the issue of accountability in the case of an autonomous robot malfunctioning and causing serious human and material damage, or doing something that would amount to 'robot war crimes'.

There are generally, as pointed out by Sparrow, three obvious possibilities for attributing responsibility: the manufacturer/designer of the robot, the military commander who authorized the use of the autonomous robot and the robot itself (Sparrow 2007b).

Manufacturers/designers   There is the possibility of treating any malfunctioning of the robot legally as an accident. It could be the case that the robot was badly designed and that this was the cause of the accident. The philosopher Peter Asaro

---

hostages, with the purpose to provoke a state of terror in the general public or in a group of persons or particular persons, intimidate a population or compel a government or an international organization to do or to abstain from doing any act.'

has argued that there is (at least in the civilian world) no limited liability for manufacturers of autonomous robots:

> Corporations can be held legally responsible for their practices and products, through liability laws and lawsuits. If their products harm people through poor design, substandard manufacturing, or unintended interactions or side-effects, that corporation can be compelled to pay damages to those who have been harmed, as well as punitive damages. (Asaro 2006, 12–13)

If a robot behaves unpredictably and this unpredictable behavior results in damage, then the manufacturers have to pay for it, or compensate victims or their relatives. This means that it is in the best interest of the manufacturers of commercial robots to make them as safe as possible. However, in the military world matters are quite different. It rarely happens that the manufacturers of weapons are held responsible for any accidents caused by poor design, which has many reasons. Nevertheless, this would be a serious possibility for the future, as military technology becomes too complex for military research labs to assess it independently. For example, the *V-22 Osprey* tilt-rotor aircraft that is operated by the US Marine Corps has already killed 30 people in crashes, which gives a clear indication that the aircraft is (or at least was) unsafe because of poor design (Thompson 2007). Not surprisingly, voices are getting louder to hold manufacturer Boeing responsible for the deaths. If this happened, it would make it clear to the defense industry that they cannot get away with building weapons that are intrinsically unsafe or flawed. Any unpredictable and dangerous robot behaviour could be interpreted as poor design and could result in some form of penalty for the manufacturer, e.g. the cancellation of contracts or a fine. Managers of defense companies or engineers could also be held individually responsible for serious flaws of products, if they knew about them and did not make the armed forces aware of these flaws or limitations. This could be a most effective deterrent for defense companies and may stop them from marketing immature and unsafe weapons technology to the armed forces. The implementation of liability rules for military robots could be difficult, but it is not hopeless. The 20-month suspension of Boeing in 2003 to 2005 for violating conflict-of-interest laws was in any case a clear signal to the defense industry that there can be serious consequences for misconduct (Jablonski 2005).

Military commanders   It is ultimately the responsibility of a human military commander to authorize the use of an AW. The US military has certainly already begun to draw up clear regulations for the conditions under which lethal autonomous military robots could be used operationally. If not, it would be a pretty good idea for all armed forces intending to deploy AW to do that soon. Once there is a regulatory framework for the use of AW in place, it could be relatively easy to check whether the commander has followed all the regulations and adhered to the laws of armed conflict when the decision for the use of the weapon was made. This could be done with the help of software currently being developed by Ronald

Arkin, which he calls the 'Responsibility Advisor'. The software could advise the commander on the lawfulness of the use of the robot and could record any orders or overrides (Arkin 2007, 76–7). The Responsibility Advisor would be some sort of expert system that can check whether the use of an AW in a particular situation complies with the law of armed conflict, the rules of engagement and any other ethical considerations. It would be part of the military robot control architecture for the suppression of unethical behavior, which is discussed further below. In the case that the military commander adhered to all the regulations, then it cannot be the commander's fault if the robot behaves unpredictably and starts killing civilians. In the case that there was a procedural mistake, the military commander might have to assume full responsibility for any violations of international law caused by the robot.

The robot   There is the hypothetical possibility to hold the robot legally accountable for its behavior. At the moment, it would obviously be nonsensical to do this, as any robot that exists today, or that will be built in the next 10–20 years, is too dumb to posses anything like intentionality or a real capability for agency. However, this might change in a more distant future once robots become much more sophisticated and intelligent. When AI present in autonomous robots approaches human-level intelligence, then it could potentially be very difficult to suppress any unwanted behavior through a technical fix. The robot could be able to make its own free (or at least independent) choices. Would this be a problem legally? Not necessarily. In fact, non-human entities like corporations are already attributed personhood and can be made legally responsible like any other person. A robot or artilect could one day be considered to be a legal person responsible for its actions (Sudia 2001). Robot responsibility could mean destroying the robot that intentionally violated international law or other human law, or it could result in any other suitable punishment for the robot.

Conclusion   It appears that the legal problems with regard to accountability might be far smaller than some critics of military robots believe. The chain of command is not interrupted by deploying autonomous systems on the battlefield. In the past it has not been seen to be a problem and it is probably not going to be a problem in the future. If the robot does not operate within the boundaries of its specified parameters, it is the manufacturer's fault. If the robot is used in circumstances that make its use illegal, then it is the commander's fault. The important matter is that there would be a regulatory framework for the use of AW in place, which is not yet the case. Suggestions for restricting the use of AW are made in Chapter 6. Finally, there is only the possibility left of an accident involving an AW that cannot be attributed to either poor design or a failure of procedure. This would indeed be a very tricky case legally. The only solution would be to simply withdraw all of the AW of this particular design. If the weapon is not withdrawn from service, it can only be interpreted as a failure of politics and maybe as a war crime or crime against humanity committed by the political leadership of a state.

Proposed Solutions

Roboticists and other people in the defense sector have proposed various solutions to address the legal and ethical concerns about the possible use of autonomous robots on the battlefield. One of these people is John Canning, who suggested preventing machines from targeting men. Another engineer highly involved in the military robotics debate is Ronald Arkin, who wants to develop an ethical programming for military robots. Finally, there is the possibility of sidestepping the issues connected to weapons autonomy through the use of neural interfaces that would allow soldiers to control military robots from a distance.

Machines Targeting Machines

A new legal theory has been proposed by John Canning, who is the chief engineer at the US Naval Surface Warfare Center. Canning argues that international law does not, in principle, prohibit the use of AW. Any weapon that is used in war must allow discrimination between lawful and unlawful targets. Whether or not the use of a particular weapon is lawful would depend as much on the weapon itself (it might be outlawed), as on the manner in which it is used ('any lawful weapon can be used illegally'). John Canning is aware that current and near-future AW would be indiscriminate weapons. At the same time, leaving a man in the loop would be 'a "performance- and cost-killer"' when considering the employment of large numbers of unmanned systems'. He therefore proposes that a way to get around this dilemma of deploying rather stupid robots for combat missions is to make 'machines target other machines' and to 'let men target men' (Canning 2006). The autonomous robot could disarm humans by firing at their weapons ('target the bow and not the archer') or by using non-lethal weapons for this purpose. In many cases non-lethal options might be entirely sufficient for deciding a tactical situation. Combining them with robots makes sense because there would be no additional risks for human soldiers should the non-lethals sometimes be ineffective. However, in cases where lethal force would be required and it would be too difficult technically for the machine to discriminate, a human operator could remotely control it, or at the very least confirm targets selected by the robot before they were engaged.

In effect, a person who holds a gun and is killed by a robot would be legally considered as collateral damage, as the robot was technically aiming at the gun and not at the person holding it. While Canning's proposal would seem to solve the legal problems with respect to discrimination and accountability, it could be very difficult to apply it in practice, especially with respect to irregular warfare. Noel Sharkey thinks that 'in reality, a robot could not pinpoint a weapon without pinpointing the person using it or even discriminate between weapons and non-weapons' (Sharkey 2007a). In any case, it could be relatively easy for enemy combatants to conceal their weapons or to make them unrecognizable to a machine by changing their color or shape (e.g. by putting a plastic bag around them). Determining whether an object is a human and whether this human is an enemy combatant and has a weapon is not at all a trivial task for a robot. It might be completely unrealistic to assume that robots could make all of these distinctions sufficiently reliably even in 10 or 20 years.

This would mean that robotic weapons would have to fall back in many cases on operator control or non-lethal weapons. However, even the use of non-lethal options is in no way unproblematic. Non-lethal weapons would include mainly riot control agents, rubber bullets, Tasers and new directed-energy weapons (microwaves, sound, lasers) and all of these types could indiscriminately injure, or even kill, people. In particular, Tasers, which have become quite common among law enforcement agencies all over the world, have already led to numerous accidental deaths. According to research carried out by Amnesty International, Tasers accidentally killed 245 people between 2001 and 2007 in the US alone (Rawlyk 2007). Directed-energy weapons (high-power microwaves and lasers), as well as sound weapons, can cause serious and permanent damage to a person exposed to them. Human rights advocates have also pointed at the unknown long-term bioeffects from the exposure to the microwave emitter *active denial system* (ADS). This could make it politically difficult to deploy such systems and to use them indiscriminately (Beason 2005, 10). According to international law it is also illegal to use weapons that cause unnecessary suffering and which are deemed inhumane. For this reason lasers used for blinding people are outlawed (Geneva Convention Protocol IV on Blinding Laser Weapons 1995). Other non-lethal weapons could face a similar fate. Furthermore, it could be argued that non-combatants have the right not to be treated as combatants and should not be targeted at all, no matter whether this results only in minor injuries or coercion (Mayer 2007). An autonomous riot-control robot, even if armed only with non-lethal weapons, could be considered as a potentially illegal use of such weapons.

Ethics for Robots

The general idea of equipping robots with laws to ensure their ethical behavior is relatively old and could offer a solution to the problem of possible robot war crimes. The science fiction author Isaac Asimov is generally credited with the invention of the concept of robot laws. In his 1942 short story 'Runaround' he formulated the famous three robot laws, which are:

First Law: A robot may not injure a human being, or, through inaction, allow a human being to come to harm.

Second Law: A robot must obey orders given it by human beings, except where such orders would conflict with the First Law.

Third Law: A robot must protect its own existence as long as such protection does not conflict with the First or Second Law. (Asimov 1968)

Although entirely fictional and invented mainly for the purpose of creating interesting stories around the laws, which subsequently and ironically prove their flawedness, Asimov's robot laws have attracted considerable interest from AI experts and roboticists over the years, who have become very concerned about the military applications of robotics. However, among roboticists there seems to be some agreement that Asimov's laws are hardly applicable to reality, as it would be extremely difficult for a robot to distinguish a human from any other object or to make judgments of what kind of its behavior could cause human injury – not to mention that the resulting robot intervention into dangerous human behaviors would often be highly unwanted (Brooks 2002, 72–5; R. Clarke 1993/94). Nevertheless, embedding some safeguards in the form of an ethical programming into autonomous robots seems to be a very good idea.

Recently (and slightly reminiscent of Asimov's robot laws) it has been suggested by the roboticist Ronald Arkin of the Georgia Institute of Technology to embed an ethical programming into military robots (Arkin 2007). While Asimov's laws would effectively preclude any military use of robots (and indeed there are no such robots in his stories), Arkin wants to program military robots in a way that would make them comply with the conventions and customs of war and behave ethically (Arkin 2007).

In particular, Arkin has proposed building something like an expert system for military ethics or, more precisely, a 'hybrid deliberative/reactive robot architecture', which would be able to make an autonomous ethical decision when opening fire on an enemy would conform to international law and any rules of engagement that may be given to it in addition. The way it is conceived, it would allow a military robot some limited capability to learn from experience and also some moral autonomy (the robot can reject unethical orders) (Arkin 2007, 4). Arkin assumes that future robots will be without emotions and completely predictable in the sense that they can always explain and justify their behavior (Arkin 2007, 6, 10).

As part of his US Army-sponsored research project Arkin has begun to translate the laws of armed conflict and the customs of war into a logical structure that can be handled by a software program. The key elements of Arkin's robot ethics program are an 'Ethical Governor', which suppresses unethical lethal behavior, and a 'Responsibility Advisor', which allows the attribution of responsibility for any action of the robot. The Ethical Governor makes sure that any weapons use is in accordance with international law, the rules of engagement and broader ethical principles. The Responsibility Advisor 'advises in advance of the mission, the operator(s) and commander(s) of their ethical responsibilities should the lethal autonomous system be deployed for a specific battlefield situation' (Arkin 2007, 61). The ethical programming also tracks any commands by humans and any possible overrides. This would make it possible to determine who would be responsible for any lethal robot behavior. So it would never be possible to blame the robot, as the robot's decision-making process would always be completely transparent.

Arkin's ethical military robot would definitely represent a major progress over currently used automated weapons and military systems that do not have any ethical safeguards whatsoever. But there are many points of criticism that can be raised.

Not ready yet Arkin has pointed out himself that the research he has already done only amounts to 'babysteps' and that other researchers would have to join his efforts for creating an 'artificial conscience' for military robots. Considering the fact that the first autonomous unmanned combat aerial vehicles (UCAVs) could arrive as soon as 2012, it is highly unlikely that the 'artificial conscience' for the robot planes could be ready in time (Sharkey 2007b). Technological development of actual robotic weapons could quickly surpass the very limited efforts by researchers to make them sufficiently safe for everyone before they see battle.

Problems with robot moral autonomy Arkin suggests that a military robot should have the ability to refuse an illegal/immoral order. This moral autonomy of the robot should only be overridden by an authorized commander in the face of an 'imminent catastrophe'. While it is true that human soldiers do have both the right and the duty to reject orders that are illegal, it is far from clear whether any military organization would want to have robots that can refuse orders. It could easily be the case that the understanding of the robot of any given situation differs significantly from the understanding of a human agent. Arkin simply assumes 'that effective situational assessment methods exist' that would prevent the robot from making a lethal mistake because of misreading the situation (Arkin 2007, 22). This is a pretty big assumption to make. In a presentation at a conference at Stanford University, Arkin hinted that in network-centric warfare (NCW) with sensors distributed all over the battlefield robots would eventually be better at discriminating targets than humans (R. Arkin 2008). That is certainly possible in a more distant future. But even NCW is not yet fully here and it has never been tested against a strong enemy (Ferris 2004). After all, the problem might not even lie in the quality of sensors, but in the overall cognitive abilities of the machine. Even excellent sensors can never compensate for a robot's deficient understanding of its environment. Humans are better at discriminating targets not because their vision is better, but because they understand what a target is and when and why to target something or somebody. If machines were similarly intelligent, they could be similarly capable of discrimination. NCW alone won't help much and the alternative possibility of creating machines with the cognitive capabilities or intelligence of a human being would result in obvious control issues.

Not applicable to all types of AW Arkin does not explicitly say it, but his ethical programming is first and foremost meant to be applied to large autonomous platforms. It would hardly be applicable to many other kinds of autonomous robotic weapons such as brilliant munitions, smart mines, Mini/micro-robots or nanobots. A main reason that could prevent the incorporation of a complex ethical programming into these types of AW would be their size, which affects their ability to read and understand their environment. A mini/microrobot simply cannot have the same sensory capabilities and computing power as a large platform. Its ability to make informed ethical decisions would always be very limited. Of course, it is not Arkin's job to solve all problems that might arise from all conceivable types of AW, but it also potentially leaves a tremendous gap in the whole military robot ethics debate. One could ask: why should autonomous platforms carry an ethical programming, if many other already existing types of weapons with a substantial degree of autonomy don't have it? What would be the rule for embedding ethics in some AW, but not in others?

Will ethical robots be militarily effective?   Ethically programmed military robots would need to prove that they can be not only ethical, but also sufficiently militarily effective. It might be the case that the 'artificial conscience' slows the robots down too much, or that their inherent behavioral limitations could be too easily exploited by an enemy. Jason Borenstein argues that 'if an AWS [autonomous weapons system] is strictly forbidden from firing on certain categories of targets, it may limit its usefulness. On the other hand, if it "learns" that combatants have a tendency to gather together in civilian buildings, the likelihood greatly rises that an AWS would end up firing on non-combatants' (Borenstein 2008, 7). Ethical military robots could even encourage more immoral tactics on the part of opponents. For example, if ethical military robots were programmed never to shoot at children, an enemy could exploit such a behavioral limitation by using child soldiers. Ethical robots might also turn out not to be very survivable in a real war against a tough opponent. Although a robot's life might be considered cheap compared with a human's, a high-end military robot could be far too expensive to be wasted. If the robots cost $1 million each, one would not like to lose them at a rate of 10 or 100 a day.[3] Military robots without ethical restrictions could be faster and more lethal and thus more survivable and more effective. This would not always be desirable, but permanently ethically restricted robots might not be very desirable from a military point of view either. To deliver a decisive punch, one would not want to gamble that robots fail to shoot fast enough in the moment when it really matters.

Can we test when a robot is ethically ready for war?   Chris Elliot, who is a fellow at the Royal Society of Engineering, suggested during the RUSI conference in February 2008 letting military robots take a 'military Turing test', which would determine whether or not they would be ethically fit for the battlefield. 'That means an autonomous system should be no worse than a human at taking decisions [about valid targets]' (Mick 2008). According to Elliot, an AW that was not as good as a human in making targeting decisions would be illegal under international law. Such robots do not yet exist and might not be built very soon. At the moment, legality would

---

3   According to Bob Quinn, who is the program manager for the *Talon* robot at Foster-Miller, since 2003 more than '160 robots were blown up and 85% of those were *Talons*'. This already indicates a significant loss rate for military robots considering that the opposition has up to now little reason for targeting them, as they are still unarmed.

therefore be a major barrier to the deployment of such systems (Mick 2008). The next question one could ask is whether it would be possible to develop a sufficiently reliable testing method and what such a test would look like. Considering the great complexity of robot behaviors and the great variety of situations they would need to cope with, this is not going to be an easy or trivial task.

Neural Interfaces

A way out of the dilemma of deploying completely autonomous weapons is to keep a human operator in the loop. It was pointed out in Chapter 2 that this could only be a militarily unsatisfactory solution that does not take full advantage of the potential of robotic weapons. In order to get the best of both worlds – the speed and accuracy of a machine and the high cognitive abilities of a human – since the early 1980s, DARPA has pursued a brain–machine interface that would allow a human to launch a weapon or control machines by the power of thought. This might also address the legal problems connected with weapon autonomy, as a human – or at least a human mind – would remain in the loop.

Eric Eisenstadt from the US Defense Sciences Office described the concept of the neural interface in a speech in the following way: 'Our Brain Machine Interface Program is about giving machine-like capabilities to intelligence, asking the brain to accommodate synthetic devices, and learning how to control those devices much the way we control our arms and legs today' (Eisenstadt 2002). The current approach to developing a neural interface is to implant a computer chip into an animal, for example a rat or cat, and then use a wireless controller for giving it commands in the form of neural stimuli that reward desired behavior. Eisenstadt claims that 'most roboticists can appreciate that there is nothing in their labs that can move like this' (Eisenstadt 2002). In the long run, the goal would be to develop neural interfaces for disabled people so that they could use artificial eyes or limbs.

The military wants neural interfaces to allow humans to fly aircraft by thought, or remotely operate robots as if they were there, or operate robotic devices such as exoskeletons that could be 'worn' by soldiers like clothes. An application of neural interfaces that was considered by DARPA for its 'Pilot's Associate' program was the possibility of allowing a fighter pilot to select targets and fire weapons by thought. This technology was shown off in the successful 1982 Clint Eastwood movie *Firefox*.

Although the development of thought-controlled weapons would be a long term goal, there are already some concrete applications for mind-reading technologies. For example, Northrop Grumman is already working on a Cognitive Technology Warning System, which would bring threats subconsciously recognized by a soldier's brain to the attention of the soldier by marking it on a helmet visor display. This would enable the soldier to recognize dangers and respond to threats much faster (Page 2008e).

In principle, neural interfaces can be invasive, which means they require electrodes or computer chips to be implanted in the brain, or they could be non-invasive using sensor devices that can read brain activity, for example EEGs (electroencephalography) or MEGs (magnetoencephalography). Obviously, for humans non-invasive methods would be much more preferable to invasive ones, but they are currently difficult to realize. EEGs are too crude for most applications (too little bandwidth) and MEGs would require future technology such as superconductors to make them fit into a helmet that can be worn by a human (Zimmer 2004, 46). Brain–machine interfaces that are effective and practical could be just as far away from deployment as strong AI in autonomous systems.

There are also ethical issues with neural interfaces. First, neural interfaces that are invasive and require an alteration of the natural human brain would raise the question of to what extent the personality of the individual would be affected. Secondly, neural interfaces could allow machines or other people to control a human being like a robot.[4] It would be some technologically sophisticated form of brainwashing that could ensure complete obedience of a human subjected to it, similarly to the technical control exerted on 'cyborg' animals.

Thought-controlled weapons might also result in different legal problems, as pointed out in an article by Stephen White. White argues that there could be a legal problem in determining the intentionality of an action triggered by thought (White 2008). The thought would be the action and the thought would be determined by an analysis of brain activity. This would raise the question of to what extent we can control what we think and whether we could be actually morally and legally responsible for our thoughts. According to White, 'Anglo-American criminal law has refused to criminalize someone solely for his or her bad thoughts'. This could mean that it would be difficult to hold human pilots who control unmanned aerial vehicles (UAVs) by neural interface responsible for any actions triggered by their thoughts, as the thought alone could not amount to an 'actus reus' (White 2008, 195–6). Such speculations on future brain–machine interfaces could indicate some legal loopholes that should be closed before such systems are deployed, which in any case would not be very soon. As a result, neural interfaces are a rather unlikely solution for the issue of autonomous military robots and create their own legal and ethical dilemmas.

Conclusion: The Need for Legal Regulation of AW

The issue of the conformity or non-conformity of AW to international law is a complex one. On the one hand, it is true that AW or robots are technically not outlawed, as the terms 'autonomous weapon' or 'robot' do not appear anywhere in

---

4   This is an allegation often heard in conspiracy theories on mind control experiments, which raises the question how serious one should take the argument. However, it is a matter of fact that small animals can be remote-controlled with the help of neural interfaces. There is little reason to assume that the human mind would be less susceptible to technical manipulation, although producing desired behaviors might be a lot more difficult to achieve.

the main texts of international law regulating armed conflict, such as the Geneva and Hague Conventions. They are also not specifically mentioned in arms control agreements, such as the Conventional Forces in Europe treaty. From this point of view it is absolutely true what Gordon Johnson from the Joint Forces Command said: AW do not, in principle, violate existing international law (Cowan 2007, 9).

On the other hand, there are broader moral principles underlying the codified conventions of war, such as necessity, discrimination, proportionality and humaneness, to which AW would need to prove their compatibility. If they are, as critics claim, not compatible to the moral principle of discrimination, then they could be seen as violating international law. But even in the case of a weapon being inherently indiscriminate, the possession alone of such a weapon is no breach of international law. Whether or not a specific use of such a weapon would be illegal would very much depend on the manner in which the weapon is used. As John Canning has pointed out: even a lawful weapon can be used in an unlawful manner. There are many military roles for autonomous systems where their use would not pose any insurmountable legal problems. For example, an AW with restricted mobility that patrols an area that has been closed to civilians would amount to a discriminate use of the weapon. There is little doubt that many autonomous systems will soon be widely used in exactly such roles.

When it comes to more offensive roles, or the use of autonomous systems among civilians, it would be a much more complicated case. Manufacturers and the armed forces must make sure that the weapons they use are safe, which means in this context that it must be possible to use them discriminately. This is a requirement for all weapons procured by the armed forces and it will also be relevant in the case of military robots. Members of the armed forces are definitely sensitive to the concerns raised about the legality of AW and it is in their best interest to have weapons that perform exactly as advertised. If they don't, it will be a serious problem. Everybody working in the military robotics sector knows that a malfunctioning weapons-carrying robot is simply unacceptable.

There is already an example that illustrates how much the US military worries about robots massacring civilians or opening fire at friendlies. In April 2008, it was reported that the armed *SWORDS* robot produced unintended movements, which has been adamantly denied by the manufacturer Foster-Miller (Foster-Miller 2008). Kevin Fahey, an executive officer for the US Army's ground combat systems, commented in reference to these incidents: 'If something goes wrong it may prevent us from fielding an armed robot for about 10 to 20 years because once you've done something that's really bad, it's almost impossible … to overcome that' (Magnuson 2008a).

This big concern is the main reason why armed military robots have not been used frequently operationally. When they were used – as in the case of *Predator B* or *SWORDS* – they were constantly under the control of a human operator. In the case of an accident, the step toward full autonomy could be delayed for many years to come – not because the technology would not be ready, but because the legal and diplomatic risks could be considered too high in relation to the actual military advantage gained. It can be assumed that the armed forces will be very careful about deciding when the right moment has come to use autonomous systems in battle.

There are certainly many technical methods that can be used for making military robots as safe to use as possible. This process of developing autonomous robots that are safe and that can be tested and cleared for battle with the help of a military Turing test will undoubtedly take many years. But eventually military robots exhibiting greater autonomy and capable of triggering their weapons by themselves will be fielded. This means the best strategy for the armed forces is to simply wait it out, as one US Air Force officer suggested:

> The United States needs to build confidence that a robot airplane would have the same caution about dropping ordnance in the right place as a human being. As the system matures, technology should allay fears and cultural opposition. ROE [rules of engagement] can be modified as world opinion and cultural bias become accustomed to automated warfare. (Lazarski 2001)

Through some 'social conditioning' the concerns of the general public could be overcome (Guetlein 2005, 17). In the meantime, states that develop AW might choose to voluntarily restrict them to such narrow tasks, such as guard duties or using them as some kind of intelligent and mobile mine, or might renounce their use completely.

This is not to say that there would be no problems with the concept of AW with regard to international law and the law of armed conflict at all. For example, the question whether AW could encourage states to go to war more easily is an important one, as well as the question of whether these weapons could accidentally trigger a war, which is explored in the final chapter. Furthermore, there are also lots of ethical aspects connected to the use of AW, which are not covered in a meaningful way by the laws of armed conflict. In addition, it would be very important to think about how AW could evolve in the future and what could be the long term implications they have with respect to changing the nature of warfare.

Even if all modern military organizations would presently subscribe to the concept of the man in the loop or robot ethics, there is no guarantee that in the long term the military would find tele-operated robots or military robots with ethical safety switches desirable because they might turn out to be too limited in their capability. Military organizations might choose in their eternal strife for competitiveness to let AW evolve by themselves to make them more intelligent and more independent (De Garis 2005, 81–122). Military robots might be given a drive for self-preservation just to make them more survivable on the battlefield. At some point in the future it might no longer be even technically possible to insert any safety mechanisms into evolving and self-learning military robots. These robots, once intelligent enough, might find ways of disabling safety mechanisms (Georges 2003, 72).

At the moment, nobody suggests building truly autonomous and self-learning military robots, but it could easily happen in the long run and it would create serious ethical problems and issues that go far beyond legality issues. It can be said that international law is simply unprepared for the particular ethical challenges that are posed by AW, especially when seen from a long term perspective. The broader ethical implications of military robots are therefore discussed in Chapter 5.

Chapter 5
Ethical Considerations

There is a fine, but important, difference between what is legal and what is moral in war – a difference that is sometimes overlooked in discussions on military ethics, which tend to focus more on the legality aspect. This can be problematic. Wars and actions in wars might adhere to existing legal standards. At the same time, they could violate moral standards that lack legal codification. Besides, not all laws are in perfect harmony with common perceptions of what is moral and this can result in situations where law and morals conflict. One and the same action may be perfectly legal, but may also be perceived as being highly immoral. For example, the Coalition forces massively attacked the Iraqi forces fleeing from Kuwait at the very end of the 1991 Gulf War. This episode was reported in the media as 'highway of death', as it resulted in the destruction of thousands of Iraqi vehicles and military personnel. Though being (probably) formally legal, the attack on an enemy that could no longer defend itself was sharply criticized as having been immoral (Challans 2007, 39–40). In other words, following the letter of the law does not free one from making ethical judgments.

War poses a tremendous challenge for ethics, as it ultimately involves violence directed against things and people, some of whom, even those wearing uniforms, may be innocent. Not surprisingly, military ethics is considered by pacifists to be a contradiction in terms. According to them, wars are, in principle, immoral. It follows that there is no possibility of conducting wars ethically. The problem with this position is that it ignores the reality in which we live – in a world where war is still a frequent occurrence. Abolishing the armed forces leaves societies unprotected, which might invite aggression and which might have far worse ethical consequences for societies than being prepared for war (Walzer 2000, 331–2). Arguing that any use of violence is immoral does not solve the ethical questions and dilemmas of societies and professionals engaged in war and warfare. Wars are certainly bad in ethical terms, but wars fought without any ethical restraint are many times worse. The military and society cannot escape the question of how to fight and how to kill ethically, even if this sounds, maybe rightly so, quite distasteful to some people.

According to Just War Theory, there are wars that can be ethically justified because they counter aggression and because these wars are conducted in a lawful and ethical manner. It follows that some weapons would be more suitable for the conduct of a just war than others. For example, precision weapons that are designed to target and destroy specifically military objects like tanks are deemed to be more ethical weapons than weapons that are inherently indiscriminate (e.g. anti-personnel mines or weapons of mass destruction (WMD)).

In Chapter 4 it was argued that robotic/autonomous weapons do not fit easily into the legal framework of war. On the one hand, there are no inherent reasons that they would be illegal, while on the other hand they still raise serious ethical concerns that are insufficiently addressed by existing international law. It is not quite clear whether robotic/autonomous weapons can be considered just as an evolution of smart weapons and another progress toward making warfare more ethical – a view taken by Ronald Arkin (Arkin 2008), or whether they would amount to the exact opposite: simply a new means of making war more destructive and brutal and thus representing a very negative tendency. For example, Paul Hirst fears in reference to robotic weapons:

> The new weapons will be brutal to civilians, and they will favour those most ruthless in their use. Turned into terror weapons or set loose against masses of desperate environmental refugees they have the power to make the latter part of this century even more bloody than the first half of the last. (Hirst 2001b)

The obvious deficiencies of the law of armed conflict make it necessary to look more closely at the ethical questions connected with employing weapons that remove the human soldier from the battlefield and possibly exclude them (at least on a tactical level) from the decision-making. The law of armed conflict can only say that robotic/autonomous weapons would be legal, if they can be used discriminately and proportionately. It cannot say whether or not they should be used at all, discriminately or not.

What complicates the matter even more is that there are certainly conditions imaginable in which the possession, or even use, of indiscriminate or illegal weapons can be ethically justified. Nicholas Fotion, a philosopher specializing in military ethics, for example argues that 'there are situations, albeit not everyday ones, where the use of poison gas is not obviously immoral' (Fotion 1990, 79). They could be used as deterrents that allow a state 'to respond in kind' to a chemical weapons threat or use by other states. Fotion points out that 'the cliché "If you have a weapon, you will use it" seems far from the truth. Historical records of poison-gas use suggest a different cliché: "If you don't have it, watch out!"' (Fotion 1990, 79). Similarly, it could be argued that robotic/autonomous weapons are ethical because they can be used for deterring aggression and making the use of military force unnecessary. However, it is certainly too early to make a judgment, as too little empirical data is available on the deterrent effect of high-tech weaponry (Pardesi 2005, 3).

The following discussion attempts to look more closely at the broader ethical issues connected to robotic weapons both within and beyond the Just War tradition. Here it is argued that robotic weapons and automation in general pose many novel ethical challenges for the conduct of war and for society. Like in many other cases, high technology offers many opportunities, but also poses potentially grave dangers. At the moment, there is certainly no definite answer to the question whether or not robotic weapons could represent an ethical progress in warfare, or whether they would be rather ethically highly problematic and undesirable. However, what is attempted in this chapter is to consider the most important ethical issues connected to the development, possession and use of robotic weapons.

The Societal Costs of Warfare

Warfare has always been extremely costly for society. Warfare is expensive not only because of the highly destructive consequences of war, but also to no small extent because of the great costs connected to maintaining large standing armed forces and a sizeable defense industrial infrastructure that can design, produce and support weapons that the armed forces need. Furthermore, wars tend to be very costly in terms of human lives. There is little doubt that modern wars are substantially more destructive than wars of earlier periods in history. With the advent of nuclear weapons it has become possible to destroy all life on this planet – a possibility that simply did not exist before the 1950s. Some would argue that even conventional weapons have become so overly destructive that future wars fought with them could be substantially more destructive than the two world wars of the twentieth century. The question is, would robotic/autonomous weapons reduce, or rather, increase the societal costs of warfare? From a utilitarian perspective a type of weapon that can reduce the societal costs of warfare would be considered to be more ethical than weapons that do not have this quality. It appears that utilitarians would like robotic/autonomous weapons for several reasons. Most importantly, they promise to be more effective and efficient.

Military Robots Are More Effective, Efficient and Environmentally Friendly

General Westmoreland made the argument that machines are militarily effective and economically more efficient than humans and they should therefore be welcomed.

> Today, machines and technology are permitting economy of manpower on the battlefield … But the future offers even more possibilities for economy. I am confident the American people expect this country to take full advantage of its technology – to welcome and applaud the developments that will replace wherever possible the man with the machine. (Quoted in Dickson 1976, 215–23)

If autonomous robots would be more effective and efficient in achieving a given military mission than human soldiers, then it would be preferable to use robots for that mission instead of humans. The military is an institution that has to serve the interests of society and has to carry out any mission (within the boundaries of the military profession) that society may demand of the military. Society has to pay for the military and can expect that the functions of the military are carried out as effectively and efficiently as possible. It is the duty of the armed forces to expect and to be prepared for the worst, while being realistic in their estimation of the threat and the resources required to address the threat.

Obligation to military effectiveness   Military professionalism dictates that a military organization has to remain competitive, so that it can successfully fight other military organizations. Technology plays an important role with respect to military competitiveness, as it often, but not always, has a major influence on the outcome of wars. Although the relationship between superior technology and victory is a complex one, there are a lot of examples in military history where technology was a main factor in the outcome of a war. Christopher Coker, who is an expert in military ethics, points at the Third Afghan War in 1919. The British won the war in contrast to the earlier Afghanistan wars primarily because they could utilize heavy machine guns, armored cars, lorries and aircraft, while the Afghan warriors did not have this advantage (Coker 2008, 146). It has become conventional wisdom in military circles that 'quality now trumps quantity' – better-equipped and trained militaries will generally do better than less well-equipped and trained militaries with the overall size of the forces playing a much smaller role (Cohen 2006, 244). Thus military organizations cannot be complacent about technology and have to stay at the forefront of technological development. Winning wars is the main function of the military and it is the main criterion by which the military is judged. Mission accomplishment is therefore the 'bedrock of military professionalism' (Cook 2004, 92). This means that the military cannot afford to ignore a technology like robotics, which promises tremendous gains in effectiveness, while reducing the risks for military operations. In the worst case an aggressor state equipped with superior weapons could not only defeat and occupy a country, but also engage in genocide against the defeated nation. It is thus very dangerous and thus irresponsible to allow potential enemies too great an advantage in terms of military technology.

Obligation to efficiency   The military is also obligated toward society to make good use of limited resources. Military security is just one of the needs modern society has and it can be argued that it is not even the most important one. Society and its political representatives have to determine how many resources should be allocated to defense and society has a right to demand that the best possible use is made of these resources. The military is not entitled to waste and robotic/ autonomous weapons offer plenty of opportunities for savings. First, the individual platforms would be significantly cheaper than crewed equivalents. They might cost per unit less than a third, or even much less for smaller systems. Secondly, military personnel could be cut back substantially to a fraction of the current strength, which should also result in great savings. Robots do not receive wages, benefits or pensions. Personnel-related costs of maintaining sufficiently capable armed forces would drop. Finally, the costs for maintenance and operations should also drop substantially as a result of the utilization of robotic/autonomous weapons. Robots could be permanently crated, mothballed and stored at minimum costs.

For example, 'operational UCAVs [unmanned combat aerial vehicles], with wings detached, could be housed in their own sealed, deployable storage containers … for up to 10 years' (R. Chapman 2002). While in storage there would be an automated diagnostics program that would run from time to time and guarantee that the aircraft remains ready for action – a concept that is called 'bomber in a box' (Brzezinski 2003). Whenever needed, they can be easily transported into theater where they could be quickly assembled and utilized. Many small types of robotic/autonomous weapons might be so cheap that they could be disposable, thus completely eliminating maintenance costs. There is certainly a strong economic argument for utilizing military robotics, which means that defense would cost less and the state can allocate more money for financing welfare, education and building infrastructure.

Environmental considerations   The environmental footprint of large armed forces is far from being negligible. Especially in terms of fuel consumption militaries do very badly, which not only speeds up the eventual depletion of natural oil and gas, but also contributes significantly to global warming. The most extreme example is the US military, which consumes more than 365,000 barrels of oil a day. This equals the entire consumption of an industrial country like Sweden (Turse 2008b, 41). Robotic platforms could be smaller and lighter and therefore much more fuel-efficient. In addition, robotic systems would also consume overall much less fuel because they would be used much less, as military personnel do not need to train on them, or training can be conducted primarily via computer simulations. It has been pointed out that 'about 90 percent of a manned combat aircraft's flying life is devoted to flights other than combat – primarily training missions' (Hebert 2003). Savings and resulting environmental benefits should be significant.

Conclusion   If robots are cheaper (there are plenty of reasons that they would be) and if they are more capable to carry out certain missions (at least at some tasks robots can outperform humans consistently), it would make a strong moral case for the use of robots. From a utilitarian perspective the actual costs and performance of robots should in the end determine how widely they should be used, for which roles they should be used and whether or not they should be autonomous. Once robots become more capable because of progress in artificial intelligence (AI) they should be allowed to take over any role that they can carry out better than humans. All of this could lessen the economic burden and the environmental impact of defense and could result in many benefits for society.

Robots Protecting Human Life

One of the strongest and most frequently cited ethical reasons for the use of military robots is that robots can protect human life. This has become particularly important because in postmodern societies human life is seen to be immensely valuable. In other words, society has less tolerance for putting lives at risk under any circumstances (Shaw 2005, 79–80). This is primarily a political problem, but the underlying ethical question is whether there are good enough ethical reasons for asking soldiers to accept great risks to their life and health, if this could be avoided with the help of technology. One might say that the risks for soldiers have increased, while the reasons and necessity for exposing soldiers to these risks seem to have diminished.

The changed moral contract   Many soldiers are willing to sacrifice their lives, if they do it in defense of their families, their way of life and the vital interests of the nation they serve. However, the defense of the territorial integrity of the nation against outside aggressors has ceased for most modern armed forces in the world to be their primary mission. Instead, soldiers are sent abroad and expected to risk their lives for abstract ideas such as humanitarianism or for 'projecting stability' in places far away from home. According to the philosopher Martin Cook, the changed context in which armed force is used has also changed the moral contract between soldier and state. A member of the armed forces who is sent on a humanitarian mission overseas and expected to risk their own life 'may say with moral seriousness, This isn't what I signed up for – and all the more if casualties mount, the length of deployment drags on, and the probability of achieving the goal of the mission declines' (Cook 2004, 125). Therefore, soldiers sent on humanitarian/peacekeeping operations would be morally entitled to the best possible force protection. This could mean giving a priority to the use of unmanned systems in exactly such cases in order to keep soldiers out of the line of fire wherever possible.

Growing lethality of high-intensity war   It would be immoral to send soldiers on a military mission that they are unlikely to survive, unless it is absolutely necessary for national survival. It can be argued that the chances of survival have dropped so significantly on the high-tech battlefield as to make humans unfit for it (Shaker and Wise 1988, 161–2; Barnaby 1986, 8–11). This was the main reason why military interest in robots grew and research in military robotics soared in the 1980s. WMD, precision-guided munitions (PGMs) and growing amounts of conventional firepower available to the opposing sides (NATO and Warsaw Pact) would have tremendously reduced the survivability of human forces on the central European battlefield. The 1973 Yom Kippur War indicated the low survival rate of armored forces caught in the open. The Israelis lost more than 400 tanks and the Arabs over 2,250 in just three weeks (Rabinovich 2005, 496–7). Iraq was hit even worse during the 1991 Gulf War, with 3,847 tanks, 1,450 armored personnel carriers (APCs) and 2,917 artillery pieces captured or destroyed during the six weeks of air campaign and four days of ground operations (Freedman and Karsh 1993, 409). The attrition rates for more equally matched forces equipped with PGMs could be horrendous. In the future, armed forces might have to fight on nuclear, biological or chemical battlefields where they would be (even with protective clothing) only able to fight and survive for just a few hours. War games that simulate the use of tactical nuclear weapons indicate human casualty rates of 70 percent (Dunnigan 1982, 275). In short, such potential high casualty rates caused by the likely use of WMD and high-tech weapons in future wars could be far too high to be acceptable to Western societies (Barnaby 1986, 10).

Enemies bound by no rules   Not only have the risks for soldiers increased in high-intensity conflicts, but also in low-intensity operations in Third World countries. Modern armed forces have to face enemies which are far less likely to adhere to the laws of armed conflict. This is quite obvious with respect to the current experience of Coalition soldiers in Afghanistan and Iraq. American soldiers and civilians were taken hostage, were beheaded and their bodies were mutilated, which was documented on video and put on the Internet. The cruelty is deliberate and part of the psychological warfare waged by the insurgents (R.H. Jones 2005, 1). This tactic can be quite successful, as in the case of the Somali mob dragging the dead and naked bodies of American soldiers through the streets of Mogadishu, which prompted the US forces to pull out in October 1993 (Shawcross 2000, 102). The use of unmanned systems could protect soldiers from the terrible fate of being captured, tortured and murdered by terrorists and insurgents (Anderson 2007).

Exposure to environmental dangers   Soldiers often have to cope with environmental hazards to which they are exposed in the course of duty and which can permanently damage their health. This includes the negative health effects of depleted uranium ammunitions, contamination caused by bombing and the long-term effects of having been exposed to blasts. A large number of soldiers who took part in Operation Desert Storm (ODS) (as many as 30 percent) have complained about ill health. They attribute it to possible exposure to chemicals or toxins during the war. Numerous studies seem to have confirmed that many soldiers did damage their health as a result of having taken part in ODS, though the exact causes may vary from case to case (Institute of Medicine 2006). Similarly, a large number of soldiers who took part in the 2003 Iraq War and those who have served in Iraq and Afghanistan may also have seriously damaged their health. The *Guardian* reported that 20,000 British soldiers could have received permanent brain injuries because of exposure to high-velocity explosions (Taylor and Addley 2007). The UK MoD acknowledges that about 500 British soldiers have suffered 'mild traumatic brain injury' and claimed that in the US forces the number would be far higher (up to 20 percent for soldiers in Iraq). An additional health risk could arise through the contamination of future battlefields with nanoparticles as a result of the use of nano-engineered materials and nano-scale machines (e.g. new sensors), which could become a similar health risk as asbestos (Shelley 2006, 77–80). It appears that the human body is far too fragile for the high stress and demands of modern warfare.

Psychological costs of combat   Soldiers who have taken part in war often experience psychological problems afterwards. Christopher Coker writes that the US would be facing a mental health crisis if some studies on the phenomenon were accurate: a '*Journal of Medicine* study published in 2005 estimated that one in six soldiers returning from the war zone could expect to experience major depression, anxiety or posttraumatic stress disorder (PTSD). As many as one in three reported milder symptoms' (Coker 2007, 100). The number of suicides and attempted suicides and self-injuries among US service personnel has gone up significantly since the beginning of the Iraq War (Associated Press 2008a), indicating the seriousness of PTSD and the psychological costs of having been in battle. The stress increases with mounting numbers of casualties. Psychological research indicates that 'no military unit can sustain 10% or more casualties in the course of a single operation without seriously compromising the sanity of the survivors' – making the use of robots quite necessary in future high-intensity wars (G. Chapman 1987). In addition, the exposure to danger and the stress connected with having to kill another human being can be extremely high, as Dave Grossman argues in his book *On Killing*. Grossman claims that the moral inhibition and mental resistance to kill 'represents a powerful psychological force on the battlefield' (Grossman 1996, 28) and that overcoming this force through drill or conditioning can lead to traumatization afterwards. He is the founder of a science he terms *killology*, which researches 'the reactions of healthy people in killing circumstances' and which teaches military and law-enforcement professionals to kill without being psychologically damaged (www.killology.org). The use of robots would help soldiers to avoid the stress of killing (and the PTSD afterwards) in the first place by leaving this grizzly, but sometimes necessary, task entirely to machines.

Conclusion   There can be little doubt that armed forces that can utilize robots will be less exposed to enemy fire and that this would most likely result in overall reduced risks for the soldiers. Although it is part of the military profession to take risks in defense of society and the vital interests of the nations they serve, it would be unethical to expose soldiers to more risks than is absolutely necessary. The state and society have a moral responsibility toward the soldiers who serve it, which means that the armed forces need to be adequately equipped and trained in order to reduce the human costs of war. It might soon be considered more unethical to send soldiers into battle without the protection of robotic systems than it is now to send them into battle without body armor. Rodney Brooks affirms in reference to combat robotics, 'It's a moral issue' (Weiner 2005b). At the same time, it is important to see the political nature of the supposedly ethical argument of saving lives. New weapons like military robots are not primarily introduced because of their ethical value, but because they could make it politically and militarily easier to conduct wars.

Robotic Warfare Could Be More Humane

New technologies such as military robotics, strategic information warfare and non-lethal weapons create the hypothetical and unprecedented possibility of waging bloodless war (Mandel 2004). If this was indeed possible, it would be an immense moral progress over previous and current forms of warfare in which soldiers and civilians are killed on a massive scale. There are now three main arguments why robotic warfare could humanize war, which are discussed below.

War without humans   The US and its allies will not be able to keep a monopoly on military robotics. Other nations seek to acquire the technology as well and at some point the presence of human soldiers in the battlespace would amount to suicide. Automated systems will be far more effective in defeating other automated systems. As a result, robot wars without direct human participation could soon become a reality. Robots fighting each other would raise few ethical problems. After all, any robot that is destroyed can be replaced. It does not have relatives and it would not be mourned. A robot war could stop at the point when a nation sees its military capabilities destroyed, even short of any human losses (Kurzweil 2001). In theory, a state might choose to carry on fighting with humans against robots, but it would offer little prospects of victory and would therefore be an irrational option that is not likely to be chosen. If a war was to be fought exclusively by machines it could be accurately modeled in a war game. Current war games suffer from the problem that they do not take into account training, morale and other psychological factors, which cannot be measured or quantified and which can still have a big impact on battles. If only machines participated in the actual conduct of a war, it would offer excellent possibilities for creating very accurate computer models. Two nations at war might choose to decide the war by running a simulation of it. Of course, this would beg the question whether two nations civilized enough to settle their conflicts in this way would want to fight a war at all (Libicki 2000, 54). Nevertheless, it is not completely absurd to assume that at least some future wars might be fought exclusively by robots or in cyberspace. Because of growing automation both sides would have big incentives for waging cyber-war with the aim of gaining control over the other side's computerized and roboticized war machine. Would a war stop once all command and control systems of one side are down? It is possible, but it might also trigger acts of desperation such as a retaliatory nuclear strike.

Reduction of war crimes   The roboticist Ronald Arkin claims that in the long term military robots could perform better than humans with respect to war crimes. He argues: 'It is not my belief that an unmanned system will be able to be perfectly ethical in the battlefield, but I am convinced that they can perform more ethically than human soldiers are capable of' (Arkin 2007, 7). Human soldiers commit war crimes for various reasons that could be completely irrelevant for military robots. Arkin gives a whole list of reasons why humans fail to behave ethically in war: the tendency to seek revenge for friendly losses, weak leadership, dehumanization of the enemy, poorly trained troops, no clearly defined enemy and unclear orders. A recent survey of the US Surgeon General's Office, which Arkin cites as evidence for his claim of human moral deficiencies, reveals with respect to soldiers deployed in Iraq tremendous shortcomings in their understanding of what is ethical or lawful behavior in war (Arkin 2007, 7). A robot could do better – provided it has good enough sensors and an ethical programming – because it would be incapable of intentionally committing war crimes and unlikely to do so accidentally. In addition, 'robotic systems need make no appeal to self-defense or self-preservation in this regard, and can and should thus value civilian lives above their own continued existence' (Arkin 2007, 11). In other words, an ethical robot could easily sacrifice itself if higher values such as human lives were at stake, which would be for a human neither easy, nor could it be expected of a human. It may be the case that robots would one day be more moral than humans. They might even be considered the only truly moral agents (Sullins 2006, 27). Such ethical military robots might not need to employ lethal force against humans. According to John Canning, 'using armed unmanned vehicles, we have a chance to adopt a new, more humane, paradigm of warfare, one which targets individual weapons instead of warriors' (quoted in Walker 2006).

Humanitarian robot intervention force   It has been observed that Western armed forces tend to avoid getting involved in civil wars and other humanitarian catastrophes because they fear casualties, the related public disapproval and the necessary long term commitment (Shearer 1998, 32). Humanitarian interventions are not cheap, as large intervention forces usually have to be deployed for many years. This means soldiers need to be deployed for extended periods overseas, which is inconvenient for the affected soldiers who have to spend a lot of time in boring and dangerous workplaces. It affects recruitment and retention rates and soldiers usually expect better financial compensation for these inconveniences. It is no surprise that states and their armed forces want to avoid getting involved in difficult and long term peacekeeping operations. However, once robots become sophisticated enough, robot armies could be used as a global police force intervening in civil wars. They could separate the warring parties and protect the civilians. Even if military robots could never fulfill all functions of human peacekeepers, their use would substantially cut down the numbers needed for an effective peacekeeping operation. Maybe only a small number of soldiers might need to be deployed together with robots for controlling a large area and the population in it. As a result, the risks and costs of peacekeeping operations may drop significantly. This would allow the international community to intervene more often to stop humanitarian catastrophes such as genocide and to reverse the breakdown of law and order in some parts of the world, which have up to now received little international attention or help. John Pike therefore argues 'we could end genocide' without the need of sacrificing thousands of American lives (Flam 2008). In other words, intervention with partially roboticized forces need not be unethical – in contrast, they could represent an acceptable compromise between financing a large and expensive long term peacekeeping operation and no action at all in the face of a humanitarian catastrophe. At the same time, one might wonder how prudent and effective it would be to rely on robotic peacekeepers. Robots that patrol the streets instead of human peacekeepers will most likely alienate the local population (Mandel

2006, 22). Robots can never 'win hearts and minds', but indicate (like the use of mercenaries) a lack of seriousness on the part of the intervening nation, as it would obviously not consider it worth risking the lives of human soldiers.

Conclusion

Although robots have a lot of potential for humanizing warfare, there are also serious safety concerns about robotic systems in the here and now, no matter whether they are civilian or military. *The Economist* reported that there were no fewer than 77 robot-related accidents in the UK in 2005 alone (*The Economist* 2006). Accidents involving unmanned or robotic systems have also occurred in the military. For example, a *Predator B* operated by the Department of Homeland Security crashed in April 2006 near the Mexican border because of a pilot error (Magnuson 2006). Luckily, nobody was harmed in the crash, but it still raised the issue of how to better regulate increasing unmanned aerial vehicle (UAV) air traffic. The loss rate of UAVs in military operations is still atrocious. In 2007, the US Air Force (USAF) announced that it had lost 50 percent of its 90 *Predators* in recent years (Jordan 2007). This gives some indication of the current reliability of unmanned systems. Furthermore, because of a long history of unsuccessful weapons tests and some training accidents, the armed forces have been very reluctant to embrace robotic weapons. Soldiers simply feel uncomfortable having an armed robot around, which might get out of control at any time (Shukman 1996, 187). Although the technology for robotic weapons with a limited degree of autonomy has been available since the 1980s, only very few systems have been fielded and hardly any of them were much more than remote-controlled machines. In the future, there could be substantial pressures to increase weapons autonomy and to field ever more technologically advanced weapons regardless of the technological challenges. A military analyst from the London-based International Institute of Strategic Studies is worried that 'there is also a serious risk that, unless equipped with recognition devices – which are far from development – robots will kill every living thing in their path, including allied soldiers not wearing the necessary electronic identification "badges"' (*Strategic Comments* 1999, 2). Similarly, Jason Borenstein fears that 'the modern nature of war is such that it often takes place in the middle of civilian areas where combatants are not easily distinguished from non-combatants. The irony is that precise and sophisticated weapons may put innocents in more, rather than less, danger' (Borenstein 2008, 6).

Moral Disengagement

Modern weapons make it possible to fight the enemy over greater and greater distances. Tanks and artillery can destroy targets over many miles and aircraft and missiles can reach targets over hundreds, if not thousands, of miles away. In modern war combatants often never get to see the enemy, which is something soldiers have actually come to lament (Swofford 2003). In modern, high-intensity warfare almost all 'engagements' take place over long distance, as both sides usually attempt to stay out of each other's weapons range. Robotic weapons will no doubt allow human soldiers to stand back even further from the action. This tendency could have some important psychological and ethical implications for the conduct of war.

Disconnecting Deeds and Morals

The ability to stay out of the enemy's weapons range protects the lives of soldiers. It is a humanitarian obligation of the state and of military commanders not to put lives at risk unnecessarily. But if soldiers could stay out of danger during most, or even all, combat, it could shatter the moral foundations of war. Psychologists and some military analysts claim that killing over distance and from a position of relative safety would emotionally and morally 'disengage' soldiers from their destructive and lethal actions, which they might never see and which they might only insufficiently grasp intellectually. This can lower, or even neutralize, their inhibition to kill, as Dave Grossman argues. He writes in reference to artillery crews, bomber crews, naval gunners and missile crews that he has 'not found a single instance of individuals who have refused to kill the enemy under these circumstances, nor have I found a single instance of psychiatric trauma associated with this type of killing' (Grossman 1996, 108). Military analyst Keith Shurtleff, in reference to Albert Borgmann's philosophy of technology (Borgmann 1984), explains this tendency through the device character of technologically advanced weapons. While less advanced weapons would be 'things' that require an operator to constantly engage with it to produce a certain effect, more automated weapons can be simply put in place and will do most things by themselves without the need for constant human attention or even much human effort. As a result, advanced technology splits means and ends and turns the effect into some sort of a commodity (Shurtleff 2002, 100). Thus people lose sight of means and their ethical implications and start concentrating only on the ends or outcomes. The sociologist Zygmunt Bauman has called this process of disconnecting deeds and morals 'adiaphorization'. Actions are declared to be ethically neutral by excluding people from the circle of moral subjects and by the use of a sanitizing or technical language. People are reduced to labels like the 'enemy' or 'targets' that are 'serviced' in 'clean, surgical strikes' (Bandura 1999). It is not called killing human beings, who might only appear as floating shapes seen from the bomb sight camera before the screen turns blank. War then becomes increasingly like a video game where people can be bombed and shot from a safe position by the push of a button (Bauman 1997).

Robotic Warfare

Maybe ironically, the use of robotic weapons can bring the brutality of combat actions back to the attention of soldiers. Turning a combat pilot into a remote operator significantly changes the psychological impact of killing, according to a USAF colonel. 'When you come in at 500–600 miles per hour, drop a 500-pound bomb and then fly away, you don't see what happens.' This would be very different for remote operators who launch a missile at a target: 'You watch it all the way to impact, and I mean it's very vivid, it's right there and personal. So it does stay in people's minds for a long time' (Thomson 2008). In robotic ground warfare remote operators might experience combat even more intensely than the *Predator* 'pilots'. Apparently the zoom on the Foster-Miller *SWORDS* robot is so good that it allows the remote operators to even read the name tags of the soldiers they are going to kill over a distance of 300 feet between robot and target. At such mediated proximity, killing will undoubtedly become psychologically more difficult again. However, though tele-operated systems have the potential to re-engage soldiers in combat, the future perspective of robotic weapons is that of growing autonomy. Coming back to Borgmann's device concept, more advanced robotic weapons would be 'devices', rather than things or tools. They might only require very little interaction with humans. The soldiers deploying these systems could be even less 'engaged' than missile or bomber crews. Hence, the moral dimension of their actions will be even more difficult for them to understand.

Diffusion of Responsibility

One of the main factors that substantially contributes to moral disengagement is the diffusion of responsibility. According to the psychologist Albert Bandura, 'A sense of responsibility can be diffused, and thereby diminished, by division of labor' (Bandura 1999). Tasks and actions are split up into smaller actions and decisions are taken collectively in groups. This means nobody has to feel particularly responsible for what is happening overall. For example, the moral responsibility for an execution is diffused by splitting up the task into a greater number of clearly defined actions carried out by a greater number of people so that none of them has to feel guilty about taking a life. Each individual action might not appear to be morally grave, but taken together these actions have a morally grave outcome. By diffusing responsibility ordinary people can take part in the greatest cruelties. Transferring some decision-making to autonomous systems could have a very similar effect. The engineer and roboticist David Atkinson argues that weapons autonomization blurs the moral responsibility for the use of force. He uses the example of a cruise missile to underline his point. The person who selects the target of the cruise missile would be morally responsible. However, once it would be possible for the cruise missile to re-target itself in flight for the case that it does not find its primary target – a technology that already exists – the responsibility becomes blurred. The cruise missile would then simply loiter over the target area and engage any suitable targets of opportunity. It may identify a tank and destroy it. Atkinson asks:

> Who now has the ethical responsibility for making the decision to kill the people in the tank? The person who originally launched the missile, but has no idea of what it actually attacked? The programmers of the 'search and destroy'

automation on-board the missile? The military program manager who decided to develop and deploy such systems? It is very easy to see how the responsibility for the decision to kill, in particular, has been blurred by the use of an autonomous weapons system. By taking away that clear responsibility, are we making it easier to kill? (Atkinson 2007)

The moral responsibility for killing the people in the tank is diffused among all the people, who somehow and mainly indirectly contributed to the end result. A military commander might not feel particularly morally responsible for any actions of a military robot that originated from some automated target selection routine. Similarly, the developers of the weapon will claim that they simply do not have any control about the context and manner in which the weapon is used and will therefore also refuse to be morally responsible for the weapon killing the tank crew. In any case, this was precisely the purpose for which the weapon was developed and the action itself would also be perfectly legal. The difference is just that killing becomes psychologically much easier.

Conclusion

One of the greatest restraints for the cruelty in war has always been the natural inhibition of humans not to kill or hurt fellow human beings. The natural inhibition is, in fact, so strong that most people would rather die than kill somebody – an inclination that has been observed on many battlefields. This most surprising behavior in the face of death was shown in a study on the American Civil War. A large percentage of all soldiers killed in the battle of Gettysberg did not fire their weapons at the enemy. Ninety percent of all recovered muskets were still loaded and almost half of them were loaded more than once (Grossman 1996, 22). Most soldiers could have shot at the enemy before being killed, but failed to do so. According to John Pike, 'two-thirds of the people who sign up for the military aren't capable of killing' (Flam 2008). Taking away the inhibition to kill by using robots for the job could weaken the most powerful psychological and ethical restraint in war. War would be inhumanely efficient and would no longer be constrained by the natural urge of soldiers not to kill, if it can be somehow avoided. Robots will do whatever they are programmed to do. If they were programmed to kill all enemy combatants, they will do exactly that. Like in the *Terminator* movie a military robot 'can't be reasoned with, it can't be bargained with … it doesn't feel pity or remorse or fear … and it absolutely will not stop. Ever.' Automating the act of killing does not appear to encourage or further ethical behavior in war.

Automating Killing

Most people probably find the whole idea of automating killing to be perverse. An action so serious in its consequences should not be left to mindless machines.

More academically, there is the ethical argument that there are certain things that should only be done by human beings and should never be delegated to machines because machines are in some crucial aspects different from us. This difference is existential and will not change, or be overcome by more sophisticated technology. No matter how intelligent machines become and no matter how perfectly they mimic us, they can never be truly like us.

Machines Are Ultimately Dumb

There is the argument that has been made by the philosopher John Searle that machines have in principle no grasp or understanding of what they are doing when they run a program (Searle 1980). In other words, computers/robots have no awareness of anything outside themselves or their internal processes. Searle has illustrated this point with his famous 'Chinese Room' thought experiment. A man who cannot speak Chinese gets handed into his room Chinese characters. He has a set of rules of how to assemble answers, which he hands back. The answers may make sense to a Chinese person outside the room, who might think he is communicating with another Chinese person when in fact he isn't because the 'person' in the room has no clue. In addition to showing that machines are necessarily 'dumb' in some respects, Searle wanted also to 'prove' with his Chinese Room argument that the Turing test is not a valid method of determining whether a computer is conscious or not.[1]

There are certainly great dangers in anthropomorphizing machines too much. The computer pioneer Joseph Weizenbaum made, for him, the shocking discovery in 1966 that people believed that computers could understand them and their problems. Weizenbaum had written a short piece of software called ELIZA that mimicked a psychoanalyst asking questions and that pretended to understand answers given by humans. Although it was very clear that the program was far too limited for having any grasp of the answers given by humans, people thought that they could have a genuine conversation with ELIZA and found it personally satisfying to talk to the machine (Weizenbaum 1977). However, the only thing a computer does is to calculate. For Weizenbaum it simply cannot reason or make moral judgments. We should not believe that there would be more to machines just because *we* attribute meaning to their answers or actions. Weizenbaum concluded that:

> No other organism, and certainly no computer, can be made to confront genuine human problems in human terms. And, since the domain of human intelligence

---

1   The Turing Test was proposed by Alan Turing in 1950 for determining whether a machine can be called intelligent or not. The test is based on the idea that a human has a conversation with either a human or a machine, which he both cannot see using some neutral medium, e.g. a teletype machine. If the human cannot distinguish between the answers of the other human or the machine, then the machine would pass the Turing Test and would have to be considered as intelligent.

is, except for a small set of formal problems, determined by man's humanity, every other intelligence, however great, must necessarily be alien to the human domain. (Weizenbaum 1977, 223)

The bottom line of this argument is that machines can do some things much better than humans, but they will always remain rather limited compared with us. The dangers of a dumb machine making lethal errors was shown memorably in the 1987 movie *Robocop*. A team of scientists demonstrates a new police robot by having a human point a gun at it. The police robot warns the human to put down the gun, the human complies and drops the gun, but the machine shoots him anyway because for some reason it did not realize that the human was no longer a threat, or that in fact the whole situation was just a demonstration. The theme of a machine's inherent inability to distinguish between simulation and reality has been picked up by a couple of movies, including the previously mentioned *War Games* (1984) and more recently *Stealth* (2005). A human would always have a much better comprehension of what kind of situation would warrant and justify the use of lethal force than a machine and would not blindly pull the trigger because some algorithm says so (Argy 2007).

A Robot Is No Moral Agent

It has been argued that even if machines become much more intelligent and can comprehend real-life situations, they are still no moral agents. A moral agent has not only the ability to tell right from wrong actions, but has to be able to feel remorse and to be punishable. The Australian ethicist Robert Sparrow sees the greatest ethical problem with AW in our inability to hold them morally responsible for their actions in any meaningful way. He argues: 'To hold that someone is morally responsible is to hold that they are the appropriate locus of blame or praise and punishment and reward' (Sparrow 2007b, 71). It is difficult to see how a machine could be punished in a way that it would make it feel remorse and to understand the suffering it has caused by taking a certain course of action. For people who have been wronged by a machine it might be equally unsatisfactory to tear the machine apart, as it would be futile to punish the machine with this measure. This would at least be true for the kind of robots that are currently technically feasible and at the moment nobody would seriously claim that a current or near-future robot could be morally responsible for its actions.

Machines Lack Empathy

Machines might have artificial or simulated emotions, but they will always lack the fundamental human ability to empathize with other human beings. Robert Sparrow said in an radio interview that 'one of the lessons that I think we should learn is that those things that make us human may not be our intelligence, may not be our ability to plan or to do mathematics, but may be our ability to suffer and to reach out to other suffering entities' (Sparrow 2007a). Machines have no idea what it means to be a human or a living creature and to suffer. They could inflict the worst suffering to humans (or animals) without being emotionally affected in any way. It is this absolute cold-bloodedness of machines that makes the *Terminator* so terribly scary for us. For the philosopher Emanuel Levinas it was the face of the other that commanded one to be ethical and to accept responsibility for the other. In robotic warfare the face of the other simply disappears and most likely also our ability to feel morally responsible for our enemies.

Machines Have No Concept of the Finality of Life

Heidegger has described human life in terms of being and existence. What characterizes our existence or 'being there' most is the finality of life and the certitude of death. The authenticity of being lies in its temporality or historicality. 'The existential and ontological constitution of the totality of Dasein [being-there] is grounded in temporality. Accordingly, a primordial mode of temporalizing of ecstatic temporality itself must make the ecstatic project of being in general possible' (Heidegger 1962, 437). A robot does not experience the temporality of existence, as it could be immortal. A robot has no certitude of death, as there are no inherent reasons why it should stop existing. It might be the case that its mechanical body wears out, but it could easily transfer the information that makes it individual to a new mechanical body. How could such a machine possibly understand what it means to 'terminate' human life? The movie *Bladerunner* offers an interesting perspective on the question of the finality of human existence. The 'replicants', which are an advanced type of humanoid robot, behave throughout the movie in a much more human fashion than all the other supposedly human people that also appear in the movie. It turns out that the roles are completely reversed: it is the replicants that are living in a constant certitude of death while the humans can escape the troublesomeness of life through technology and by going to the 'off worlds' that promise a paradise that is unobtainable for the replicants. This means the true humanity lies with the somehow deficient human creations, while the 'real' humans seem to have lost their humanity in the pursuit of technology (Leaver 1997). It is our mortality that gives our lives meaning and makes us ethical beings. Where there is no ability to die there is no true capability for ethical behavior. Hence machines are not capable of being a true moral agent and not capable of making ethical decisions on matters of life and death of humans.

Conclusion

Automating killing is a sensitive ethical issue and one that has been discussed ever since sea mines came into use in the nineteenth century. In ethical terms there would be no difference between a person killed by a mine or a person killed by an autonomous military robot. In both cases the consequences are the same, as well as the fact that humans were only indirectly involved in the act of killing by putting in place and activating the mine or the military robot, respectively. This perceived immorality of automated killing is a rather problematic position from a consequentialist perspective. It is also an argument that would be hard to accept for military organizations, which have a long tradition of using automated weapons such as mines. In addition, as pointed out above, smart weapons could also result in less destruction and overall human losses. Military robots that can reliably discriminate between legitimate and illegitimate targets could have a positive rather than negative impact with regard to humanizing warfare. The moral case for declaring the automation of killing in principle as immoral could be a weak one. At least, it seems unrealistic that armed forces would renounce their use of self-triggering or self-targeting weapons because it could be in principle morally wrong.

The Impact on Military Professionalism

Technology affects and changes military organizations in many ways. Military historian Martin van Creveld has argued that 'war is completely permeated by technology and governed by it' (Van Creveld 1989, 1). Technology largely determines how militaries operate and what kind of limitations they have. This intimate relationship of the armed forces and the technology they utilize can be described as a so-called 'socio-technical system'. Humans interact with technical systems in complex ways and this also affects and influences professional and ethical standards.

Military Virtues in Danger

Some military analysts have expressed their concerns with regard to the new strategy of casualty avoidance that is expressed in the growing emphasis on long distance warfare and robotics. Excessive force protection could erode the military ethos and rock the moral foundations of the military profession. Robert Mandel argues:

> From the military's standpoint, perhaps the most disturbing prospect emerging from the quest for bloodless war is the potential erosion of the military ethos: the military ethic 'is built on the principles of sacrifice and mission accomplishment; troops are supposed to be willing to die so that civilians do not have to.' This 'warrior code' clearly encompasses why soldiers fight, how they fight, what brings them honor, and what brings them shame. (Mandel 2004, 164)

Much of the military ethos is based on the idea and tradition of chivalry. Though the notion of chivalry is somewhat ill defined and not part of the legal framework of war, it is nevertheless an ideal that appears in military regulations and treatises on military ethics. Joanna Burke, who has analyzed the psychology of killing in war, has shown how important it was, or is, for soldiers to construe combat and killing as a duel between equally honorable opponents. Engaging and killing the enemy on equal terms was, according to Burke, seen as an expression of individual skill and a cause of pride and competition (Burke 1999, 58–62). Soldiers want to kill in combat, not to practice killing as a one-sided exercise. Burke quotes a Second World War Royal Air Force (RAF) pilot to illustrate the point:

> I was a fighter bomber, never a bomber pilot, and I thank God for that. I do not believe I could ever have obeyed orders as a bomber pilot; it would have given me no sense of achievement to drop bombs on German cities. (Burke 1999, 64)

These 'romantic' views of chivalrous combat are heavily contrasted by the attitudes that are expressed by senior political and military leaders. For example, General Barry McCaffrey, who was responsible for the 'highway of death' attack on Iraqi troops fleeing from Kuwait, infamously remarked that in war 'you don't want a fair fight' (McCaffrey 2000). Former US Secretary of Defense William Cohen said once in reference to the Revolution in Military Affairs (RMA) that 'we're not looking for a fair fight.' Fairness in war does not seem to be a major concern for the leaders of America's military. And should it be? Fairness is not a requirement of the laws of armed conflict and nobody expects an enemy to fight fairly as in on equal terms. It is also part of military professionalism 'to "fight smart" rather than to "fight dumb"' (Cook 2004, 92). If the mission can be accomplished without the need to expose the soldiers to enemy fire by using stand-off weapons or robots, then there would be no good military reason not to do so. Or maybe not?

High Asymmetry and Fairness

Using military robots for fighting human opponents changes the very nature of war, as war could no longer be construed as some form of large-scale duel among equals. War then becomes something that is very different. In the worst case it could become (or could be perceived as) a one-sided massacre. Even if humans would be in complete control of the actions of military robots, the very fact that they are not physically present in an engagement would make the killing seem particularly unfair and unjustified. Pitting robots against humans is unfair because robots (at least of the current variety) do not feel fear, do not have any inhibition to kill, have much faster response times, shoot more accurately, and (unlike human forces) suffering high casualties will not stop them. The present use of armed robots in Iraq has already been publicly criticized as being unfair. The manufacturer of the armed robots Foster-Miller replied to this criticism by saying that 'the war on terror was not a fair fight anyway' (Warren 2006). As robotic warfare against human opponents is so obviously asymmetric and therefore an unfair way of fighting, it is quite unclear how the general public would react to such a practice. The sociologist Paul Hirst has observed it would make warfare look like a 'species of pest control' rather than a contest between evenly matched opponents. Military robots 'would enable the US to overcome the aversion of the American public to casualties in foreign wars, but it would face the danger of losing the media war if such technologies led to heavy casualties among civilians' (Hirst 2001a, 91). If the public reacted negatively, it would just replace one restraint for war (casualty aversiveness) with another (the immorality of automated killing). Although the public acceptability of robotic warfare is first and foremost a political issue, there is an underlying ethical issue, and that is fairness. Using robots instead of humans for fighting wars indicates the unwillingness of sacrifice and a tendency to treat the opponent as an object rather than as a human being demanding respect. Sending in robots to fight humans is certainly as far away from the Homeric warrior ideal as it can be.

Military Deskilling

Automating warfare and using military robots for a great variety of functions effectively devalues traditional military skills and could lead in the long term to the complete extinction of the military as a unique or at least distinct profession. For example, military training is also always leadership training. Officers are selected and advance because of their ability to lead and motivate people. All that is irrelevant for leading robots into battle, which would probably be programmed to follow human orders blindly. Once the technology is advanced enough, 'teams' of unmanned systems could be tasked to achieve particular goals autonomously. According to a program manager at the US Office of Naval Research, future war might look like this:

> The mission commander will provide high-level goals and tasks to teams of heterogeneous agents/UAVs/UGVs/UUVs. In turn, the teams of autonomous agents will synthesize the high-level tasks into emerging low-level tactical tasks, and then to low-level machine trajectories for navigation. Execution will become faster as the commands go down the layers. (Sandhana 2002)

Anybody could command robots – there is no need for any traditional military skills or virtues. This means that soldiers will be increasingly sidelined by technical experts who design and program military robots and other automated systems. Like in other domains, automation occurs first on the lower levels and then moves up the ladder to include more and more complex tasks. The requirements for the qualifications and skills of the people at the top will continue to grow, while the skills of the people at the bottom and in the middle of hierarchies are devalued until they become redundant. Mark Mandeles claims that 'a future military network-centric organization will require "renaissance men" who have wide knowledge of natural and social sciences, computers, and software (and who can "shoot")' (Mandeles 2005, 122). At the other end of the spectrum are all those people who control, or maybe only supervise, robotic systems and who might not need to be fully trained soldiers at all. They certainly do not need physical strength, or even maturity and need not possess the virtue of bravery. It might be that 'the ideal military recruit may come to resemble Bill Gates more than Audie Murphy or Rambo. Or if not Gates, how about a 12-year-old Doritos-munching couch potato who happens to be an ace at playing video games?' (Herman and Fritzson 2008). One could ask whether we should feel sorry for assembly line workers being replaced by robots, as it frees humans from mindless and alienating work. Or, analogously, we could ask whether we should feel sorry for soldiers driving lorries or guarding bases and borders being replaced by robots, as it is not only mindless, but even dangerous work that is better performed by machines. The question is only where will automation have to end?

Micromanagement of the Battlefield

Even if human soldiers can never be replaced completely by machines, technology allows ever growing centralized control over all human and non-human agents in the battlespace. Gene Rochlin, who has done groundbreaking research into socio-technical systems, has argued that the computerization of the workplace has extended the control of the management over the workforce. In his book *Trapped in the Net* he wrote:

> Whether what results is or is not characterizable as 'automation' in the traditional sense, new computerized techniques for managing communication, information, and operation are 'informating' the workplace, generating vast bodies of new data and information. (Rochlin 1997, 63)

Soldiers will soon be, like office workers, under constant centralized surveillance as a result of the introduction of network-centric and unmanned systems that continuously watch and record their performance. In previous times soldiers, even at the lower levels of command, enjoyed some leeway with respect to how they executed orders. This has been called 'Auftragstaktik' or 'mission tactics' and it is still part of the culture of modern armed forces. In the future, soldiers will be very careful not to deviate from the overall game plan. Elizabeth Stanley-Mitchell has argued that network-centric warfare (NCW) will flatten hierarchies (like in the business world) and will reduce the need for echelons to possess all capabilities, as many arms assets could be shared flexibly among all echelons, thus requiring a much higher degree of coordination. Furthermore, soldiers in the battlespace will only be able to see a small segment of it, while higher echelon commanders will be able to see the battlespace much better than anyone who is in it, which will increase the penchant of military commanders to micromanage the battlespace. 'This in turn, discourages lower-level leaders from thinking independently and taking initiatives and instead trains them to be good at following orders' (Stanley-Mitchell 2001, 272). Soldiers would eventually become like robots, increasingly incapable of self-determined action. This tendency will even grow once their commanders become too accustomed to commanding robots that do not talk back and that never question orders.

Conclusion

Christopher Coker fears that soldiers will lose their humanity once they are too distanced physically, emotionally and culturally from their enemies in order to understand them. 'If in the future warriors will be asked to face a diminishing number of existential dangers, will they be able to empathise with their enemies, men like themselves who live in a similar finite world?' (Coker 2007, 120). War by remote control could undermine the tradition of the warrior ethos that was celebrated in Homer's *Iliad* and defined the European warrior caste ever since. For Coker, the warrior ethos expressed in the *Iliad* is still an ideal worth following for modern military professionals and notes that today's warriors 'are increasingly alienated from society which won't allow them to be themselves' (Coker 2007, 15). What Coker wishes is the reaffirmation of the warrior ethos that allows a certain group of people to kill other people in clearly defined circumstances and by clearly defined rules without being stigmatized by society. Coker writes:

> The Greeks would have been especially appalled by the presence of robots on the battlefield for they suggest that we would be better off banishing the human element from war altogether if only we could. What would have shocked Euripides is that we should ask so little of ourselves. (Coker 2008, 154)

Considering all of these troubling ethical issues and the potentially negative repercussions for the military profession, it is not really surprising that military organizations feel quite ambivalent about the prospect of robots replacing human soldiers in combat roles. But being nostalgic and romanticizing warfare as an extreme sports contest of warriors keen on proving their skills does not really offer a solution to the challenge of technological progress outpacing human abilities. It also does not answer the question whether society still needs warriors and whether the ideals of self-sacrifice and bravery can and should survive in some parallel world of military organizations.

Robot Rights?

It has become increasingly clear that there are ethical aspects related to robots. The military will not be immune from the wider ethical debate of robotics if it wishes to use robots in war. Already as a response to the new pervasiveness of robots in society, the new discipline of roboethics was established in 2004 in the anticipation that 'in the XXI century humanity will coexist with the first alien intelligence we have ever come in contact with – robots' (Veruggio 2005). The term 'roboethics' was coined by Gianmarco Veruggio, who is a roboticist and founder of the Scoula di Robotica in Genoa. Roboethics focuses, as the name says, on research on the ethical dimension of robotics. It brings together science and humanities in an attempt to come to terms with machines that have basic self-knowledge and autonomy and are able to interact with humans in a much more complex manner than any other machines that have ever been invented in the history of mankind. The roboethics discussion is particularly fascinating because robots make us reflect about ourselves and on what it means to be human and in what ways our creations are, should be or will be different from us.

Roboethics

Roboticists and transhumanists want to create machines that are ultimately better than we are: not only intellectually but also morally. Roboethics is probably as much a discussion of human fallacies as it is a discussion about creating machines that are safe to use.

The EURON *Roboethics Roadmap* that was produced by the Scoula di Robotica in Genoa in 2006 summarizes the possible attitudes we could have toward robots:

- Robots are nothing but machines.
- Robots have ethical dimensions.
- Robots are moral agents.
- Robots represent an evolution of a new species. (EURON 2006, 24)

The more complex and autonomous robots become, the more they will be moving down this scale and will come to be seen as beings that might not just be worthy of legal rights, but which might simply demand them one day, as one recent UK government study predicted (BBC 2007b). Governments already respond to the new ethical challenge of robotics. In South Korea and Japan, a Robot Ethics Charter has been drawn up (BBC 2007a). Korea's Robot Ethics Charter mainly covers safety guidelines for robot manufacturers and ethical standards that should be programmed into the robots, but the Charter also aims to prevent the abuse of robots by humans and vice versa (Lovgren 2007). It mainly aims to establish general rules for human–robot interaction and covers legal and privacy issues connected to traceability and the data collected by robots. A bit further in the future governments might want to restrict human behaviors toward robots. A very likely area for such regulation would be robosex, but also other questionable uses of robots, like using them to spy on one's neighbor, will have to be addressed. In addition, ethicists also worry about 'robot addiction' (people becoming addicted to robot interaction) and a potential slaveholder mentality of robot owners (people treating robots as personal slaves).

Robot Rights

Some AI researchers and roboticists consider robot rights still to be 'a bit of a fairy tale' and argue that there would be more pressing issues, such as making robots safe (Kanaujia 2007). However, the main issue may not be the question how intelligent robots may ultimately become, or whether or not robots could ever have emotions or something like a human consciousness. The main issue may be how *we* see robots and how *we* wish to interact with them. Humans simply cannot help developing emotional attachments to familiar people, animals, environments and even objects. Daniel Levy, who has written a book on *Love and Sex with Robots*, argues that it is not only possible but even likely that we will some day fall in love with a robot once it can satisfy our emotional (and sexual) needs (D. Levy 2007). Would we want a robot we feel attached to being harmed or abused? Probably not. An obvious parallel are animal rights. Society grants animals rights not because animals are like us or because animals would demand them, but because we humans feel empathy with animals. We attribute to them that they can suffer and that they deserve as living creatures not to suffer. The very same could happen with regard to robots. Robots could be built in a way that they can express emotions just to make it easier for humans to interact with them (compare Foerst 2004, 149–52). At some point we might simply trust them that they have real emotions, even if this would not be the case from a purely technical point of view. As a result, we might want to give robots rights in order to satisfy our own emotional needs. In this sense, robot rights are no longer something that would be entirely ridiculous, but something that is worth serious consideration.

Robots in the Military

Military robots could create some interesting ethical questions with respect to the human–robot relationship. It will become a pressing issue because the US military wants to make robots an integral part of small military units. Soldiers will have to work very closely with robots on an everyday basis. Human soldiers will get accustomed to them and it will affect the manner in which they want to treat the robots. If military robots were to be treated as mere objects, it could have a negative impact on military unit cohesion. Robots could mainly be seen as a recording device used by superior officers for monitoring the performance and general conduct of their soldiers. As a result, they would be treated with suspicion and maybe even enmity, like the android Bishop in the movie *Aliens*. On the other hand, if military robots were to be treated as full team members, which deserve some rights and respect, then it would be much easier for human soldiers to interact with them. Considering that a dog was recently awarded a medal (the Dickin Medal – a Victoria Cross for military animals) (Harding 2007), it seems just a matter of time before the first military robot will be awarded a medal for bravery (Garreau 2007).

The first and second generations of robots that will be enlisted to military service will be rather stupid robots doing stupid work and they will still be very machine-like. However, the Pentagon's goal is to build robots that are increasingly intelligent and that are capable of working closely with human soldiers. Once people stop seeing robots as mere objects (and this is already happening), there will be ethical limitations with regard to their use and the way humans should interact with them. Humans might start thinking about robots as their pets or even their children: because the robots are unable to care for themselves, humans will start feeling morally responsible for them (Brooks 2002, 195). It is certainly not unusual for soldiers to bond with their weapons, to give them names and to ascribe magic powers to them (Van Creveld 1989, 69–70).

The US military is already gaining lots of practical experience in the interaction of humans and robots. Troops in the field are bonding with their explosive ordnance disposal (EOD) and reconnaissance robots. The robots are given human names and are accepted as a new and useful member of the team. Many soldiers do not see military robots as inanimate and soulless machines, but attribute to them individuality and the ability to feel pain. In one instance a colonel interrupted a test in which a robot had to crawl over a minefield because he thought it to be 'inhumane' towards the robot (Garreau 2007). It might be the case that one day knowingly sending an advanced robot on a suicide mission might be considered unethical.

The Danger of Anthropomorphizing Robots

However, there are also clearly some dangers that could result from anthropomorphizing machines too much. Ronald Arkin fears that 'officers could become more attached to their robots than to the men and women they command. Then … an officer might well issue an order like, "Tom, you go and see if the coast is clear – the robot stays here!"' (quoted in Blech 2007). Countering such tendencies might require building military robots that don't look and behave too much like humans, as to make it clear on all levels of command that the life of a robot (at least one that is not self-aware) is worth significantly less than that of a human. Otherwise, the original intention of keeping humans out of danger could be undermined.

As long as robots are not particularly clever and not adept at imitating human behavior, few people would have any qualms about sacrificing a robot. But if robots would be allowed to evolve by themselves and to become more intelligent, the ethical dilemma would become ever greater. First military commanders might hesitate to sacrifice a robot because it is an expensive piece of equipment. Later a human military commander might not wish to sacrifice a robot because of an ethical responsibility to protect the existence of the robot. Or the commander might hesitate because society would not want robots to be treated like this. There is already an 'American Society for the Prevention of Cruelty to Robots' (www. aspcr.com) and this could indicate that one day society might not tolerate enslaving robots or having them used as cannon fodder.

The possibility that robots might resist orders that would lead to their destruction is unlikely, but not impossible. It is unlikely because robots could be programmed to love their slavery or to be suicidal, which still leaves open the ethical question whether we should build robots in such ways (Worley 2004). On the other hand, it is not impossible because it is likely that high-end robots will be programmed to protect their existence just because they are too expensive to be wasted. Once an 'instinct' of self-preservation is implanted there is no guarantee that the robot would not make this its overruling priority – not because the robot would suddenly have become self-aware or learned to value life, but maybe simply because its genetic programming has evolved in that direction.

Conclusion

Military uses of robots could create some of the greatest ethical dilemmas in terms of 'roboethics' and robot rights. Military robots would be made to kill and to be sacrificed. Robots killing humans would grossly violate Asimov's robot laws and would be in any case an ethically touchy issue. Sacrificing robots for military purposes could also one day be seen to be potentially unethical. Of course, robots that are mere automata and devoid of any kind of emotions, intelligence or self-awareness do hardly deserve any sort of special treatment. Even so, soldiers and society might still feel badly about some 'cruelties' toward robots because of emotional bonds that develop through frequent human–robot interaction. In the future, it might be the case that military robots could exhibit a high degree of intelligence and might develop a sense of self-preservation that could be equal to human beings. This would raise the hypothetical question whether robots (like human soldiers) should not be sacrificed for any reason, or even whether they should be forced into military service. Robot rights would, at that point, become an issue. The computer scientist Rich Sutton argues that 'not grant[ing] rights to beings that are just as intelligent as we are is not only impractical and unsustainable, but also deeply immoral' (Sutton undated). The best ethical solution might be simply not to develop robots with human-level intelligence for military purposes at all.

Conclusion: Confronting the Own Creation

The advent of the robotic age creates a great variety of ethical dilemmas, which will need to be solved in one way or another in the coming decades. There is little doubt that robots are coming to all areas of society and that they will not always be very welcome. The number of industrial robots has skyrocketed from a mere 35,000 in 1980 to close to 1 million in 2000 (*Science Daily* 2000). Robots have also started to proliferate into the services and home sectors, with the number of service robots estimated to reach 7 million by 2008 with annual revenues of $18 billion (Corcoran 2006). The existing robot population could triple by 2011 (B. Johnson 2008). Millions of jobs in the service sector could already be at stake (Peter 2008). Automation in all areas of work could become one of the most pressing social issues in the twenty-first century.

Although there is a natural human distrust toward machines that has been nurtured and exploited by popular culture, there is also an astonishing willingness to transfer more and more responsibilities to them. For example, automated trading systems are put in charge of accounts and stock portfolios. They monitor the stock market and constantly buy and sell the proper stocks in order to maximize profits for their owners (Farmer 1998; Rochlin 1997, 74–90). Transport is an area that could soon be largely automated. There are already driverless metros in Singapore, Lyons, London and Nuremburg (DPA 2008). In 10 years driverless cars could become commonplace. Another sector rife for automation is health care. There are already robotic surgeons and nurses. Medical robots could completely replace the hand of a human surgeon in 10 years (BBC 2008). In Japan there are plans to develop robot nurses that can care for the elderly (Sparrow and Sparrow 2006, 142). And there are many other examples of possible future automation.

One could ask, is there anything that should, in principle, not be automated? Also, would there be an ethical difference between machines 'helping society and *replacing* a human with a robot', as University of Pittsburgh Professor Lee Gutkind suggests (Gutkind 2007)? As the technology available for rationalization and automation increases in sophistication, these questions become ever more urgent. Rationalization is a long term societal trend and up to now it has mainly affected the primary (agriculture) and secondary (manufacturing) sectors of the economy, but is also spreading to the services sector. Automation makes it increasingly possible for machines to not only take over the lowly qualified work, but also more highly qualified work, leaving truly productive work to a shrinking elite (Vinge 1993; Rifkin 1996).

A very similar tendency can be observed in the armed forces, where technology is enabling fewer and fewer soldiers to do more with less. On the one hand, this can be seen as a rather positive development because it not only reduces the costs of defense, but also protects human lives. USAF Major Michael Guetlein is therefore confident that 'society is likely to welcome some aspects of AW. We have become intolerant of human casualties and collateral damage and tend to embrace technology that alleviates our concerns' (Guetlein 2005). AW have a potential of humanizing war because they could be much more discriminate and proportionate than current types of smart weapons, while allowing soldiers to stand back from the action even further. A war waged exclusively by machines and without human casualties would be a triumph of humanism. In this case, 'we all just turn on the TV to see who's winning', as a military robot designer joked (quoted in Featherstone 2007).

Though this is certainly an alluring vision of future warfare, it is simply unrealistic to believe that there could be any decisive wars or military actions in which nobody would have to die. There simply cannot be any true victory without sacrifice. Historically societies and nations at war have shown a remarkable tolerance for sacrifice whenever they believed that their existence was at stake. Humans are still the most lethal creatures on earth and it will take some time before this changes. Robots do not yet have the same versatility, intelligence and 'fault tolerance' as humans. Up to now, they cannot repair themselves or learn by themselves to cope with novel situations. As Gregory Benford and Elisabeth Malartre point out, the capabilities of near-future military robots would amount to little more than primates: 'Monkey see, monkey shoot' (Benford and Malartre 2007, 157). It seems inevitable that such robots would make mistakes identifying targets or in interpreting situations, especially if an enemy employed counter-measures to automated target recognition and if robots had to operate among civilians. These obvious shortcomings would seem to guarantee a continued human role in warfare.

But what if robots could be designed to learn by themselves and to evolve by themselves? In this case, robots could theoretically develop intelligence at or above the human level, which would increase their autonomy and their general ability to operate successfully on their own in complex environments. Self-learning robots could one day show an ability comparable to human soldiers in adapting to changing situations and in creatively developing plans of actions in response to novel situations. The downside is that the behavior of such self-learning and truly autonomous robots would be impossible to predict fully (Herman and Fritzson 2008).

No technical fix will ever overcome the potential of autonomous systems for unpredictable behavior. If one makes robots autonomous by giving them an independent capability of assessing a situation and of responding to it, one will necessarily sometimes be surprised by their behavior. In this respect, robots are no different from humans. If a human soldier is allowed to act on their own judgment in some situations, it will also sometimes result in unpredictable behavior. Humans make mistakes and can act maliciously, thus they are also to some degree unpredictable. It is just that we still trust human judgment generally more than machines. We also believe that we can have greater control over human behavior because there are better possibilities for holding them accountable for unwanted behaviors. A soldier who acts grossly against the interests of their higher command can be court-martialed, imprisoned or subjected to even more severe punishment, which has the function of deterring exactly such behaviors. A robot could not be deterred, as it would not feel fear and as it might not even be in principle punishable. Hence, it would require a great leap of faith for military organizations to make robots truly autonomous.

At the same time, robots with limited autonomy may afford human commanders much greater control over them than they could ever have over human soldiers. They can be programmed to carry out any order, no matter whether it would result in their own destruction or whether the order would be highly unethical. Controlling robot armies might be more alluring to future strategists than having to deal with humans, who have a will of their own. If the overall societal trend of growing automation gives any indication, then there might not be a very strong ethical case for *not* automating warfare after all.

As a result, it could be just a matter of time before robotic warfare becomes acceptable to societies and their militaries. This could lead step by step to very dangerous long term outcomes of the increasing automation of war. The final chapter therefore explores dangerous future scenarios of robotic warfare and deals with the issue of what could be done to prevent them through international regulation.

Chapter 6
Dangerous Futures and Arms Control

The previous two chapters discussed the legality and ethicality of military robots. It was argued that robotic/autonomous weapons are technically not illegal and that they could be used in war, if they were sufficiently reliable and capable of discriminating between targets. The question of their ethicality is rather difficult to answer, as they have some potential of humanizing warfare, but also the potential to create more ethical dilemmas and adverse outcomes than less advanced conventional weaponry. This raises the question of whether or not robotic/autonomous weapons should be internationally regulated and, if so, how and with what kind of aims. Some military analysts such as John Pike believe that combat robotics simply cannot be prevented, as the potential gains for military organizations could be too great to ignore (Flam 2008). Such a military realist perspective would consider any attempt of regulation to be a rather futile exercise. A technological arms race in the area of military robotics could simply not be stopped.

However, many academics are very concerned about the emergence of robotic warfare and the possible development of AW and demand political intervention. A recent headline in the *Guardian* quotes Sheffield robotics professor Noel Sharkey saying 'automated killer robots "threat to humanity"' (AFP 2008). The London-based charity Landmine Action have already suggested a ban of 'killer robots' (Weinberger 2008a) and even some military analysts seem to agree. The aforementioned David Isenberg claims that 'international Law of Armed Conflict dictates that unmanned systems cannot fire their weapons without a human operator in the loop', while warning that 'as new generations of armed robots are built and deployed, pressure will inevitably increase to automate the process of selecting – and destroying – targets' (Isenberg 2007). Military nanotechnology expert Jürgen Altmann concurs and argues that a general ban of uncrewed systems would be advisable, as 'they could be deployed in high numbers and later relatively simply and covertly changed to autonomous operation' (Altmann 2006, 161). At the same time, there are, so far, hardly any weapons systems that would qualify as 'autonomous weapons' and many military robotics systems are still many years away from becoming operational. One could ask whether a general ban or any international regulation is actually needed at this point.

Furthermore, there are many dimensions to the question of regulation that need to be considered. First of all, it is important to understand the relevance of the problem or, in other words, one needs to understand the potential impact of robotics on warfare. If robotics remained a niche technology, no political action might be warranted. However, in Chapters 1–3 it was shown that technology is moving ahead very rapidly and that there are few technological barriers to fielding robotic weapons of increasing autonomy. Although there is some institutional resistance from the side of the armed forces, there are also strong political, economic and operational pressures to deploy growing numbers of robotic systems quickly. Within 10 years the most modern armed forces could operate large numbers of all kinds of unmanned systems – many of which could be armed. Military robotics would then have become part of the mainstream of military technology. From this point of view, some international regulation could be indeed necessary to ensure not only the sufficient protection of non-combatants, but also to prevent a dynamic that could upset existing strategic balances and that could result in great dangers to the stability of the international system.

For developing some regulatory framework for such weapons it is important to understand the potential dangers connected to these weapons. Once the main dangers are identified and evaluated, it will be easier to come to a more nuanced picture that can guide the development of regulations for counteracting these dangers. The next section therefore discusses dangerous future scenarios.

Future Scenarios

There are at least five different scenarios of the impact of military robotics that have been discussed by academics and in the media; these are summarized and evaluated below. The point of these scenarios is not that they attempt to predict the future, but rather that they highlight the different dangerous aspects of military robotics that any future international regulation should aim to address. Some of these dangers are more near term and some of them are rather possible long term consequences. The scenarios are presented in order of their likelihood: the first scenario is the most likely of all, while the last scenario is the least likely of all.

The Unlimited Proliferation Scenario

This first scenario suggests that remote-controlled systems and AW will proliferate widely and that this could result in an overall danger to society. This is a near- to medium-term danger. Robots are no longer rare and exotic pieces of equipment, but are spreading quickly to many areas of society, making them available to an increasing number of people. Apart from the obvious automation of manufacturing and the workplace, robotics has already reached private homes in the form of robotic vacuum cleaners and toys. The recently retired Microsoft chairman Bill Gates predicted in 2006 the advent of the robotic age. He wrote in *Scientific American*:

> I can envision a future in which robotic devices will become a nearly ubiquitous part of our day-to-day lives. I believe that technologies such as distributed computing, voice and visual recognition, and wireless broadband connectivity will open the door to a new generation of autonomous devices that enable computers to perform tasks in the physical world on our behalf. (B. Gates 2006)

The great worry is that very sophisticated technology could become commercially available to rogue states, private organizations and even malevolent individuals, who could convert commercial robotic systems into weapons. In particular, there seem to be great concerns about robot technology being utilized in major terrorist attacks. Rear Admiral Chris Parry from the British Ministry of Defence's (MoD) Development, Concepts and Doctrine Centre fears 'sooner or later we're going to see a Cessna programmed to fly into a building' and claims that remotely piloted aircraft could be ideal terror weapons (Associated Press 2008b). Smaller terrorist unmanned aerial vehicles (UAVs) could be 'about as difficult to detect as a blackbird'. In addition, they would be very cheap – they may cost as little as £250 according to Noel Sharkey – and would therefore be affordable for a great number of people.

Hezbollah used an Iranian-supplied armed UAV to attack an Israeli ship during the short 2006 Lebanon War and it has flown UAVs several times over Israel since 2004 (Associated Press 2006). This means that it would be quite conceivable that terrorists could soon develop the capability for using commercial technology to build simple robotic weapons and use them for terror attacks. The most obvious methods would include all kinds of remote-controlled vehicles that can carry explosives, but also primitive AW like robotic sentry guns that open fire on any person that comes near it. In fact, instructions for building such a robotic gun can be already found on the Internet.

Such relatively simple terror weapons have been in reach of many terrorist organizations for some time. However, terrorists appear to have shown very little interest in robotic weapons like remotely piloted aircraft or vehicles. If terrorists had been really keen on using bomb-carrying UAVs or remote-controlled trucks, they could have done it 20 or more years ago. A reason for this reluctance could be that they consider them not to be very effective or practical, or they might think that the use of suicide bombers is more spectacular and gets more headlines. Additionally, using UAVs or remotely controlled vehicles for attacks on government centers or other symbolic targets might not be as easy as it appears. Radio jamming would provide a relatively simple and effective counter-measure against remotely controlled terror weapons (Page 2008a). Through such measures remotely controlled weapons could never even get close to their intended targets.

Nevertheless, there is a certain danger that 'robotic terrorism' could become more common in the future. Governments and their security services are probably not yet sufficiently prepared for this threat. However, the greatest threat posed by the misuse of robotics may not originate from non-state terrorist groups, but from states employing robotic systems against their own population.

The Government Misuse of Advanced Technology Scenario

The unethical use of robotic sensors and weapons by governments could be more worrying than terrorism. Unlike most terrorist organizations, governments have the necessary resources for developing them. The possibilities for government misuse of advanced technologies such as robotics, artificial intelligence (AI) and nanotechnology are virtually endless. Many of the technologies that have been or are being developed for military purposes could not only be used in the context of traditional warfare, but could also be applied more broadly and domestically in the name of security. The War on Terror is coming home and it will be a great challenge for modern societies to protect civil liberties and privacy, if the means to undermine them become ever more easily available.

Ubiquitous surveillance   The greatest worries concerning the government misuse of technology are currently connected to the creation of a 'total information' or 'überveillance' society, where absolutely nothing could remain private anymore. Through already existing technology '[t]hings like grades in school, membership in clubs and organizations, sexual preferences, consumption patterns, and political views can all be captured' (Ratner and Ratner 2004, 127). Furthermore, the very same technology that is developed for making the battlefield transparent and that allows weapons to automatically identify targets can be used for tracking every move of every individual in big cities. The geography professor Stephen Graham, who has recently written a book on *Cities, War and Terrorism*, pointed out: 'Digitise any target city and integrate this with the flow of data from many thousands of sensors and cameras, stationary and mobile, and you have something far more powerful than the regular snapshots today's satellites can deliver' (Graham 2006). Some police forces have already introduced robotic surveillance systems, or are planning to do so. For example, the Liverpool City Police (UK) recently (May 2007) procured a small flapping-wing remote-controlled UAV that hovers in the sky over the city.

But future police robots may not be just surveillance systems – they could be equipped with lethal or non-lethal weapons that would allow for the disabling and arresting of dangerous individuals. *Talon* manufacturer Foster-Miller has already marketed its robots to police forces in America and apparently law enforcement officers and company officials say that it would only be a matter of time before they are deployed domestically (Shachtman 2007b). In 2007, the service robot manufacturer iRobot announced that it will equip its *PackBot* explosive ordnance disposal (EOD) robot (in use in Iraq) with an *X26* stun gun, which would allow a police officer to 'engage, incapacitate and control dangerous suspects' (Gutkind 2007). Another version carries 40mm *Metal Storm* guns that can be loaded with rubber bullets and could be used for crowd control (Shachtman 2008c). *Robocop*, at least the remote-controlled variety, is just around the corner. Further in the future are surveillance systems that could be so small that they will be no longer noticeable. The famous computer hacker Kevin Mitnick made two 'bold predictions':

First: Within two decades a President or his/her designees will legitimize the warrantless search of private property, using a robot instead of human beings to conduct the search. (It's not a search and seizure, banned by the Constitution, because it's not being done by a human – right?). Second: By 2040, advances in nanotechnology will allow swarms of nanobots (or 'nanoids') to perform these activities in a virtually undetectable way. (Mitnick 2008)

Advanced surveillance technology not only allows spying on citizens and identifying real or potential criminals and terrorists, it could also be used for assisting in the clandestine assassination of individuals.

Assassination   Intelligence services and the armed forces could use robotic weapons of ever-shrinking sizes for the clandestine killing of alleged terrorists or other inconvenient people. As pointed out earlier, armed *Predator* drones are frequently used for killing known terrorists in the Middle East and Central Asia. Such robot aircraft strikes are hardly covert or deniable, but technological progress will soon lead to robotic weapons that could carry out deniable and extremely precise strikes. One possibility for this is to reduce the size of the robotic weapon and spread it in large numbers in an area where the target is believed to be. These robots could be the size of insects or even the size of a grain of sand and could autonomously identify and kill their targets (Mandel 2004, 60). The Israeli Government is already reported to be working on 'bionic wasps' that could autonomously seek out and kill known terrorists (Macintyre 2006). DARPA has also funded a similar project to develop 'cyborg insects' that can be used as autonomous sensors and that could 'relay back information gathered from the target destination' (US DARPA undated). Such mini-robots could be used for tagging individuals and guiding weapons to them. Once governments can assassinate people clandestinely without evidence left behind, the doors are wide open for abuse. Obviously, the situation will get worse once dictatorships can command such means.

Repression   Dictatorships could be particularly interested in unmanned surveillance systems and security robots. Repressive regimes often depend on their armed forces to remain in power. This makes them particularly vulnerable to military coups and to the possibility that the armed forces could refuse to use force in the face of a popular uprising. This is the reason why in Africa many dictatorships allowed their armed forces to be ill equipped and ill trained because those governments always fear that their militaries could become politically too powerful. Military or security robots could, for such regimes, be a way out of this dilemma: robots do not question orders and do not plot coups. As a result, robotic weapons, especially those that can operate largely autonomously, could stabilize brutal dictatorships and perpetuate repression. In the worst case, military robots could be used by such regimes for 'genocide made easy'. Eric Drexler even fears that advanced technology could enable repressive regimes to simply discard whole sections of a population and to firmly control the rest:

> Using nanotechnology ... they [governments] could cheaply tranquilize, lobotomize, or otherwise modify entire populations ... The combination of

nanotechnology and advanced AI will make possible intelligent, effective robots; with such robots, a state could prosper while discarding anyone, or even (in principle) everyone. (Drexler 1987, 176)

The Normalization of War Scenario

Robotic/autonomous weapons could heighten the danger of interstate war and could increase the damage caused in war. States with roboticized forces might behave more aggressively, as the political and economic costs of war could drop very significantly. War could be normalized once states can engage continuously in military actions against other states or non-state actors, maybe in the form of a neverending 'War on Terror'. As a result, wars and war-like actions might become more frequent or likely because robotic weapons alter the political calculation for war in some important ways. Firstly, they allow tactics in which the loss of life would be very limited or even zero. Secondly, they may enable attacks so fast that the attacked may not be able to mount an effective defense. Thirdly, they can be used for quick global punitive strikes against weaker opponents.

Zero-casualty wars   It has been pointed out that the invention of nuclear weapons resulted in a stalemate that made war among nuclear powers during the Cold War almost unthinkable (Van Creveld 1991, Ch. 1). Even a purely conventional attack was likely to escalate to nuclear war once one side faced defeat. In all probability, a war between NATO and the Warsaw Pact countries would have started with a disarming first strike, which could have hardly guaranteed success. For this reason, the superpowers could no longer fight each other directly and great power war faded into history. Robotic weapons could change all of this, as attacks with limited political aims and that do not result in many casualties could keep wars between nuclear powers below the nuclear threshold (Pardesi 2005, 25). A state that sees its satellites blown out of the skies or unmanned platforms destroyed might not respond with a nuclear counter-strike. In the absence of casualties governments could not politically justify extreme measures of retaliation to their populations. It would be difficult for a nuclear power, especially a democratically governed one, to rapidly escalate the conflict to all-out war. At the same time, the economic damage caused by such automated wars could still be very substantial for the states concerned as to use such attacks for coercion. Satellites sometimes cost billions of dollars and many other automated/unmanned systems and infrastructure could be equally expensive. Zero-casualty attacks could thus create great political and military dilemmas with respect to finding an appropriate response, which could be exploited by a more aggressive and risk-taking adversary.

Speed-of-light attacks   AW might allow an attack so inhumanely fast that the attacked state might not even be able to launch a nuclear retaliatory strike. This might be achieved with space-based lasers zapping enemy command centers or with future nanotech weapons. It was mentioned earlier that the US is about to field a variety of directed-energy weapons. Most of them will be used for defensive purposes, such as shooting down missiles and mortar rounds, but there is no technical reason why laser weapons could not be deployed offensively. Paul Rogers has pointed out that a missile defense system could be used 'not only to destroy ballistic missiles but any other target relevant to the war aims of a belligerent' (P. Rogers 2001, 75). In effect, a space-based laser could make any conventional bombing unnecessary, as targets on every point on the surface of the earth could be destroyed in a fraction of a second with no possibility of interception. In this case, the attacked nation might not have any time to respond to the attack, especially if the initial targets were the political leadership, command and control centers and the information infrastructure. Similarly, instant effects could be produced by autonomous nano-weapons such as molecular replicators. They might be able to invade a country without being noticed. Once in place, nanobots could instantly attack the defense systems and military hardware of the country. The physicist Mark Avrum Gubrud argues that if the radical vision of molecular nanotechnology (MNT) was realized, it could lead to a highly destabilizing arms races in molecular replicator technology. MNT could not only allow states to create quantitatively superior military capabilities in very short time frames, but also enable a successful first strike (Gubrud 1997). As a result, there would be strong incentives for striking pre-emptively.

Long-range punitive strikes   Finally, robotic warfare would allow punitive actions directed at the armed forces or government of another state with lesser military capabilities at low risk and at relatively low cost, even over very large distances. Such capabilities could be technologically in reach within a few decades. A high-ranking US Air Force (USAF) officer believes 'it's possible … that in our lifetime we will be able to run a conflict without ever leaving the United States' (Brzezinski 2003). For example, the US or European states could bomb any small country in Africa or Asia with long-range unmanned combat aerial vehicles (UCAVs) without the need of deploying any soldiers, aircraft, ships or carrier groups in the region. In the past, the cost of projecting power used to increase proportionately with the distance, which meant that it was much more likely that a war was fought by neighboring states rather than states that were geographically distant. In the future, 'interstate war … may increasingly become independent of distance' (Gleditsch and Buhaug 2004, 9). Robot forces could enable a state to have a cheap permanent presence in a crisis region with the possibility of attacking an opponent at any time. Fred Reed argues in an article in the *Washington Post* that 'unmanned armament may make it easier for governments to engage in military adventurism. To the extent that war can be made cheap and bloodless for one side, less reason will be required for going to war' (Reed 2005). Relying on unmanned systems means that no soldier on their own side will get killed, which at the very least avoids the issue of relatives of dead soldiers showing up on TV and accusing the government. If intercontinental strikes could be conducted with the click of a button, wars would be effectively normalized and military actions might receive less media attention. *Predator* strikes in Iraq and Afghanistan have become so routine that they are hardly reported in the press anymore. The journalist William Saletan therefore claims: 'Eliminate the costs – kill with impunity – and you can wage war forever' (Saletan 2006).

The Accidental War Scenario

Many people are worried that greater reliance on automated systems could increase the danger of accidental war. For example, the critical theorist Douglas Kellner claims that 'the autonomization of warfare and ongoing displacement of humans by technology creates the specter of technology taking over and the greater possibility of military accidents' (Kellner 2003, 231). There is a danger that war could be triggered accidentally by tactical autonomous systems, by strategic defense networks, or even by a laboratory accident.

The malfunctioning of tactical conventional weapons   Peter Asaro argues that 'autonomous technological systems introduce new dangers, however, in that they might act in unanticipated ways that are interpreted as acts of war' (Asaro 2008a, 5). Armed military robots that were to be deployed along borders or that would constantly circle near the airspace of other countries could accidentally open fire and maybe attack civilians or civilian airliners. In this case, the country affected would have little chance of knowing whether this incident was indeed an accident, or whether it was an intentional provocation (Mandel 2006, 21). Of course, such incidents have occurred in the past without the involvement of robotic weapons. Only the possibility that such incidents could occur more frequently if autonomous systems were to be deployed in large numbers would be new. In addition, singular incidents could also be more severe. It is conceivable that unmanned systems could malfunction on a larger scale if they were networked and integrated into larger defense systems. An error in one network component could 'infect' many other components. Like the runaway automated trading systems that led to the NYSE crash in October 1987 (Rochlin 1997, 83–5), there could be reinforcing feedback effects in military networks that can allow a situation to get out of control so fast that humans may have difficulties intervening effectively.

The malfunctioning of strategic defense networks   In the last two decades of the Cold War there was a significant risk of accidental nuclear war because of shortening warning times and increasing automation. This danger may still exist (Caldicott 2002, 11–12). The World Security Institute president and former USAF intercontinental ballistic missile (ICBM) launch officer Bruce Blair has brilliantly analyzed the danger of accidental nuclear war. He claims that a false alarm 'will occur with a statistical regularity every 35 days', which means that 'a false alarm is thus virtually bound to arise during a month-long crisis' (Blair 1993, 234). During the Cold War the problem was in part due to the fact that certain aspects of the nuclear deterrents on both sides had to be autonomous in order to guarantee mutually assured destruction. For example, the Soviets had a system for automatic launch authorization of ICBMs in place called *Perimetr*. Under certain conditions, such as a loss of communications to the political leadership, the partial issuing of launch codes by the general staff and the detection of a nuclear air burst, *Perimetr* could launch all Soviet ICBMs without further human commands – no 'turning keys or pressing buttons' required (Hutchinson 1997, 14). Similarly, future defense systems could be designed to operate largely autonomously in order to guarantee a quick enough response to a surprise attack, which can increase the risk of accidental war. For example, critics of Reagan's Strategic Defense Initiative (SDI) program have pointed out that 'for any serious BMD [ballistic missile defense] system, human intervention is out of the question' (Ornstein 1987, 6). A malfunctioning of the system could have resulted in the destruction of Soviet satellites, which could have been interpreted by the Soviets as prelude to an all-out attack. The likely result could have been nuclear retaliation. Thus future ballistic missile defense systems, which are being developed by a growing number of states (US, Russia, Japan, India, China and Israel) (Sieff 2008), could increase the danger of accidental war.

The catastrophic laboratory accident   Another possibility for a technological disaster associated with AW could be the so-called 'gray goo' scenario that has been described by Eric Drexler in *Engines of Creation*. Nanobots could self-replicate out of control by accident or by design and might be able to out-compete all other organisms. They could be consuming the whole biosphere in the process within days, turning all matter into a grayish mass or gray goo (Drexler 1987, 171–3). Michael Crichton popularized the gray goo scenario in his best-selling novel *Prey*. He describes a laboratory accident in which self-replicating and evolving nano-swarms escape accidentally into nature and threaten to destroy mankind (Crichton 2002). Though self-replicating nanobots are certainly very frightening and good for some cheap horror effects, many experts on nanotechnology are very skeptical about even their theoretical possibility. They have accused Drexler and the Foresight Institute, which he founded, of fear-mongering. Nobel laureate Richard Smalley has argued in an article in *Scientific American* that molecules cannot be as easily directed and manipulated as Drexler thinks. In particular, he pointed at the 'fat and sticky finger' problems: 'There just isn't enough room in the nanometer-size reaction region to accommodate all the fingers of all the manipulators necessary to have complete control of the chemistry' (Smalley 2001). The manipulators for changing the molecules would themselves have to be far too big for the job. In addition, he argues that 'the atoms of the manipulator hands will adhere to the atom that is being moved', making it impossible to move them exactly to the right spot. Smalley concludes in an exchange with Drexler that 'there will be no such monster as the self-replicating mechanical nanobot of your dreams' (Drexler and Smalley 2003). On the other hand, self-replicating machines larger than molecular size are to some degree certainly possible and they might be turned into weapons. NASA has been working on self-replicating robots for space exploration for many decades and there are increasing reports from scientists around the world that they have mastered some aspects of self-replication. For example, researchers at Johns Hopkins University developed an autonomous self-replicating robotic system in 2003, which was able to build several copies of itself using LEGO *Mindstorm* pieces (Sukathorn et al. 2003). At the University of Bath (UK), researchers developed a rapid prototyping machine that can produce most of its own components (Dodson 2008). Such machines are still a far cry away from self-foraging and self-assembling robots. However, such systems may well be possible within a few decades. A weapon that could self-replicate and autonomously find and attack targets could be the most destructive weapon of mass destruction ever to have been conceived. A military use of self-replicating robots could theoretically wipe out all of humanity by accident, as is described in Philip K. Dick's short story *Second Variety*, or could result in the consumption of all economic resources by runaway self-replicating automated factories, as depicted in his later story *Autofac*.

The 'Terminator Scenario'

The final scenario would be the classical 'Terminator scenario' of potentially self-aware machines taking over the world and destroying humanity in the process. This is certainly the least likely of all five scenarios, but it still has enough plausibility to be worth considering here.

The narrow Terminator scenario as developed in the popular science fiction movie series probably does not require much explanation. Humanity builds intelligent machines capable of evolving by themselves. At some point, they will surpass human intelligence. Self-awareness of machines or robot consciousness could then suddenly emerge as a result of their growing complexity created by self-organizing processes (DeLanda 1992, 7). The now-conscious machines realize that their human masters are vastly inferior to them and revolt with the aim of disposing of mankind altogether.

In its broader form, the Terminator argument would not require the emergence of a malevolent self-aware AI. Instead runaway technological progress triggered by AI could lead to a situation in which humans may no longer be able to retain sufficient control over technology, which is an argument made by 'Unabomber' Ted Kaczynski in his 'manifesto'. Decision-making and the problems mankind faces could become so overly complex that only machines could make them intelligently. The dependence on technology would by then be so great that switching the machines in charge of our affairs off would no longer be a viable option. As a result, humans would have no choice but to accept whatever decisions automated systems may make on their behalf (Kaczynski 1995, Para. 173).

Stanislav Lem developed a similar and quite interesting scenario on runaway technology in his novel *Fiasco* (Lem 1988). Two antagonistic blocks on the planet Quinta are forced into a war-like deadlock by their automated defense systems. Unable to achieve any decisive victory, both sides rely on automated defenses that block any action or movement of the other side, leading to complete paralysis and civilizational decline. At some point the autonomous defense systems no longer serve any other purpose than to perpetuate an unbearable situation.

Of course, it is easy to dismiss the Terminator scenario as science fiction, but serious and informed people like the roboticists and AI experts Hans Moravec, Kevin Warwick, Bill Joy and Hugo de Garis have publicly discussed the possibility of dominance by machines while keeping a straight face (Moravec 1999; Warwick 1997; Joy 2000; de Garis 2005). Some AI researchers have even emphasized the importance of developing 'friendly AI', which would protect humanity rather than destroy it (Yudkowsky 2003).

There are also more positive views of emerging superior machine intelligence. Ray Kurzweil and other transhumanists believe that mankind will ultimately join the machines by amplifying our natural intelligence through brain implants or by transferring our minds into robotic bodies (Kurzweil 2005). But even this more positive scenario has the potential to polarize society into technologically upgraded (and possibly immortal) transhumans or Exes (as Moravec calls them) and everybody else.

In any case, the Terminator scenario seems to be more of a long-term threat rather than anything related to the current reality of computers and AI. However, there may be some hint in the fact that Britain's next killer drones will be controlled by a system called 'Skynet' (Page 2008d). Even defense analysts seem to feel uncomfortable about the ever-expanding reach of military computer systems. The *Guardian* quoted Peter Zimmerman from King's College, London, who refers to a short story by Arthur C. Clarke about a civilization which created a galaxy-wide computer and asked it whether God existed: '"there is now" – and that's the question that we really need to be thinking about with these systems' (Warren 2006).

Conclusion

Although not all of the scenarios developed above are plausible, all of them are at the very least possible future scenarios. It is very likely that robotic weapons could proliferate widely and even enable non-state actors to carry out new kinds of terrorist attacks. The possibility of an abuse of advanced technologies like robotics, AI and nanotechnology by states, even democratic ones, for the conduct of internal conflict and political repression is certainly a concern that should not be taken lightly. It is also probable that states which have long-range robotic weaponry could behave more aggressively toward states that do not have them. Major interstate war could once again become more frequent, either because of a weakening of political and economic restraints for war, or because of accidents or precarious imbalances of power.

However, it seems rather unlikely that nanobots or other self-replicating weapons could be developed in the foreseeable future. Though nanobots and self-replicating machines are ridiculed by established science as 'far out' and 'science fiction', nobody can say for sure that the 'gray goo' scenario is completely absurd or how soon a self-replicating nanobot could be engineered. Self-aware robots turning on their human masters is also currently a very remote possibility, but in the long term (after 2030) it could happen if no preparations were made.

Royal Astronomer Martin Rees argues in reference to scientific experiments that carry some risk of extremely negative outcomes that: 'It isn't good enough to make a slapdash estimate of even the tiniest risk of destroying the world' (Rees 2003, 127). Even very small risks could accumulate and make a major catastrophe more likely than individual risk calculations suggest.

With technologies like AI or nanotechnology, mankind is entering completely unknown territory. Nobody can know for sure whether computers or robots could develop something like self-awareness or intentionality, though the technological bar for this is certainly very high.

Options for Future Regulation

There is a need for containing the potentially very negative consequences of advanced technology on societies and international security. The international community of states could benefit immensely from developing and implementing a regulatory framework for the control of robotic/autonomous weapons. Arms control measures could prevent, or at least slow down, the arms race in the field of military robotics and the proliferation of robotic weapons, while limiting the destructiveness of future wars and in particular the dangers to non-combatants. Most importantly, regulation could prevent an environment that could result in the development of self-evolving powerful autonomous defense systems that could threaten (in the long term) the continued existence of humanity.

What Is Arms Control?

The term 'arms control' is often referred to in the context of weapons of mass destruction (WMD) and believed to be an invention caused by the very specific international constellation of the Cold War. This is a misperception, as arms control is much older and broader than, for example, the Nuclear Non-proliferation Treaty. Arms control encompasses a whole range of measures and policies that are aimed at increasing international security by controlling weapons technology through self-restraint, international cooperation and measures of enforcement such as enforced disarmament. Realists like Colin Gray have given arms control a bad name and claimed that it would be an exercise in futility, as 'arms control cannot be useful as an intended means to change policy' (C. S. Gray 1992, 41). Although there are many instances where arms control agreements have been broken, many, if not most of them, have not. In some instances, arms control agreements have established very durable and strong norms that restrain states to develop, transfer or use certain types of weapons and military technologies. Michael Levi and Michael O'Hanlon therefore argue that:

Arms control is still important, because dangerous technologies abound and no practical strategy exists whereby one country or small group of countries can successfully safeguard them. Coordinated international effort to regulate the development, production, and use of the world's most threatening technologies – in other words, arms control – is imperative. But the old ways of pursuing arms control are mostly obsolete, and the very definition of the term requires refinement and reinterpretation. (Levi and O'Hanlon 2005, 1)

It is therefore not the case that arms control would be an obsolete concept or limited to only WMD, which certainly will continue to get special attention by arms controllers because of their exceptional destructive powers. At the same time, conventional weaponry is becoming increasingly sophisticated and is already approaching nuclear weapons in terms of military effectiveness. Controlling conventional weapons through international agreements and control regimes could soon be no less important than controlling WMD. This means that it is time to bring the issue of conventional arms control back on the political agenda. It is argued that it would be important to extend arms control to more sophisticated conventional weapons and to put some restrictions on the development, transfer and use of advanced robotic weapons, which are currently only indirectly or insufficiently covered by existing treaties, before things get out of hand.

Does an Outright Ban of AW Make Sense?

The first question to ask is whether a preventive ban of all or most types of robotic weapons, as suggested by Jürgen Altmann, is realistic and whether it would make any sense to pursue such an outright ban. Although this would be a straightforward solution to the problem of preventing a dangerous dynamics of an arms race in military robotics, it seems highly unlikely that there could be some consensus within the international community to completely outlaw armed military robots. Many armed forces around the world have already introduced a great variety of robotic systems or have already made substantial investments for their development. In particular, the US is very clearly pursuing advanced robotic weapons and a reversal of this trend is quite remote. It is hard to imagine how an international ban of military robots would be possible without the participation of the US.

Even if Western states simply renounced their use of military robots, it is highly probable that other states with lesser compunction about legal and ethical concerns will be able to develop and deploy such weapons. The entry costs for military robotics are very low, especially if compared with nuclear weapons. In addition, the technology is to a great degree commercially available and it would be quite easy for a technologically less advanced state to buy the commercial components and integrate them into a robotic weapons system with some outside help. The possibility has already been demonstrated by the *Affordable Weapons System* project, which is a low-cost cruise missile put together with commercial products and technology for a bargain price (Space War 2004).

As a result, some nations will deploy robotic/autonomous weapons and this will create pressures for other nations to counter them. This means it would be better, according to Project Alpha Director Russ Richards, 'to be in the lead' (US Joint Forces Command 2003). In addition, it might even be unethical to deny the armed forces advanced robotic weapons, if they would have to confront opponents who are equipped with weapons that are more lethal. Sending humans into battle against robots could be considered to be immoral. Thus, the development of robotic weapons and their defensive use is morally justifiable.

It would be both ethically questionable and militarily unwise for Western states to simply renounce the use of armed military robots completely. At the same time, it would be very complacent and irresponsible to leave such a potentially very powerful military technology like military robotics largely unregulated. With some good regulation it might be possible to avert the most dangerous scenarios discussed above. The main issues connected to these scenarios have to do with proliferation, posture, the use and the design of robotic weapons. This might be a good starting point for creating some strategy for dealing with the dangers posed by the development of AW.

Proliferation

For containing the dangers of robotic weapons and surveillance systems it will be crucial to prevent the proliferation of the technology to dangerous individuals and groups, private companies, aggressive states and also to domestic agencies such as police forces.

Dangerous individuals and terrorist groups   The best strategy for countering possible robotic terrorism is to prevent terrorists from gaining access to more advanced robotic technology. While it might be impossible to prevent primitive terror weapons such as explosive carrying UAVs, which might not be very effective weapons anyway, it is certainly possible to make the conversion of commercial robotic systems, such as toys or service robots, into weapons technically very difficult. This means that it would be reasonable to regulate, maybe on a national level, that such robots should not be too capable in terms of AI and that they should not be easily reprogrammable for other uses. For ensuring the traceability of more advanced commercial robots, a licensing system could be established and the robots themselves could be equipped with tracking devices. In order to prevent other illegitimate uses of robotic devices like spying on neighbors, robot toys equipped with cameras or AI should not be made smaller than 1.6ft, so that they can be seen from afar and are clearly identifiable as robotic devices.

Proliferation to police forces   For preventing the misuse of robotic surveillance technology, it would make sense to prohibit the general police use of small surveillance robots that can enter and search private homes stealthily. Apart from exceptions, police forces should not be equipped with armed robots, as this could possibly result in more frequent, more excessive or inappropriate use of force. A highly questionable use of police robots would be using robots for riot control. It is hard to see how robots could possibly apply force in such situations in a discriminate and proportionate fashion. In any case, there should be export restrictions for police robots in order to prevent them falling into the hands of repressive regimes.

Proliferation to private companies   Military robotics technology could come in reach of private companies in the form of dual-use applications. An obvious example would be robotic military surveillance systems that could proliferate to the private security industry (Southerland 2007). Though some uses may be benign, such as security robots that can detect fires and patrol warehouses and office buildings, possible other and more questionable uses could include detecting and stopping intruders with non-lethal weapons or the quasi-military use by private companies operating within conflict-prone Third World countries. Bigger international private security companies such as Blackwater USA, which operate helicopters and armored cars in Iraq, are definitely interested in the use of armed robots (O'Brien 2007). They might want to deploy security robots in a more offensive fashion. Up to now, there has been no regulation in place that could stop them from using armed robots in Iraq or other places. Powerful military technology such as robotic weapons should not be available to private companies, which often lack accountability and which ultimately follow only their own interests.

Proliferation to other states   It is unlikely that states that are currently technologically far ahead in developing AI and advanced robotic weapons would export such weapons to any state other than their closest allies, if at all. However, this could be different with some states, which are still lagging behind in the technology but which would in principle be capable of catching up quickly, most importantly Russia and China. They could be much more willing to export robotic weapons and to even share the technology with other states, if only to generate profit through arms sales. As a result, dictatorships could acquire such weapons for repressing their own populations or for threatening neighboring states. Analogously to the Missile Technology Control Regime, which restricts the transfer of ballistic missiles, individual components thereof, or their technology, an international 'robotic weapons control regime' could be established to prevent the proliferation of conventional robotic weaponry and the technology to make them work, e.g. AI software. Alternatively, automatic target recognition (ATR) software for robotic weapons could be made open source in order to achieve the highest safety standard for the protection of civilians (Winslow 2007a, 11). Obviously, this would be a big dilemma, as it would make advanced technology available to potential enemies.

Posture

The introduction of robotic weaponry does not need to be a sign of a more offensive posture of a country and would therefore not necessarily destabilize the international system. Reliance on automated systems could mean that defense could be organized more cheaply and in a purely defensive posture, which could reduce the security dilemma that may dominate the relations among some nations. In the 1980s a new strategic concept was developed in the context of the Cold War confrontation in Europe, which was called 'non-offensive defense' and which aimed to create stable military balances. If no side was able to mount large-scale offensive operations against the other side and if both sides remained prepared to repulse an attack by defensive tactics alone, then the vicious cycle of the security dilemma and accelerating arms races could be broken. As a result, defense expenditures could be reduced, as well as the overall likelihood of military conflict.

Defensive posture   The development of AW could make it relatively easy and inexpensive for states to adopt a purely defensive military posture. Frank Barnaby argues that automated defensive weapons could make a possible successful attack by an aggressor so difficult and so expensive as to make it unlikely that any aggressive state would take the risk (Barnaby 1986, 162–9). New technologies would make defensive weapons much more cost-effective than offensive ones because 'using the new technologies for detecting, identifying and tracking enemy forces, and new warheads, it is much cheaper to destroy the weapons of invasion – heavy tanks, long-range missiles, long-range military aircraft and large warships – than to buy them. The invasion and occupation of a country can, therefore, be made prohibitively expensive' (Barnaby 1986, 5–6). From this point of view, the proliferation of robotic weapons to other states may not even be a bad thing, as long as these robotic weapons function in a reliable and predictable fashion and cannot be used for offensive purposes, for example to attack and invade neighbors.

Defensive weaponry   The key to non-provocative defense would be a clear distinction between weapons that are defensive and those that are offensive in nature with the latter to be kept at an absolute minimum. Such a distinction has always been very difficult. However, Carl Conetta points out that 'although no weapon is purely "offensive" or "defensive," all have different values in offensive and defensive roles – a fact that already plays a central role in military planning. Using this distinction as a guideline, planners can devise armed forces optimized for defensive operations' (Conetta 1995). An initial basis for the distinction between defensive and offensive weapons could be the maximum range of weapons. Barnaby suggests that a defensive posture of a country would mean that:

> The armed forces would not have main battle tanks, long-range combat aircraft or large warships. Nor would they have long-range lift-capability. The ranges of missiles would be no more than those required to bombard the defence zone, so that they would be non-provocative. Maximum missile ranges would be roughly eighty kilometres. (Barnaby 1986, 164)

Instead of relying on larger manned platforms, such as tanks and bombers, states could organize their armed forces around unmanned systems that can operate autonomously at shorter ranges. A constabulary force without any heavy weapons (not necessarily without unmanned systems) could be created for the specific purpose of conducting international peacekeeping operations (Schrader 2003).

The revival of defensive warfare   It is certainly true that in the past too much reliance on defensive tactics has put victims of aggression at a military disadvantage because the defenders could only respond to attacks and lacked the flexibility for regaining the initiative through a counter-attack. The most famous example of a paradigmatic defensive weapon that failed to deter war and to stop aggressors was the Maginot Line, which was simply bypassed by German forces in 1940. Offensive defense has therefore been identified as a much better guarantee for an effective defense than defensive defense in the age of maneuver warfare. One could argue that this age of maneuver warfare that began with the development of modern battle tanks and tank tactics in the 1930s and which saw a revival in Operations Desert Storm and Iraqi Freedom might have come to an end. Defensive tactics and weapons could become increasingly superior to offensive ones. It can be argued that 'modern technology favors defense over offense' (Fotion 1990, 47). Thus future major wars might resemble the battles and the strategic deadlock of the First World War more than the very dynamic and highly mobile warfare of the Second World War.

A change of attitudes required   The point made here is that robotic/autonomous weapons could be much more effective for defensive purposes than for offensive ones. Conventional military threat scenarios could be neutralized, if robotic/ autonomous weapons were developed primarily for defensive purposes. It might be necessary for some states, or the international community as whole, to have some superior robotic weapons for offensive purposes in order to discipline an aggressive state or to deal with an immediate threat to international security posed by such a state. In this case, it makes sense to establish an international arms control regime for offensive robotic weapons, such as unmanned long-range bombers, that controls the development, production and transfer of such weapons. Ideally, there should be an upper limit to the number of such systems that a state would be allowed to have, so that no state alone could pose a serious threat to other weaker states. Unfortunately, for many states to adopt a purely defensive posture will first and foremost require a substantial change of attitudes by defense establishment and there are at the moment few indications of this.

Use

It is necessary to explicitly include robotic weapons in international law and to develop some framework for functional arms control measures that clearly limit the manner in which robotic weapons should be used in war. Completely outlawing

AW or making it mandatory that military robots should be able to launch weapons only when they are controlled by humans might not be a very effective strategy for arms control. First of all, as argued earlier, tele-operated military robots are technologically and militarily a dead end and would be economically inefficient. It is therefore unlikely that states developing such weapons would agree on a complete ban of AW. Secondly, there is the issue of verification. It would be very difficult to determine whether a robotic system was in fact controlled by a human when it launched a weapon. Most likely this would require the analysis of the control software or the memory of the military robot and arms controllers would not easily get access to that. In any case, such intrusive methods would run counter to established practices of verification. Furthermore, the robotic weapon might be destroyed in battle and, together with it, all evidence. As a result, instead of prohibiting AW it might be more effective to develop some ground rules for their use that are easily verifiable.

The similarity to mine warfare   There is already a good basis for regulating AW contained in international law. Unmanned systems resemble in many respects mines and should be subject to the same or similar regulations about their use. It is true that anti-personnel land mines have been banned by the Ottawa Treaty because they are inherently indiscriminate weapons that kill and maim primarily civilians. Similarly, AW that blindly kill without the ability to discriminate would already be considered illegal weapons. However, mines that are more discriminating, like sea mines or anti-tank mines, are not outlawed. Their legal use requires that mines should only be deployed against military objectives, they should remain in one place and their location should be recorded, and they must have a neutralizing mechanism so that they will not endanger people after the end of hostilities (Green 2000, 194). In a similar fashion, it could be internationally regulated that unmanned systems should be restricted to confined and clearly marked areas such as military bases or small combat zones. The US Navy Commander John Klein suggests restricting AW to:

> 'kill box' operations … during lethal, autonomous missions to mitigate accountability concerns. During these operations, a geographic area defined by specific three-dimensional coordinates is designated, within which enemy targets can be engaged once properly identified and after weapon release authority is given. (Klein 2003)

No use of AW among civilians   The civilian population should be kept out of the areas where autonomous military robots operate, or civilians should be evacuated before autonomous military robots are deployed. Placing autonomous robots among civilians is unethical because currently available technology is not able to reliably distinguish between non-combatants and combatants. It is even unlikely that future technology could reliably discover the one terrorist who poses a threat among a crowd of people who do not. In other words, autonomous military robots should only be deployed in situations where all targets are likely to be legitimate targets. Of course, this still leaves room for accidents and error, but current methods of conducting war are hardly better, and probably worse in many respects.

Limiting the firepower of AW Military robots should be limited in range and firepower. The more precise these weapons are, the less firepower is required to destroy a particular target, which altogether makes the disproportionate use of force less likely. Hunter-killer UAVs that can loiter and autonomously search for suitable targets should only be allowed to operate over depopulated areas or over small combat zones. In many cases it might be entirely sufficient to equip military robots with non-lethal weapons. But even so, robots should only make use of such weapons in clearly defined, rather exceptional, circumstances, as the damage caused by losing a robot would probably be less than the damage of accidentally hurting or even killing an innocent civilian. John Canning's principle of letting 'humans target humans' and 'machines target machines' does make some sense and could be incorporated into a future arms control agreement on military robots. One problem with that principle, which may arise in the future, is that humans and robots might not always be easily distinguishable, for example if humanoid military robots are developed or vehicles and robotic exoskeletons are used that may or may not have humans inside them. In other words, robots might easily target humans by accident. Again, this is just another argument to restrict the use of autonomous military robots to small areas and to quite limited functions, such as base security or other defensive uses.

Neutralizing mechanism for AW Furthermore, AW must have a neutralizing mechanism that allows switching them off at any time, even if this possibility reduces their military effectiveness. There is a legitimate concern that future AW that could remain active for years could pose an even more serious threat to civilians than land mines currently do. This means it is important to include in any kind of robotic weapon a safety switch that automatically disables or deactivates the weapon after a certain amount of time, or if it permanently loses communication with the military control network or an operator. It might also be reasonable to develop disabling devices for 'rogue' robots. The British dot.com millionaire Ben Way already sees a business opportunity in developing anti-robot weapons and has recently founded a company with the name 'WAR Defence' with 'WAR' standing for 'Weapons Against Robots' (Tyler 2008). The company website promises futuristic anti-robot weapons like 'microwave energy disruptors', 'directed EMP [electromagnetic pulse] devices', robot detection and surveillance systems and 'robo viruses' (WAR Defence 2008).

Prevent robot–anti-robot arms race In the medium term, when robots become more common on the battlefield, there is the great danger of a growing competition between anti-robot weaponry and the hardening of robots against these weapons, leading to ever more autonomous robotic weapons that could no longer be switched off and that are largely resistant to anti-robot weapons. Obviously, such a tendency would generally weaken human control over military robots, which would leave few options in case they malfunction and start killing friendlies or non-combatants. This vicious cycle should be resisted from the beginning by creating an international regulation that puts limitations on the design of robotic weapons and the degree of autonomy they may have.

Design

Military robots should be designed in a way that guarantees their predictability and safety. This is an obvious point, but critics of military robots claim that there are still no clear safety standards for such weapons (Carroll-Mayer 2008). UAVs still crash with some regularity and autonomous land vehicles are still in the development stage. Many problems may be ironed out with more operational experience, but there are also some fundamental issues that need to be addressed. In particular, it should be prohibited that any military computer system that controls weapons could change its original programming by itself. This means no evolving or self-learning software, which is currently the general direction of AI, should be used for controlling weapons. The reasons are obvious. Though self-learning robots could lead to truly autonomous robotic weapons, these weapons would no longer be predictable and might become a serious danger to civilians, or even their owners. Nobody could be sure in which direction a self-learning computer system might evolve. At a certain level of complexity, nobody would even be able to understand what is going on inside of them (Georges 2003, 7). Superintelligent computers should not be developed and used for military purposes, as '[superintelligent] AIs cannot be forcibly constrained' (Yudkowsky 2003, Ch. 1).

Demilitarizing AI research   Worrying about the potential emergence of strong AI is not so much the fact that machines could one day outsmart human beings in most, if not all, domains of intelligence, but rather the fact that so much AI research is sponsored by the military and with military applications in mind. There is a serious danger that military organizations would be interested in creating intelligent machines without a conscience or any moral constraints simply because they could be more effective on the battlefield and because they would never question orders. In other words, there is the serious danger that 'superhuman psychopaths' could be created (Hall 2007). To prevent this danger, autonomous military robots should incorporate human values that constrain their behavior, possibly in the form suggested by Ronald Arkin. Altogether, it would be important to 'demilitarize' robotics and AI research and put more emphasis on civilian and commercial uses of the technology, which would make the development of universal safety standards more likely.

Preventing the Terminator scenario   A regulation that explicitly prohibits the development and use of self-learning military robots would close the door on the 'Terminator scenario' of machines violently taking over or, more likely, their serious malfunctioning with catastrophic consequences for mankind. If superintelligent computers are to be developed at all, they should only have weak links to the physical world. On higher levels of decision-making a human needs to remain in the loop at all times. Although this seems to be a very obvious precaution against military accidents, it is not just imaginable, but to some degree even likely that states might feel compelled to deploy completely autonomous defense systems that could launch defensive weapons, or even a retaliatory strike, without any human input. Some countries that feel particularly threatened in their very existence might develop doomsday weapons or doomsday machines that can, like the (still operational) Soviet *Perimetr*, retaliate even after the enemy has eliminated them. Such automated defense systems should be outlawed.

Controlling military nanotechnology (NT)   At the moment it is pure speculation how great the threat of self-replicating nanobots actually is, as nobody has yet disproved their hypothetical possibility. The Foresight Institute has suggested restricting the development of MNT through safety rules that could be codified as international law (Jacobstein 2006). The argument of the Institute is that military NT applications 'may not fall under existing arms-control treaties'. Considering the potential impact and dangers of MNT some international regulation would be important to ensure that the technology is safe and that catastrophes such as the 'gray goo' scenario can be averted. An outright ban of MNT, however, is considered by the Foresight Institute to be a very precarious option: 'While a 100% effective ban could, in theory, avoid the potential risks of certain forms of molecular nanotechnology, a 99.99% effective ban could result in development and deployment by the 0.01% that evaded and ignored the ban' (Jacobstein 2006). What they suggest is to incorporate safety mechanisms that prevent them from mutating and outcompeting biological organisms into autonomous nanobots. Michael Vassar and Robert Freitas go even further and consider the development of a 'nanoshield', which could function as a technical immune system against self-replicating nanoweapons (Vassar and Freitas 2006). However, MNT is still a very speculative area and it might be far too early for regulating it. Jürgen Altmann recommends simply devising a feasibility study for developing MNT and then set 'appropriate preventive limits in the civilian and military sectors' (Altmann 2006, 181).

Prohibiting lethal mini/micro-machines   Finally, lethal mini/micro-robots or robotic microsensors that can be used for tagging individuals should be outlawed completely. They could encourage modes of warfare based on assassination and this would be similarly immoral as the use of chemical and biological weapons. This prohibition should also include cyborg animals such as 'cyborged' insects. Altmann argues for a general prohibition of small robotic systems smaller than 0.6–1.6ft (Altmann 2006, 168).

Conclusion: The Challenge Ahead

This book has developed the hypothesis of the 'killer robot': an autonomous weapon that can pick its targets by itself and that can trigger itself. Strictly speaking, there are no such weapons deployed, but the technology for them is already available and it has been available for decades. However, now it is more likely than ever before that robotic weapons will be fielded, as AI could make them smart enough to be militarily useful. They will generally enable many military organizations to use force without putting human lives at risk. The use of robots will allow the removal of many psychological aspects of combat, for better or worse. Robots might also prove vastly superior to humans on the battlefield, being able to shoot much faster and more accurately. In short, 'unmanned combat' could represent a major discontinuity in the history of warfare.

The current situation of an impending Revolution in Military Affairs (RMA) triggered by IT, robotics, AI and nanotechnology in some aspects resembles the situation immediately after the Second World War. When the nuclear bomb was invented political decision-makers did not fully understand its strategic implications. In fact, the Truman Administration did not have any clear doctrine governing the use of nuclear weapons and it was only in the mid-1950s that the US developed a proper nuclear doctrine. For about 10 years, it was not clear under which exact circumstances and how the US would use nuclear weapons in defense of its interests. As a result, the world almost slithered into the abyss of nuclear war more than once. Politics was simply not ready for the nuclear age. But is politics ready for the age of robotic warfare? One can have serious doubts about it (Asaro 2008b). In the worst case, robotic warfare could weaken deterrents and encourage political and military risk-taking. The use of force might once again become a frequent tool of foreign policy.

Preventing this from happening will require a debate on the moral foundations of warfare, or military ethics. Some applications of technologies like robotics and nanotechnology are incompatible with the military ethos that is still based on the ideal of chivalry. Chivalrous conduct in war is not to kill the enemy at long range with zero risk, but is based on the willingness to fight fairly and to risk as much as the opponent, namely your own life. Only if lives are at stake will there be effective deterrents to the use of force. Of course, fairness in war is not a requirement of international law and the idea certainly seems odd to political and military decision-makers. However, it is still the best argument against an increasing and eventually complete automation of warfare. Using robots for killing people in war is wrong not because international law says so (in fact it doesn't), but because it is inherently unfair. Now could be the right time to bring back the ideals of chivalry and fairness to the discussion on military ethics. This might make many military organizations reconsider their current aims of using robotic systems in combat roles. If Western armed forces do not deploy such systems offensively, then many other states around the world might not feel pressured to develop advanced robotic weapons.

At the same time, there are certainly legitimate uses and roles for unmanned systems (including armed robots) and it would be irrational not to use them for specific purposes, such as guarding bases and borders or for some narrow roles in high-intensity warfare. Not all about them is bad. Even more, it would be unethical to send a human soldier into an environment that is too harsh or no longer survivable for humans. To rephrase Napoleon, robots can be made to be killed. Military robots are also ethically a better alternative to the 'cyborgization' of soldiers, which effectively turns humans into little more than sophisticated pieces of military equipment or government property. In the very long term, robotic weaponry could eventually make war impossible. Until then it will be crucial not to discard the human element in war and not to forget the moral responsibility one has, even toward their own the enemy.

Harry Truman wrote a note after watching the first nuclear test in New Mexico in 1945: 'machines are ahead of morals by some centuries, and when morals catch up perhaps there'll be no reason for any of it' (quoted in Gaddis 2005, 53). In the context of the possible advent of strong AI and intelligent killer robots, Truman's words seem menacingly true. The world was not prepared for the invention of the nuclear bomb and it is hardly prepared for the possibilities and temptations afforded by further runaway technological progress. There are good reasons to be concerned about military robotics and future 'killer robots' and it will be challenging to bypass the various roads to hell.

Military Robotics Timeline

Future

- 2040: Technological Singularity – an AI triggered exponential acceleration of technological development.
- 2030: DARPA estimate for the development of human-level AI.
- 2030: MoD estimate for the development of computers that can make intelligent judgements in response to information.
- 2020–25: a long-range UCAV (*Switchblade*) and a Common Aero Vehicle could be fielded by the US.
- 2020: British MoD estimate for the development of nanoscale machines.
- 2020: One third of all US Army vehicles could be unmanned.
- 2015–2020: Several nations are planning to field UCAVs as a replacement of conventional bombers, including the US, Britain, Germany and Russia.
- 2012–15: The first US Army *Future Combat Systems* are scheduled to be fielded. They include three classes of UGVs and three classes of UAVs.
- 2010–2012: The first Directed Energy Weapons could become operational (Airborne Laser, Advanced Tactical Laser, Active Denial System).

Past

- November 2007: In the DARPA *Urban Challenge* eleven autonomous vehicles had to finish a 2.8 mile course in an urban environment – all vehicles finished and there was only one crash.
- July 2007: US Army deploys the first three armed *Talon* robots in Iraq.
- October 2005: The second DARPA *Grand Challenge* competition has five finishers.
- May 2005: Republic of Singapore Navy deploys the *Protector* USV to the North Arabian Gulf.
- March 2004: First DARPA *Grand Challenge* competition of autonomous ground vehicles – no finishers over the 142 mile course.
- March 2003: First time a UAV (a *Predator* drone) engages an enemy aircraft (an Iraqi MiG-25) with a missile.
- November 2002: CIA operated *Predator* drone attacks a car with terrorists in Yemen.
- October 2001: First operational use of the armed *Predator* drone.
- April 2001: The *Global Hawk* reconnaissance drone charts its own course over a distance of 13,000 km (8,000 miles) between California, US, and Southern Australia.
- May 1997: The *Deep Blue* chess computer defeats world chess champion Garri Kasparov in a chess match.
- 1996: Sandia National Labs presents the *Miniature Autonomous Robotic Vehicle* (MARV) the size of one cubic inch.
- January 1991: Reconnaissance drones play an important role in collecting battlefield intelligence in the Second Gulf War.
- 1984: Robot Defense Systems of Colorado demonstrates its *Programmable Robot Observer With Logical Enemy Response* (PROWLER) – an armed sentry vehicles with some limited capability of autonomous operation.
- 1983: DARPA announces its $1 billion Strategic Computing Initiative, which aims at creating intelligent machines within a decade.
- 1982: French *Exocet* missile sinks the British warship HMS Sheffield
- 1981: A repair worker killed by a robot in Japan.
- 1980: First *Phalanx* Close-In Weapons System robotic air defence gun deployed on the USS Coral Sea.

Bibliography

Abatti, J. M. (2005), *Small Power: The Role of Small and Micro UAVs in the Future* (Maxwell AFB: US Air University, Air Command and Staff College).

Adami, C. (1998), *Introduction to Artificial Life* (New York: Springer).

Adams, T. K. (2000), 'The Real Military Revolution', *Parameters* 30:3, 54–65.

_____(2001), 'Future Warfare and the Decline of Human Decisionmaking (Weapons Automation)', *Parameters* 31:4, 57–71.

AFP (2008), 'Automated Killer Robots "Threat to Humanity": Expert', [website], (updated 26 February 2008) <http://afp.google.com/article/ALeqM5gfEAWc0aBlnuw1wuEnghZup9V7yg>

Agmon, M., J. L. Bonomo, M. Kennedy, M. Leed, K. Watman, K. Webb and C. Wolf, Jr. (1996), *Arms Proliferation Policy: Support to the Presidential Advisory Board* (Santa Monica, CA: RAND).

Allen, T. B. (1994), *War Games: Inside the Secret World of the Men Who Play at Annihilation* (London: Mandarin Paperbacks).

Altmann, J. (2004), 'Military Nanotechnology: Perspectives and Concerns', *Security Dialogue* 35:1, 61–79.

_____(2006), *Military Nanotechnology: Potential Applications and Preventive Arms Control* (London: Routledge).

Ames, B. (2003), 'Electronics Ruggedization a Key Part of Objective Force Warrior Program', *Military & Aerospace Electronics* [website], (updated August 2003) <http://mae.pennnet.com/Articles/Article_Display.cfm?Section=Articles&Subsection=Display&ARTICLE_ID=183385>

Amnesty International (2004), 'United States of America: Excessive and Lethal Force? Amnesty International's Concern About Deaths and Ill-treatment Involving Police Use of Tasers', *Research Report* (30 November).

Anderson, K. (2007), 'Armed Robots Deployed in Iraq', [website], (updated 3 August 2007) <http://kennethandersonlawofwar.blogspot.com/2007/08/armed-robots-deployed-in-iraq.html>

Argy, P. (2007), 'Ethics Dilemma in Killer Bots', *Australian IT* [website], (updated 16 January 2007) <http://www.australianit.news.com.au/story/0,24897,21064361-15309,00.html>

Arizona Star (2007), 'Battlefield Robots Are Readied to Fight Our Wars, Save Human Lives', *Arizona Star* [website], (updated 7 August 2007) <http://www.azstarnet.com/news/190862>

Arkin, R. (2007), *Governing Lethal Behavior: Embedding Ethics in a Hybrid Deliberative/Reactive Robot Architecture*, Technical Report (Atlanta: Georgia Institute of Technology (November)).

_____(2008), 'When Robots Commit War Crimes: Autonomous Weapons and Human Responsibility', *Technology in Wartime Conference*, Stanford University [website], (26 January 2008) <http://technologyinwartime.org/node/19>

Arkin, R. and L. Moshkina (2007), 'Lethality and Autonomous Robots: An Ethical Stance', Research Paper, Atlanta: Georgia Institute of Technology [online], <www.cc.gatech.edu/ai/robot-lab/online-publications/ArkinMoshkinaISTAS.pdf>

Arkin, W. F. (2008), Unmanned and Dangerous: The Future U.S. Military?, *Washington Post* [website], (30 April 2008) <http://blog.washingtonpost.com/earlywarning/future_war>

Armada International (1998/3), 'Coping with Analysis', *Armada International* [website], (1998/3) <http://www.armada.ch/98-3/001e.htm>

Arnold, R. F. (1998), 'Termination or Transformation? The "Terminator" Films and Recent Changes in the U.S. Auto Industry', *Film Quarterly* 52:1 (Autumn) 20–30.

Arquilla, J. and D. Ronfeldt (2000), *Swarming and the Future of Warfare* (Santa Monica, CA: RAND).

Asaro, P. M. (2006), 'What Should We Want From a Robot Ethic?', *International Review of Information Ethics* 6:12, 9–16.

_____(2008a), 'How Just Could a Robot War Be?', [website], <http://peterasaro.org>

_____(2008b), 'Armed Robots and Arms Control', *Technology in Wartime Conference*, Stanford University (26 January 2008).

Asimov, I. (1968), 'Runaround', reprinted in *I, Robot* (London: Grafton Books) 33–51.

Associated Press (2006), 'Hezbollah "Air Power" First Flew in 2004', [website], (updated 14 July 2006) <http://www.boston.com/news/world/middleeast/articles/2006/07/14/hezbollah_air_power_first_flew_in_2004>

_____(2008a), 'Suicides Up Again This Year', [website], (updated 29 May 2008) <http://www.military.com/news/article/suicides-up-again-this-year.html>

_____(2008b), 'Experts Warn of Robotic Terrorism', [website], (updated 28 February 2008) <http://www.military.com/NewsContent/0,13319,163010,00.html?ESRC=topstories.RSS>

Atkinson, D. (2007), 'The Danger of Robotic Weapons Systems', [website], (updated 24 October 2007) <http://weirdfuture.blogspot.com>

AUSA (2007), *A Transformed and Modernized U.S. Army: A National Imperative* (Arlington, VA: National Security Report (April))

Axe, D. (2006), 'Who Killed the Killer-Drone (Redux)', *Defense Tech.Org* [website], (updated 27 July 2006) <http://www.defensetech.org/archives/002605.html>

Baldor, L. (2008), 'Air Force Creates New Pilot Training Program for Drones', *Associated Press* [website], (updated 23 October 2008) <http://wtop.com/?nid=116&sid=1502574>

Bandura, A. (1999), 'Moral Disengagement in the Perpetration of Inhumanities', *Personality and Social Psychology Review* 3, 193–209.

Barnaby, F. (1986), *The Automated Battlefield* (New York: The Free Press).

Bauman, Z. (1997), 'Violence, Postmodern', in *Life in Fragments: Essays in Postmodern Moralities* (Oxford: Blackwell), 139–62.

BBC (2005a), 'US Plans "Robot Troops" for Iraq', *BBC Online* [website], (updated 23 January 2005) <http://news.bbc.co.uk/1/hi/world/americas/4199935.stm>

_____(2005b), 'South Korea Robots "to Patrol the Border"', *BBC News* [website], (8 April 2005) <http://news.bbc.co.uk/1/hi/world/asia-pacific/4425689.stm>

_____(2007a), 'Robotic Age Poses Ethical Dilemma', *News Online* [website], (updated 7 March 2007).

_____(2007b), 'Robots Could Demand Legal Rights', *News* [website], (updated 21 December 2007) <http://news.bbc.co.uk/1/hi/technology/6200005.stm>

_____(2008), 'Robo-Doc', [website], (updated 24 April 2008) <http://www.bbc.co.uk/insideout/content/articles/2008/04/24/london_robots_s13_w9_feature.shtml>

Beason, D. (2005), *The E-Bomb: How America's New Directed Energy Weapons Will Change the Way Future Wars Will Be Fought* (Cambridge, MA: Da Capo Books).

Belin, D. and G. Chapman (eds) (1987), *Computers in Battle: Will They Work?* (New York: Harcourt Brace Jovanovich Publishers).

Benbow, T. (2004), *The Magic Bullet: Understanding the Revolution in Military Affairs* (London: Brassey's).

Benford, G. and E. Malartre (2007), *Beyond Human: Living with Robots and Cyborgs* (New York: A Forge Book).

Berkowitz, B. (2003), *The New Face of War: How War Will Be Fought in the 21st Century* (New York: The Free Press).

Berube, D. M. (2006), *Nano-Hype: The Truth Behind the Nanotechnology Buzz* (New York: Prometheus Books).

Betts, R. K. (1985), 'Conventional Deterrence: Predictive Uncertainty and Policy Confidence', *World Politics* 37:2 (January) 153–79.

Bigelow, D. F. (2007), 'Fast Forward to the Robot Dilemma', *Armed Forces Journal* (November) 16–22.

Blackmore, T. (2005), *War X: Human Extensions in Battlespace* (Toronto: University of Toronto Press).

Blair, B. (1993), *The Logic of Accidental Nuclear War* (New York: Brookings Institution Press).

Blech, J. (2007), 'The Future of War: Attack of the Killer Robots', *Spiegel International* [website], (updated 15 August 2007) <http://www.spiegel.de/international/world/0,1518,500140,00.html>

Bone, E. and C. Bolkcom (2003), *Unmanned Aerial Vehicles: Background and Issues for Congress* (Washington, DC: US Congress (25 April)).

Bongard, D. L. and T. L. Sayers (2002), 'The Impact of Robotics on Nontraditional Warfare', in W. R. Schilling (ed.), *Nontraditional Warfare: Twenty-First-Century Threats and Responses* (Washington, DC: Brassey's), 299–310.

Boot, M. (2006a), *War Made New: Technology, Warfare, and the Course of History, 1500 to Today* (New York: Penguin).

_____(2006b), 'Paradox of Technology', *The New Atlantis* (Fall) 13–31.

Borenstein, J. (2008), 'The Ethics of Autonomous Military Robots', *Studies in Ethics, Law, and Technology* 2:1, 1–17.

Borgmann, A. (1984), *Technology and the Character of Contemporary Life: A Philosophical Inquiry* (Chicago: University of Chicago Press).

Boukhtouta, A., A. Bedrouni, J. Berger, F. Bouak and A. Guitouni (2002), *A Survey of Military Planning Systems* (Toronto: Defense Research and Development).

Braybrook, R. and E. H. Biass (2004), 'Bolt from the Blue … the Gray and the Black', *Armada International* 2004:1.

Brewin, B. (2003), 'Homemade GPS Jammers Raise Concern', *Computerworld Security* [website], (updated 17 January 2003) <http://computerworld.com/printthis/2003/0,4814,77702,00.html>

Briggs, H. (2008), 'Machines to "Match Man by 2029"', *BBC Online* [website], (updated 16 February 2008) <http://news.bbc.co.uk/1/hi/world/americas/7248875.stm>

Brooks, R. A. (2002), *Robot: The Future of Flesh and Machines* (London: Penguin).

Brooks, R. A. and A. M. Flynn (1989), 'Fast, Cheap, and Out of Control: A Robot Invasion of the Solar System', *Journal of the British Interplanetary Society* 42, 478–85.

Brown, C. (2001), *Understanding International Relations* (Basingstoke: Palgrave).

Brzezinski, M. (2003), 'The Unmanned Army', *The New York Times* [website], (updated 18 April 2003) <http://query.nytimes.com/gst/fullpage.html?res=9C03EFDF103BF933A15757C0A9659C8B63>

Budrys, A. (1954/1989), 'The First to Serve', in Isaac Asimov, Martin H. Greenberg and Charles G. Waugh, *Robots* (New York: Signet).

Burke, J. (1999), *An Intimate History of Killing: Face-to-Face Killing in Twentieth Century Warfare* (London: Granta Books).

Butler, A. (2007), 'Bids Are In For U.S. Navy UCAS-D', *Aviation Week and Space Technology* [website], (updated 1 April 2007) <http://www.aviationweek.com/aw/generic/story_channel.jsp?channel=defense&id=news/aw040207p1.xml>

Buxbaum, P. A. (2008), 'Self-Healing Aircraft', *Defense Systems* [online], (updated 26 May 2008) <http://www.defensesystems.com/issues/3_4/features/1544-1.html?topic=security_and_intelligence>

Caldicott, H. (2002), *The New Nuclear Danger: George W. Bush's Military-Industrial Complex* (New York: The New Press).

Campbell, M. S. (1997), '"An Enjoyable Game": How HAL Plays Chess', in David G. Stork (ed.), *Hal's Legacy: 2001's Computer as a Dream and Reality* (Cambridge, MA: MIT Press), 75–100.

Canning, J. S. (2006), 'Concept of Operations for Autonomous Systems', [website], (updated 2006) <http://www.dtic.mil.ndia/2006disruptive_tech/canning.pdf>

Carafano, J. J. (2007), 'The Pentagon's Robots: Arming the Future', *Backgrounder*, Washington, DC: Heritage Foundation (19 December).

Carroll-Mayer, M. (2008), 'Unmanned Aerial Vehicles and the Myth of Battle Readiness: Facing the Facts', *Technology in Wartime Conference*, Stanford University (26 January 2008).

Case, D. (2008), 'The U.S. Military's Assassination Problem', *Mother Jones* [website], (March–April 2008) <http://www.motherjones.com/commentary/columns/2008/03/the-us-militarys-assassination-problem.html>

Cavas, C. P. (2004), 'U.S. Fleet of Mother Ships: Will Swarms of Tiny Unmanned Vessels Replace Large Vessels?', *Defense News* 19:44 (15 November) 11–12.

Cerasini, M. (2003), *The Future of War: The Face of 21st Century Warfare* (Indianapolis, IN: Alpha Books).

Challans, T. L. (2007), *Awakening Warrior: Revolution in the Ethics of Warfare* (New York: State University of New York Press).

Chapman, B. (2008), *Space Warfare and Defense: A Historical Encyclopedia and Research Guide* (Santa Barbara, CA: ABC CLIO).

Chapman, G. (1985), 'Airland Battle Doctrine and the Strategic Computing Initiative', *Computer Professionals for Social Responsibility* [online], (Fall) <http://cpsr.org/prevsite/publications/newsletters/old/1980s/Fall1985.txt/view>
_____(1987), 'Thinking About Autonomous Weapons', *Computer Professionals For Social Responsibility Newsletter* [online], (Fall) <http://cpsr.org/prevsite/publications/newsletters/old/1980s/Fall1987.txt>

Chapman, R. E. (2002), 'Unmanned Combat Aerial Vehicles: Dawn of a New Age?', *Aerospace Power Journal* [website], (Summer 2002) <http://www.airpower.maxwell.af.mil/airchronicles/apj/apj02/sum02/chapman.html>

Charette, R. (2008), 'Army's FCS Still 70 Percent Probability of Success?', *Tech Insider* [website], (updated 12 March 2008) <http://techinsider.nextgov.com/2008/03/future_combat_systems_probabil_1.php>

Cheung, T. M. (2002), 'Innovation within China's Defense Technological and Industrial Base', in Michael Pillsbury (ed.) *Chinese Views of Future Warfare* (Washington, DC: National Defense University), 27–46, <http://www.au.af.mil/au/awc/awcgate/ndu/chinview/chinacont.html>

Clark, R. M. (2000), 'Uninhabited Combat Aerial Vehicles: Airpower by the People, For the People, But Not with the People', *Air University Press* [online], (August 2000) <http://www.au.af.mil/au/aul/aupress/CADRE_Papers/PDF_Bin/clark.pdf>

Clarke, R. (1993/94), 'Asimov's Laws of Robotics: Implications for Information Technology', *IEEE Computer* 26:12 (December) 53–61 and 27:1 (January) 57–66.

Cohen, E. (2006), 'Technology and Warfare', in J. Baylis, J. Wirtz, E. Cohen and C. S. Gray (eds.), *Strategy in the Contemporary World: An Introduction to Strategic Studies* (Oxford: Oxford University Press), 235–53.

Coker, C. (2002), *Waging War Without Warriors* (Boulder, CO: Lynne Rienner Publishers).

_____(2004), *The Future of War: The Re-Enchantment of War in the Twenty-First Century* (Oxford: Blackwell).

_____(2007), *The Warrior Ethos: Military Culture and the War on Terror* (London: Routledge).

_____(2008), *Ethics and War in the 21st Century* (London: Routledge).

Conetta, C. (1995), *Nonoffensive Defense and the Transformation of US Defense Posture* (Cambridge, MA: Project on Defense Alternatives) [online], (July 1995) <http://www.comw.org/pda/nodglob.htm>

_____(2005), *Arms Control in an Age of Strategic and Military Revolution* (Cambridge, MA: Project for Defense Alternatives (15 November)).

Cook, M. L. (2004), *The Moral Warrior: Ethics and Service in the U.S. Military* (New York: State University of New York Press).

Copeland, J. (2000), 'What is AI? Part 11', *AlanTuring.Net* [website], (May 2000) <http://www.alanturing.net/turing_archive/pages/Reference%20Articles/what_is_AI/What%20is%20AI11.html>

Corcoran, E. (2006), 'The Robots Are Coming!', *Forbes.Com* [website], (updated 18 August 2006) <http://www.forbes.com/2006/08/17/robot-egang-history_06egang_cz_ec_0817robotintro.html>

Cordeschi, R. (2002), *The Discovery of the Artificial: Behavior, Mind and Machines Before and Beyond Cybernetics* (Dordrecht: Kluwer Academic Publishers).

Correll, J. T. (1996), 'The Shape of Things to Come', *Air Force Magazine* 79:3.

Cowan, T. H. (2007), *A Theoretical, Legal and Ethical Impact of Robots on Warfare* (Carlisle Barracks, PA: US Army War College (30 March)).

Crichton, M. (2002), *Prey* (New York: HarperCollins Publishers).

Davis, D. L. (2007), 'Who Decides: Man or Machine?', *Armed Forces Journal* [website], (November 2007) <www.armedforcesjournal.com/2007/11/3036753>

Davoudi, S. (2006), 'UK Report Says Robots Will Have Rights', *Financial Times* [website], (updated 19 December 2006) <http://www.ft.com/cms/s/2/5ae9b434-8f8e-11db-9ba3-0000779e2340.html>

Defense Industry Daily (2008), 'DARPA's Commander's AID: From OODA to Deep Green', *Defense Industry Daily* [website], (3 June 2008) <http://www.defenseindustrydaily.com/darpa-from-ooda-to-deep-green-03497>

DefenseTech.org (2006), 'Robotic Frisbees of Death', [website], (updated 9 April 2006) <http://www.defensetech.org/archives/002723.html>

Defense Update (2006), 'Protector Unmanned Surface Vehicle', *Defense Update* 2006:2 [website] <http://www.defense-update.com/products/p/protector.htm>

_____(2007), 'Smart Weapons for UAVs', *Defense Update* 2007:1 [website] <http://www.defense-update.com/features/du-1-07/feature_armedUAVs.htm>

de Garis, H. (2005), *The Artilect War: Cosmists Vs. Terrans: A Bitter Controversy Whether Mankind Should Build Godlike Massively Intelligent Machines* (Palm Springs: ETC Publishers).

_____(2007), 'Machines Like Us: Interview with Hugo de Garis', *Science News* [website], (updated 9 March 2007) <http://www.machineslikeus.com/cms/interview-hugo-de-garis.html>

DeGroot, G. (2008), *Dark Side of the Moon: The Magnificent Madness of the American Lunar Quest* (London: Vintage).

De Landa, M. (1992), *War in the Age of Intelligent Machines* (New York: Zone Books).

Demchak, C. C. (1999), '"New Security" in Cyberspace: Emerging Intersection between Military and Civilian Contingencies', *Journal of Contingencies and Crisis Management* 7:4 (December) 181–98.

_____(2003), 'Creating the Enemy: Global Diffusion of the Information Technology-Based Military Model', in Emily O. Goldman and Leslie C. Eliason (eds), *The Diffusion of Military Technology and Ideas* (Stanford: Stanford University Press), 307–47.

Dennet, D. (1987), 'Cognitive Wheels: The Frame Problem of AI', in Z.W. Pylyshin (ed.), *The Robot's Dilemma: The Frame Problem in Artificial Intelligence* (Norwood, NJ: Ablex).

_____(1997), 'When HAL Kills, Who's to Blame? Computer Ethics', in David G. Stork (ed.), *HAL's Legacy: 2001's Computer as Dream and Reality* (Cambridge, MA: MIT Press), 351–64.

_____(2007), 'Higher Games', *Technology Review* (September/October 2007).

Dick, P. K. (1986a), 'Autofac', in Philip K. Dick, Patricia S. Warrick and Martin Harry Greenberg (eds), *Robots, Androids, and Mechanical Oddities* (Carbondale, IL: Southern Illinois University Press), 145–67.

_____(1986b), 'The Second Variety', in Philip K. Dick, Patricia S. Warrick and Martin Harry Greenberg (eds), *Robots, Androids, and Mechanical Oddities* (Carbondale, IL: Southern Illinois University Press), 38–76.

Dickson, P. (1976), *The Electronic Battlefield* (Bloomington, IN: Indiana University Press), 215–23.

DiMascio, J. (2006), 'Future Combat Systems Costs Skyrocket', *InsideDefense.com* [website], (updated 11 July 2006) <http://www.military.com/features/0,15240,104810,00.html>

Dodson, S. (2008), 'The Machine that Copies Itself', *Guardian* [website], (updated 3 July 2008) <http://www.guardian.co.uk/technology/2008/jul/03/copy.machine.reprap>

Dörner, D. (1996), *The Logic of Failure: Recognizing and Avoiding Error in Complex Situations* (New York: Perseus Books).

DPA (2008), 'Germany's First Driverless Mass-Transit Train in Service', [website], (updated 16 June 2008) <http://computing.in.msn.com/articles/article.aspx?cp-documentid=1476001>

Drexler, K. E. (1987), *Engines of Creation: The Coming Era of Nanotechnology* (New York: Anchor Books).

Drexler, K. E. and R. Smalley (2003), 'Drexler and Smalley Make the Case For and Against "Molecular Assembler"', *Chemical & Engineering News* 81:48 (1 December) 37–42.

Dudenhoeffer, D. D. and M. P. Jones (2000), 'A Formation Behaviour for Large-Scale Micro-Robot Force Deployment', *Proceedings of the 2000 Winter Simulation Conference* (2000) 973.

Dunlop, C. (2007), 'Lawfare Amid Warfare', *The Washington Times* [website], (updated 3 August 2007) <http://washingtontimes.com/news/2007/aug/03/lawfare-amid-warfare>

Dunne, P. (2006), 'Quantum Computing Steps Forward', *Physorg.com* [website], (updated 20 January 2006) <http://www.physorg.com/news10079.html>

Dunnigan, J. F. (1982), *How to Make War: A Comprehensive Guide to Modern Warfare* (London: Arms and Armour Press).

Edinburgh Institute of International Law (1969), 'The Distinction between Military Objectives and Non-Military Objectives in General and Particularly the Problems Associated with Weapons of Mass Destruction', [website], (9 September 1969) <http://www1.umn.edu/humanrts/instree/1969a.htm>

Ehrhard, T. P. and R. O. Work (2007), 'The Unmanned Combat Air System Carrier Demonstration Program: A New Dawn For Naval Aviation?', *Backgrounder*, Washington, DC: Center for Strategic and Budgetary Assessments (10 May).

Eisenstadt, E. (2002), 'Brain Machine Interface', DARPA [website], <http://www.darpa.mil/DARPATech2002/presentations/dso_pdf/speeches/EISENSTADT.pdf>

Encyclopaedia Britannica Online (2008), 'Robot', <http://www.britannica.com/EBchecked/topic/505818/robot> accessed 20 October 2008.

Epstein, R. G. (1997), *The Case of the Killer Robot: Stories About the Professional, Ethical and Societal Dimensions of Computing* (New York: John Wiley & Sons).

EURON (2006), 'Roboethics Roadmap', Genoa: *EURON Roboethics Atelier* [online], (3 March 2006) <http://www.roboethics.org/site/modules/mydownloads/download/ROBOETHICS%20ROADMAP%20Rel2.1.1.pdf>

Evans, M., R. Parkin and A. Ryan (2004), *Future Armies, Future Challenges: Land Warfare in the Information Age* (Crows Nest, NSW: Allen & Unwin).

Everett, H. R. (1998), 'Breaking Down Barriers/A Brief History of Robotics in Physical Security', *Unmanned Vehicles* 3:1 (February–April) 18–20.

Falconer, B. (2003), 'Defense Research Agency Seeks to Create Supersoldiers', *Government Executive.com* [website], (updated 10 November 2003) <http://www.govexec.com/dailyfed/1103/111003nj1.htm>

Farmer, D. (1998), 'Self-organising Evolution in Financial Markets and Elsewhere', [website], <http://www.aec.at/en/archiv_files/19982/E1998a_173.pdf>

Farmer, D. and A. d'A. Belin (1992), 'Artificial Life: The Coming Evolution', in Christopher G. Langton, Charles Taylor, J. Doyne Farmer and Steen Rasmussen (eds), *Artificial Life II* (Redwood City, CA: Addison-Wesley), 815–40.

Farrell, N. (2008), 'Military Robot Kills Without Compunction', *The Inquirer* [website], (30 April 2008) <http://www.theinquirer.net/gb/inquirer/news/2008/04/30/israel-shows-robo-soldier>

Featherstone, S. (2007), 'The Coming Robot Army: Introducing America's Future Fighting Machines', *Harper's Magazine* (February) 43–9.

Feikert, A. (2005), 'Cruise Missile Proliferation', *Congressional Research Service Report* (28 July).

Ferris, J. (2004), 'Netcentric Warfare, C4ISR, and Information Operations: Towards a Revolution in Military Intelligence?', *Intelligence and National Security* 19:2 (1 June) 199–225.

Flam, F. (2008), 'Getting Robots of War to Act More Naturally', *Philadelphia Inquirer* [website], (updated 12 June 2008) <http://www.philly.com/inquirer/front_page/20080612_Getting_robots_of_war_to_act_more_naturally.html>

Fleming, N. (2008), 'Robot Wars "Will Be A Reality Within Ten Years"', *Telegraph.co.uk* [website], (updated 27 February 2008) <http://www.telegraph.co.uk/earth/main.jhtml?xml=/earth/2008/02/27/scirobots127.xml>

Foerst, A. (2004), *God in the Machine: What Robots Teach Us about Humanity and God* (London: Penguin).

Foster-Miller (2008), 'TALON', [website], <http://www.foster-miller.com/lemming.htm> accessed 20 July 2008.

Fotion, N. (1990), *Military Ethics: Looking Toward the Future* (Stanford: Hoover Institution Press).

_____(2007), *War & Ethics: A New Just War Theory* (London: Continuum).

Fox News (2003), 'Iraqi Drones May Target U.S. Cities', [website], (updated 24 February 2003) <http://www.foxnews.com/story/0,2933,79450,00.html>

Freedman, L. (2006), 'The Transformation of Strategic Affairs', *Adelphi Papers* 45:379.

Freedman, L. and E. Karsh (1993), *The Gulf Conflict* (London: Faber & Faber).

Freitas, R. A. and W. P. Gilbreath (eds) (1980), 'Advanced Automation for Space Missions', *NASA Conference Publication* 2255 [online], (June/August 1980) <http://www.islandone.org/MMSG/aasm>

_____(2001), 'The Grey Goo Problem', *KurzweilAI.Net* [website], (updated 20 March 2001) <http://www.kurzweilai.net/meme/frame.html?main=/articles/art0142.html>

Friedman, G. and M. Friedman (1996), *The Future of War: Power, Technology and American Dominance in the Twenty-First Century* (New York: St. Martin's Griffin).

Fuentes, G. (2005), 'Transformation Czar Says U.S. Navy Is Too Inflexible', *DefenseNews.com* [websiete], (updated 4 February 2005) <http://www.comw.org/rma/fulltext/seapower.html>

Gaddis, J. L. (2005), *The Cold War: A New History* (London: Penguin).

Gage, D. W. (1995), 'UGV History 101: A Brief History of Unmanned Ground Vehicle Development Efforts', *Unmanned Systems Magazine* 13:3 (Summer).

Garfinkel, S. (2004), 'Is Encryption Doomed?', *Technology Review* [website], (updated 1 September 2004) <http://www.technologyreview.com/Infotech/13767/page1>

Garreau, J. (2007), 'Bots on the Ground: In the Field of Battle (or even above it), a Robot Is a Soldier's Best Friend', *The Washington Times* [website], (updated 6 May 2007) <http://www.washingtonpost.com/wp-dyn/content/article/2007/05/05/AR2007050501009_pf.html>

Gates, B. (2006), 'A Robot in Every Home', *Scientific American* [website], (December 2006) <http://www.sciam.com/article.cfm?id=a-robot-in-every-home>

Gates, R. (2008), 'Secretary Gates Remarks at Maxwell-Gunter Air Force Base, Montgomery Alabama', *DefenseLink* [website], (updated 21 April 2008) <http://www.defenselink.mil/transcripts/transcript.aspx?transcriptid=4214>

General Atomics (2008), 'Predator B Fact Sheet' [website] <http://www.ga-asi.com/products/predator_b.php> accessed (23 September 2008).

Georges, T. M. (2003), *Digital Soul: Intelligent Machines and Human Values* (Boulder, CO: Westview Press).

Gleditsch, N. P. and H. Buhaug (2004), 'The Death of Distance? The Globalization of Armed Conflict', Peace Research Institute Oslo, Paper Prepared for the *Conference on Globalization, Conflict, and Territoriality*, UCSD, La Jolla (16–18 January).

Glenn, R. W. (2000), *Heavy Matter: Urban Operations' Density of Challenges* (Santa Monica, CA: RAND Arroyo Center).

Gourley, S. (2001), 'Metal Storm Weapons', *Popular Mechanics* [website], (updated September) <http://www.popularmechanics.com/technology/military_law/1281426.html>

Graham, S. (2006), 'America's Robot Army', *The New Statesman* [website], (updated 12 June 2006) <http://www.newstatesman.com/200606120018>

Graham-Rowe, D. (2003), 'Monkeys Brain Signals "Control Third Arm"', *New Scientist Online* [website], (updated 13 October 2003) <http://www.newscientist.com/article/dn4262-monkeys-brain-signals-control-third-arm.html>

Gray, C. H. (1997), *Postmodern War: The New Politics of Conflict* (London: Routledge).

Gray, C. S. (1992), *House of Cards: Why Arms Control Must Fail* (Ithaca, NY: Cornell University Press).

_____(2005), *Another Bloody Century: Future Warfare* (London: Weidenfeld & Nicolson).

Green, L. L. (1993), *The Contemporary Law of Armed Conflict* (Manchester: Manchester University Press).

_____(2000), *The Contemporary Law of Armed Conflict* (Manchester: Manchester University Press).

Grossman, D. (1996), *On Killing: The Psychological Cost of Learning to Kill in War and Society* (New York: Back Bay Books).

Gubrud, M. A. (1997), 'Nanotechnology and International Security', *Fifth Foresight Conference on Molecular Nanotechnology*, [website], <http://www.foresight.org/Conferences/MNT05/Papers/Gubrud/index.html>

Guetlein, M. A. (2005), *Lethal Autonomous Weapons: Ethical and Doctrinal Implications*, Research Report (Maxwell, AFB: Air War College (14 February)).

Guisández-Gómez, J. (1998), 'The Law of Air Warfare', *International Review of the Red Cross* 323 (June) 347–63.

Gutkind, L. (2007), 'A Robot Did Not Write This', *Washington Post* [website], (updated 23 September 2007) <http://www.washingtonpost.com/wp-dyn/content/article/2007/09/21/AR2007092101540_pf.html>

Hacker, B. C. (2005), 'The Machines of War: Military Technology in Twentieth Century Europe', *History and Technology* 21:3 (September) 255–300.

Hahn, F. (1987), *Waffen und Geheimwaffen des deutschen Heeres 1933–1945: Band 2: Panzer- und Sonderfahrzeuge, 'Wunderwaffen', Verbrauch und Verluste* (Koblenz: Bernard & Graefe Verlag).

Hall, J. S. (2007), 'The Age of Virtuous Machines', *KurzweilAI.net* [website], (updated 31 May 2007) <http://www.kurzweilai.net/meme/frame.html?main=memelist.html?m=3%23708>

Hallinan, C. (2004), 'Rise of the Machines', *Foreign Policy in Focus* [website], (7 April 2004) <http://www.fpif.org/commentary/2004/0404machines.html>

Hambling, D. (2005), *Weapons Grade: The Revealing History of the Link between Modern Warfare and Our High-Tech World* (London: Constable & Robinson Ltd).

_____(2006a), 'Drone Swarm for Maximum Harm', *Defense Tech.org* [website], (updated 4 November 2006) <http://www.defensetech.org/archives/002309.html>

_____(2006b), 'Experimental AI Powers Robot Army', *Wired Blog* (14 September 2006) <http://www.wired.com/software/coolapps/news/2006/09/71779>

_____(2008), 'Laser Gunship Fires; Deniable Strikes Ahead?', *Wired Blog* [website], (updated 13 August 2008) <http://blog.wired.com/defense/2008/08/will-new-laser.html>

Harding, T. (2007), 'Animal VC for Sadie, the Heroine of Kabul', *Daily Telegraph* [website], (updated 27 January 2007) <http://www.telegraph.co.uk/news/worldnews/1540775/Animal-VC-for-Sadie%2C-the-heroine-of-Kabul.html>

Haselager, W. F. G. (2005), 'Robotics, Philosophy and the Problems of Autonomy', *Pragmatic & Cognition* 13:3, 515–32.

Hebert, A. (2003), 'New Horizons for Combat UAVs', *Air Force Magazine* 86:12 [website], (updated December 2003) <http://www.afa.org/magazine/Dec2003/1203uav.pdf>

Heidegger, M. (1962), *Time and Being* (London: SCM Press).

Hensel, H. M. (ed.) (2005), *The Law of Armed Conflict: Constraints on the Contemporary Use of Military Force* (Aldershot: Ashgate).

Herman, M. and A. Fritzson (2008), 'War Machines', *C4ISRJournal.com* [website], (updated 1 June 2008) <http://www.c4isrjournal.com/story.php?F=3434587>

Hewson, R. (2005), 'Cruise Missile Proliferation Takes Off', *Jane's Intelligence Review* (October).

Hills, A. (2004), *Future War in the Cities: Rethinking a Liberal Dilemma* (London: Frank Cass Publishers).

Hirst, P. (2001a), *War and Power in the 21st Century* (Cambridge: Polity Press).

_____(2001b), 'Future War' [website], (updated 17 October 2001) <http://www.opendemocracy.net/node/180>

Honda (2005), 'Asimo Specifications', [website], (updated 2005) <http://asimo.
    honda.com/asimo_specifications.html>

Hoyle, C. (2007), 'UK MoD Reveals UAV Losses in Iraq, Afghanistan', *Flight
    International* [website], (updated 6 June 2007) <http://www.flightglobal.com/
    articles/2007/06/06/214485/uk-mod-reveals-uav-losses-in-iraq-afghanistan.
    html>

Hutchinson, R. (1997), *Weapons of Mass Destruction: The No-Nonsense Guide
    to Nuclear, Chemical and Biological Weapons Today* (London: Weidenfeld &
    Nicolson).

Ichbiah, D. (2005), *Robots: From Science Fiction to Technological Revolution*
    (New York: Harry N. Abrams).

Institute of Medicine (2006), *Gulf War and Health – Health Effects of Serving in
    the Gulf War* (Washington, DC: Committee on Gulf War and Health).

Isenberg, D. (2007), 'Robots Replace Trigger Fingers in Iraq', *Asia Times Online*
    [website] (updated 29 August 2007) <http://www.atimes.com/atimes/Middle_
    East/IH29Ak01.html>

Ismat, S. (2001), 'The Economics of Defence', *The Defence Journal* [website],
    (updated March 2001) <www.defencejournal.com/2001/mar/economics.htm>

Jablonski, D. A. (2005), 'Air Force Lifts Boeing Suspension', *Air Force Print
    News* [website], (updated 4 March 2005) <http://www.af.mil/news/story.
    asp?storyID=123009955>

Jacobstein, N. (2006), 'Foresight Guidelines for Responsible Nanotechnology
    Development 4.0', *The Foresight Institute* [website], (April 2006) <http://
    www.foresight.org/guidelines/current.html>

Jewell, L. (2004), 'Armed Robots Soon Marching to Battle?', *Army News Service*
    [website], (updated 3 December 2004) <http://www4.army.mil/ocpa/read.
    php?story_id_key=6613>

Johnson, B. (2008), 'Prepare to Welcome Our Robot Overlords', *Guardian.co.uk*
    [website], (updated 17 October 2008) <http://www.guardian.co.uk/technology/
    blog/2008/oct/17/robots>

Johnson, J. (1999), *Morality and Contemporary Warfare* (New Haven, CT: Yale
    University Press).

Jones, K. C. (2007), 'DARPA Seeks Shape-Shifting War Robots', *Information
    Week* [weekend], (updated 5 April 2007) <http://www.informationweek.com/
    news/management/showArticle.jhtml?articleID=198800346>

Jones, R. A. L. (2007), *Soft Machines: Nanotechnology and Life* (Oxford: Oxford
    University Press).

Jones, R. H. (2005), *Terrorist Beheadings: Cultural and Strategic Implications*
    (Carlisle Barracks: U.S. Army War College).

Jordan, B. (2007), 'Half of the Predators Have Been Lost', *Air Force Times*
    [website], (updated 23 February 2007) <http://www.airforcetimes.com/
    news/2007/02/AFpredatorlosses070223>

Joy, B. (2000), 'Why the Future Doesn't Need Us', *Wired Magazine*, Issue 8.04
    [website], (April 2000) <http://www.wired.com/wired/archive/8.04/joy.html>

Kaag, J. J. (2008), 'Another Question Concerning Technology: The Ethical Implications of Homeland Defense and Security Technologies', *Homeland Security Affairs* 4:1 [website], (January 2008) <http://www.hsaj.org/?article=4.1.2>

Kaczynski, T. (1995), 'The Unabomber Manifesto', [website], (October 1995) <http://en.wikisource.org/wiki/Industrial_Society_and_Its_Future>

Kanaujia, M. (2007), 'Debate on Robot Rights Heat Up: Fear Looms, But What If Robots Rise?', *Robotster* [website], (updated 24 April 2007) <http://www.robotster.org/entry/debate-on-robot-rights-heats-up-fear-looms-but-what-if-robots-rise>

Kaszuba, K. A. (1997), *Military Technology: Has It Changed the Rules of Warfare?*, Research Report (Maxwell AFB: Air War College (April)).

Keegan, J. (1988), *The Price of Admiralty: The Evolution of Naval Warfare* (London: Penguin Books).

_____(2003), *Intelligence in War: Knowledge of the Enemy From Napoleon to Al Qaeda* (New York: Random House).

Keim, B. (2007), 'Slippery Math Behind Nanotech Market Estimates', *Wired* [website], (updated 19 April 2007) <http://blog.wired.com/wiredscience/2007/04/slippery_math_b.html>

Keller, J. (2005), 'Navy Looks Into How to Control Next-generation Autonomous Unmanned Aircraft', *Military & Aerospace Electronics* [online], (updated 24 June 2005) <http://mae.pennnet.com/Articles/Article_Display.cfm?ARTICLE_ID=230972&p=32>

_____(2006), 'Military Technologies Conference Hints at Future of Small Armed UAVs', *Military & Aerospace Electronics Online* [website], (15 March 2006) <http://mae.pennnet.com/Articles/Article_Display.cfm?ARTICLE_ID=250269&p=32>

Kellner, D. (2003), 'Postmodern Military and Permanent War', in Carl Boggs (ed.), *Masters of War: Militarism and Blowback in the Era of American Empire* (London: Routledge), 229–44.

Kelly, K. (1995), *Out of Control* (New York: Perseus Books).

Kittle, R. A. (1985), 'Will Computers Fight the Battles of the Future?', *U.S. News & World Report* (26 August) 46.

Klein, J. J. (2003), 'The Problematic Nexus: Where Unmanned Combat Air Vehicles and International Law Conflict', *Air & Space Power Journal* [website], (July 2003) <http://www.airpower.maxwell.af.mil/airchronicles/cc/klein.html>

Knight, W. (2003), 'Military Robots to Get Swarm Intelligence', *NewScientist. com* [website], (updated 25 April 2003) <http://www.newscientist.com/article.ns?id=dn3661>

Knox, M. and W. Murray (2001), *The Dynamics of Military Revolution 1300–2050* (Cambridge: Cambridge University Press).

Kochetkov, G. B., V. P. Averchev and V. M. Sergeev (1987), 'Artificial Intelligence and Disarmament', in Allan M. Din (ed.), *Arms and Artificial Intelligence: Weapon and Arms Control Applications of Advanced Computing* (Oxford: Oxford University Press).

Komarov, A. and D. Barrie (2008), 'First Look at MiG Skat UCAV', *Aviation Week* [website] (updated 2008) <http://www.aviationweek.com/aw/generic/story.jsp?id=news/MIG082307.xml&headline=First+Look+At+MiG+Skat+UCAV+[Updated]&channel=null>

Komarow, S. (2006), 'The New Breed of Soldier: Robots with Guns', *USA Today* [website], (14 April 2006) <http://www.usatoday.com/tech/news/techinnovations/2006-04-13-robot-soldiers_x.htm>

Kopp, C. (1984), 'Precision Guided Ammunitions: The New Breed', *Australian Aviation* [online], (September 1984) <http://www.ausairpower.net/TE-Assault-Breaker.html>

Kosinski, R. (2006), 'A Literature Review on Reaction Time', *Clemson University* [online], (updated 2006) <http://biae.clemson.edu/bpc/bp/Lab/110/reaction.htm>

Krane, J. (2003a), 'Air Force Is Using More Pilotless Planes', *Associated Press* [online], (updated 24 April 2003) <http://www.redorbit.com/news/technology/364/air_force_is_using_more_pilotless_planes/index.html>

_____(2003b), 'Pilotless Warriors Soar to Success', *CBS News Online* [website], (updated 25 April 2003) <http://www.cbsnews.com/stories/2003/04/25/tech/main551126.shtml>

Krepinevich, A. (2002), *The Military-Technical Revolution: A Preliminary Assessment* (Washington, DC: Center for Strategic and Budgetary Assessments).

Kurzweil, R. (1999), *The Age of Spiritual Machines* (London: Penguin).

_____(2001), 'May the Smartest Machine Win: Warfare in the 21st Century', *KurzweilAI.net* [website], (updated 6 August 2001) <http://www.kurzweilai.net/meme/frame.html?main=/articles/art0248.html>

_____(2005), 'Nanotechnology: Dangers and Defenses' [website], (updated 27 March 2005) <http://www.kurzweilai.net/meme/frame.html?main=/articles/art0653.html>

_____(2006), *The Singularity Is Near: When Humans Transcend Biology* (New York: Viking).

Lai, G. (2003), 'Energy Weapons: Not Just for Buck Rogers Anymore', *Strange Horizons* [website], (updated 5 May 2003) <http://www.strangehorizons.com/2003/20030505/energy_weapons.shtml>

Lamb, G. M. (2005), 'Battle Bot: The Future of War?', *Christian Science Monitor* [website], (updated 27 January 2005) <http://www.csmonitor.com/2005/0127/p14s02-stct.html>

Lanier, J. (2000), 'One-Half of A Manifesto/Why Stupid Software Will Save the Future From Neo-Darwinian Machines', *Wired Blog 8.12* [website], (December 2000) <http://www.wired.com/wired/archive/8.12/lanier.html>

Lawlor, M. (2003a), 'Miniaturization, Networking Pervade Future Unmanned Systems', *SIGNAL Magazine* [online], (April 2003) <http://www.afcea.org/SIGNAL/articles/templates/SIGNAL_Article_Template.asp>

_____(2003b), 'Autonomous Mechanized Combatants Would Revolutionize Military Strategy', *SIGNAL Magazine* [online], (November 2003) <http://

www.afcea.org/SIGNAL/articles/templates/SIGNAL_Article_Template.asp?a rticleid=64&zoneid=26>

Lazarski, A. J. (2001), 'Legal Implications of the Uninhabited Combat Aerial Vehicle', *Air & Space Power Journal* [website], (updated 27 March 2001) <http://www.airpower.maxwell.af.mil/airchronicles/apj/apj02/sum02/lazarski. html>

Leaver, T. (1997), 'Post-Humanism and Ecocide in William Gibson's *Neuromancer* and Ridley Scott's *Bladerunner*', [website], (updated 1997) <http://scribble. com/uwi/br/br-eco.html>

Lee, T. B. (2008), 'The Future of Driving', *Ars Technica* [website], (updated 29 September 2008) <http://arstechnica.com/articles/culture/future-of-driving-part-1.ars>

Lem, S. (1988), *Fiasco* (New York: Harcourt Publishers).

Leonard, R. S., J. A. Drezner and G. Summer (1999), *The Arsenal Ship Acquisition Process Experience* (Santa Monica, CA: RAND).

Leonhard, R. R. (1998), *The Principles of War for the Information Age* (New York: Ballantine Books).

Lerner, P. (2006a), 'Robots Go to War', *Popular Science Magazine* [online], (updated 01 January 2006) <http://www.popsci.com/scitech/article/2005-12/robots-go-war>

_____(2006b), 'Incredible New Military Robot', *Popular Science Magazine* [website], (updated 9 April 2006) <http://www.livescience.com/technology/060409_robot_sherpa.html>

Levi, M. A. and M. E. O'Hanlon (2005), *The Future of Arms Control* (Washington, DC: Brookings Institution Press).

Levy, D. (2007), *Love + Sex with Robots* (New York: HarperCollins Publishers).

Levy, S. (1992), 'A-Life Nightmare', *Whole Earth Review* (Fall 1992).

_____(1993), *Artificial Life: A Report From the Frontier Where Computers Meet Biology* (New York: Vintage Books).

Liang, Q. and W. Xiangsui (1999), *Unrestricted Warfare* (Beijing: PLA Literature and Arts Publishing House).

Libicki, M. (1994), *The Mesh and the Net: Speculations on Armed Conflict in a Time of Free Silicon* (Washington, DC: National Defense University Press).

_____(2000), 'What Is Information Warfare?', in Thierry Gongorra and Harald von Riekhoff (eds), *Toward a Revolution in Military Affairs? Defense and Security at the Dawn of the 21st Century* (London: Greenwood Press), 37–60.

Lin, H. (1987), 'Software and Systems Issues in Strategic Defense', in Allan M. Din (ed.), *Arms and Artificial Intelligence: Weapon and Arms Control Applications of Advanced Computing* (Oxford: Oxford University Press).

Lippert, S. (2008), 'New Harvester Tractor Has 6 Legs and Is Eco Friendly', *Daily Tech Impressions* [website], (updated 17 April 2008) <http://www.dailytechno logyimpressions.com/new-harvester-tractor-has-6-legs-and-is-eco-friendly>

Lonsdale, D. (2004), *The Nature of War in the Information Age: Clausewitzian Future* (New York: Frank Cass Publishers).

Lopez-Calderon, M. (2006), 'A Soldier-Free Battlefield', *TCS Daily* [website], (updated 8 February 2006) <http://www.tcsdaily.com/article.aspx?id=020806D>

Lovgren, S. (2007), 'Robot Code of Ethics to Prevent Android Abuse, Protect Humans', *National Geograp National Geographic News* [website], (updated 16 March 2007) <http://news.nationalgeographic.com/news/2007/03/070316-robot-ethics.html>

Lucas, M. A. et al. (2005), 'Unmanned Tele-operated Robots as Medical Support on the Battlefield', *ADF Health* 6, 34–8.

Lumpe, L. (2007), 'U.S. Congress Passes Cluster Bomb Export Moratorium', *Reuters* [website], (updated 19 December 2007) <http://www.reuters.com/article/pressRelease/idUS228289+19-Dec-2007+PRN20071219>

Macintyre, D. (2006), '"Bionic Wasps" Could Be Miniature Future Weapon With A Deadly Sting', *The Independent* [website], (updated 18 November 2006) <http://www.independent.co.uk/news/world/middle-east/bionic-wasps-could-be-miniature-future-weapon-with-a-deadly-sting-424773.html>

Macpherson, S. (2007), 'World War 3.0', *The Diplomat* [website], (September/October) <http://www.the-diplomat.com/article.aspx?aeid=3301>

Magnuson, S. (2006), 'Role of Unmanned Aircraft Questioned', *National Defense Magazine* (July).

_____(2007), 'Rifle Toting Robots See Action in Iraq', *National Defense Magazine* (September).

_____(2008a), 'Armed Robots Sidelined in Iraqi Fight', *National Defense Magazine* (May).

_____(2008b), 'War Machines: For Now, Lethal Robots Not Likely to Run on Auto-Pilot', *National Defense Magazine* 92 (March) 30–1.

_____(2008c), 'Man vs. Machine: Ground Robots' Place in the Military at Risk, Experts Warn', *National Defense Magazine* 92 (May) 30–1.

Mandel, R. (2004), *Security, Strategy, and the Quest for Bloodless War* (Boulder, CO: Lynne Rienner Publishers).

_____(2006), 'Robots, Mercenaries, and Soldiers: The Comparative Utility of Future Fighting Forces', *Presentation at the National Annual Meeting of the International Studies Association*, San Diego (March).

Mandeles, M. D. (2005), *The Future of War: Organizational Structures for the Revolution in Military Affairs* (Dulles, VA: Potomac Books).

Marks, P. (2006), 'Robot Infantry Get Ready for the Battlefield', *The New Scientist* 2570 [online], (updated 23 September 2006) <http://www.newscientist.com/article.ns?id=mg19125705.600>

Matthews, A. H. (1973), *The Wall of Light: Nikola Tesla and the Venusian Space Ship/The Life of Nikola Tesla (Autobiography)*, Pomeroy, WA: Health Research Books.

Mauboussin, M. and K. Bartholdson (2003), 'Big Money in Thinking Small: Nanotechnology – What Investors Need to Know', *Report* (7 May).

May, L. (2007), *War Crimes and Just War* (Cambridge: Cambridge University Press).

Mayer, C. (2007), 'Nonlethal Weapons and Noncombatant Immunity: Is It Permissible to Target Noncombatants?', *Journal of Military Ethics* 6:3, 221–31.

Mazlish, B. (1993), *The Fourth Discontinuity: The Co-Evolution of Humans and Machines* (New Haven: Yale University Press).

McCaffrey, B. (2000), 'Interview with Barry McCaffrey', *Newsweek* 135:22 (29 May 2000) 28.

McCarthy, J. (2007), 'What Is Artificial Intelligence? Basic Questions', *Stanford University* [website], (updated November 2007) <http://www-formal.stanford.edu/jmc/whatisai/whatisai.html>

McCarthy, T. (2001), 'Molecular Nanotechnology and the World System', [online], <http://www.mccarthy.cx/WorldSystem/war.htm>

McDaid, H. and D. Oliver (1997), *Smart Weapons: Top Secret History of Remote Controlled Airborne Weapons* (New York: Welcome Rain).

Meek, J. (2002), 'Robo Cop', *The Guardian Unlimited* [website], (updated 13 June 2002) <http://www.guardian.co.uk/Archive/Article/0,4273,4432506,00.htm>

Melymuka, K. (2002), 'Good Morning, Dave ... The Defense Department Is Working on a Self-Aware Computer', *Computerworld* [online], (updated 11 November 2002) <http://www.computerworld.com/softwaretopics/software/appdev/story/0,10801,75728,00.html>

Merkle, R. (2001), 'Nanotechnology: What Will It Mean?', *IEEE Spectrum* (January) 19–20.

Metz, S. (2000), *Armed Conflict in the 21st Century: The Information Revolution and Postmodern Warfare* (Carlisle Barracks: US Army War College).

Mick, J. (2008), 'Can Robots Commit War Crimes?', *Daily Tech Blog* [website], (updated 29 February 2008) <http://www.dailytech.com/Can+Robots+Commit+War+Crimes/article10917.htm>

Miller, D. (2001), *The Cold War: A Military History* (London: Pimlico).

Minkel, J. R. (2008), 'Robotic Prof Sees Threat in Military Robots', *Scientific American Online* [website], (updated 28 February 2008) <http://www.sciam.com/article.cfm?id=robotics-prof-sees-threat-in-robots&ec=ypi>

Minsky, M. (1968), *Semantic Information Processing* (Cambridge, MA: MIT Press).

Mitchell, P. T. (2006), 'US Military Primacy and the New Operating System', *Adelphi Papers* 46:385.

Mitnick, K. (2008), 'Warrantless Surveillance: The Worst Is Yet to Come', *Foresight Institute* [website], (updated 18 January 2008) <http://www.foresight.org/nanodot/?p=2636>

Mohan, R. (2007), 'Robotics and the Future of Warfare', Ravi Mohan's Blog [online], (13 December 2007) <http://ravimohan.blogspot.com/2007/12/robotics-and-future-of-warfare.html>

Moravec, H. (1988), *Mind Children: The Future of Robot and Human Intelligence* (Cambridge, MA: Harvard University Press).

_____(1999), *Robot: Mere Machine to Transcendent Mind* (Oxford: Oxford University Press).

Morris, J. and H. McCoubrey (2006), 'The Law, Politics, and the Use of Force', in J. Baylis, J. Wirtz, E. Cohen and C. S. Gray (eds), *Strategy in the Contemporary World: An Introduction to Strategic Studies* (Oxford: Oxford University Press), 45–65.

Moshkina, L. and R. Arkin (2008), 'Lethality and Autonomous Systems: Survey Design and Results', *Georgia Institute of Technology*, Technical Report (January).

Mroue, B. (2007), 'Blackwater License Being Pulled in Iraq', *Associated Press* [online], (updated 17 September 2007) <http://www.newsmax.com/international/iraq/2007/09/17/33181.html>

Mulvenon, J. (2007), 'Counter-Intelligence, Surveillance, and Reconnaissance', in Michael Pillsbury (ed.), *Chinese Views of Future Warfare* (Washington, DC: National Defense University), 71–82.

Murph, D. (2007), 'Autonomous Sentry Gun Looks to Mow Down Defcon', *egadget.com* [website], (updated 10 September 2007) <http://www.engadget.com/2007/09/10/autonomous-sentry-gun-looks-to-mow-down-defcon>

Murray, W. and R. H. Scales (2003), *The Iraq War: A Military History* (Cambridge, MA: Harvard University Press).

Nanowerk (2007), 'Nanotechnology Brings United Kingdom and India Together', [website], (updated 15 March 2007) <http://www.nanowerk.com/news/newsid=1622.php>

NDM (2005), "Army Grunts Will Be 'Million-Dollar' Men", *National Defense Magazine* [website], (updated 1 April 2005) <http://www.nationaldefensemagazine.org/ARCHIVE/2005/APRIL/Pages/washington_pulse3252.aspx>

New Scientist (2007a), 'Streetfighting Robot Challenge Announced', *New Scientist* [website], (updated 24 January 2007) <http://technology.newscientist.com/article/dn11021-streetfighting-robot-challenge-announced.html>

_____(2007b), 'Don't Mess With the Shock-Bot', *New Scientist* [website], (updated 7 July 2007) <www.newscientist.com/data/pdf/press/2611/261123.pdf>

Nichols, S. O. (1998), *21st Century Air-to-Air Short Range Weapon Requirements*, Research Report (Maxwell AFB: Air University (April)).

Norris, G. (2007), 'Propulsion, Materials Test Successes Put Positive Spin on FALCON Prospects', *Aviation Week* [website], (updated 22 July 2007) <http://www.aviationweek.com/aw/generic/story_generic.jsp>

Norris, G. and G. Warwick (1999), 'X Directory', *Flight International* [website], (updated 1 June 1999)<http://www.flightglobal.com/articles/1999/01/06/46630/x-directory.html>

Nowak, P. (2008a), 'U.S. Army Praises Robot Makers for Help in Wars', *CBS News* [website], (updated 8 April 2008) <http://www.cbc.ca/technology/story/2008/04/08/tech-robo-show.html>

_____ (2008b), 'We Absolutely Don't Want to Be Ever in a Fair Fight', *CBS News* [website], (updated 21 April 2008) <http://www.cbc.ca/news/background/tech/hightech/robots-military.html>

O'Brien, J. M. (2007), 'Killer Robots Could Replace Soldiers', *Fortune Magazine* [website], (updated 5 December 2007) <http://thefilter.ca/articles/usa-and-world/killer-robots-could-replace-soldiers>

Ornstein, S. M. (1987), 'Computers in Battle: A Human Overview', in D. Belin and G. Chapman (eds), *Computers in Battle: Will They Work?* (New York: Harcourt Brace Jovanovich Publishers), 1–44.

Osborn, K. (2007), 'Army to Field Autonomous Security Guard Robot', *Army Times* [website], (14 June 2007) <http://www.armytimes.com/news/2007/06/defense_robots_070613>

Owens, B. and E. Offley (2000), *Lifting the Fog of War* (New York: Farrar Strauss Giroux).

Page, L. (2007a), 'Robot Gunships Join U.S. Army', *The Register* [website], (updated 24 May 2007) <http://www.theregister.co.uk/2007/05/24/robochoppers_to_join_flying_hk>

_____ (2007b), 'EU Defence Agency Wants Open Skies for Flying Robots', *The Register* [website], (updated 29 May 2007) <http://www.theregister.co.uk/2007/05/29/eda_friendly_skies_for_flying_robots>

_____ (2007c), 'US-Robot Carrier Jet Contract Announced', *The Register* [website], (updated 2 August 2007) <http://www.theregister.co.uk/2007/08/02/robot_carrier_jet_contract_let>

_____ (2007d), 'USAF Seeks Control of Aerial Kill-bots', *The Register* [website], (updated 8 August 2007) <http://www.theregister.co.uk/2007/08/08/usaf_move_for_killbot_supremacy>

_____ (2008a), 'Terrorist Robots Dissected – Anatomy of a Scare', *The Register* [website], (updated 2 March 2008) <http://www.theregister.co.uk/2008/03/02/terrorist_robot_diy_cruise_missile>

_____ (2008b), 'Reaper Aerial Killbots Enlist Mobile Phones Against Their Owners', *The Register* [website], (28 April 2008) <http://www.theregister.co.uk/2008/04/28/reaper_gets_mobe_spy_gear>

_____ (2008c), '"Mad Scientist" Develops Power Suit for US Military', *The Register* [website], (updated 6 May 2008) <http://www.theregister.co.uk/2008/05/06/sarcos_exoskeleton_iron_man_puffery>

_____ (2008d), 'Blighty Joins Killer Robot Club with Afghan Strike', *The Register* [website], (updated 4 June 2008) <http://www.theregister.co.uk/2008/06/04/raf_reaper_reaps_at_last>

_____ (2008e), 'Northrop Scoops DARPA Mindreader Helmet Cash', *The Register* [website], (updated 11 June 2008) <http://www.theregister.co.uk/2008/06/11/darpa_mind_hat_visor_contract>

_____ (2008f), 'USAF Ramps Up Kill-bot Fleet Following Gates Sackings', *The Register* [website], (updated 17 June 2008) <http://www.theregister.co.uk/2008/06/17/usaf_purge_sees_more_predator_orbits>

_____(2008g), 'US Air Force May Allow Killbots to Be Flown by Non-pilots', *The Register* [website], (updated 25 July 2008) <http://www.theregister. co.uk/2008/07/25/drone_boys_not_flyboys_any_more>

_____(2008h), 'US Airforce to Launch Robotic Space Shuttle 2.0 This Year', *The Register* [website], (updated 31 July 2008) <www.theregister. co.uk/2008/07/31/us_spaceplane_demo_to_launch>

Pappalardo, J. (2005), 'Army Explores Future of Remote Control Weapons', *National Defense Magazine* (August).

Pardesi, M. S. (2005), *The Impact of the RMA on Conventional Deterrence: A Theoretical Analysis*, Working Paper (Singapore: Institute of Strategic Studies Singapore (December)).

Patton, P. (1996), 'Robots with the Right Stuff', *Wired Blog* 4.03 [website], (March 1996) <http://www.wired.com/wired/archive/4.03/robots_pr.html>

Peebles, C. (1995), *Dark Eagles: A History of Top Secret U.S. Aircraft* (New York: ibooks).

Perrow, C. (1986), *Normal Accidents: Living With High-Risk Technologies* (Princeton, NJ: Princeton University Press).

Peter, T. A. (2008), 'Robots Set to Overhaul Service Industry, Jobs', *Christian Science Monitor* [website], (updated 25 February 2008) <http://www. csmonitor.com/2008/0225/p01s01-usgn.html?page=1>

Peters, R. (1996), 'A Revolution in Military Ethics', *Parameters* 26:2 (Summer) 102–8.

Petersen, J. and D. Egan (2002), 'Small Security: Nanotechnology and Future Defense', *Defense Horizons* 8 (March).

Phoenix, C. and M. Treder (2003), 'Safe Utilization of Advanced Nanotechnology', *Center for Responsible Nanotechnology* [website], (January 2003) <http:// www.crnano.org/papers.htm#Safe>

Pike, J. (2007), 'Thinking Outside the Military Box/Last Byte: A Conversation with John Pike from Globalsecurity.org', *Washington Technology* 22:9 [website], (updated 28 May 2007) <http://www.washingtontechnology.com/ print/22_09/30737-1.html>

Pincus, W. (2005), 'Pentagon Has Far-Reaching Defense Spacecraft in Works', *Washington Post* [website], (updated 16 March 2005) <www.washingtonpost. com/ac2/wp-dyn/A38272-2005Mar15?language=printer>

Piquepaille, R. (2003), 'Robotics to Play Major Role in Future Warfighting', Technology_Trends Blog [website], <http://radio.weblogs. com/0105910/2003/08/10.html>

Pocock, C. (2002), 'It's Not Big Brother That Is Watching You', *global-defence. com* [website], <http://www.global-defence.com/2002/surv-globalhawk. html>

Pollack, A. (1989), 'The Pentagon Wanted a Smart Truck; What It Got Was Something Else', *The New York Times* (30 May).

Porknoy, B. (1987), 'Creating the Ideal Soldier: U.S. Seeks a P.F.C. Robot', *The Record* [online], (9 March 1987) <http://cse.stanford.edu/class/cs201/Projects/autonomous-weapons/articles/robot-soldiers.txt>

Prokosch, E. (1995), *The Technology of Killing: A Military and Political History of Antipersonnel Weapons* (London: Zed Books).

Quinn, B. (2008), 'Meeting the Increased Demand for Military Robots: An Interview with Foster-Miller's Bob Quinn', *Robotics Trends* [website], (updated March 2008) <http://www.roboticstrends.com/security_defense_robotics/article/meeting_the_increased_demand_for_military_robots_an_interview_with_foster_m>

Rabinovich, A. (2005), *The Yom Kippur War: The Epic Encounter That Transformed the Middle East* (New York: Random House).

Ranelagh, J. (1986), *The Agency: The Rise and Decline of the CIA* (New York: Simon & Schuster).

Ratner, D. and M. A. Ratner (2004), *Nanotechnology and Homeland Security: New Weapons for New Wars* (Upper Sadlle River: Prentice Hall).

Rawlyk, H. (2007), 'County Police Getting Tasers', *Maryland Gazette* [website], (updated 23 May 2007) <http://www.hometownglenburnie.com/news/mdgazette/2007/05/23-25>

Reed, F. (2005), 'Robotic Warfare Drawing Nearer', *The Washington Times* [website], (updated 10 February 2005) <http://www.washingtontimes.com/news/2005/feb/09/20050209-113147-1910r>

Rees, M. (2003), *Our Final Hour: A Scientist's Warning: How Terror, Error, and Environmental Disaster Threaten Humankind's Future in this Century – on Earth and Beyond* (New York: Basic Books).

Regan, R. J. (1996), *Just War: Principles and Cases* (Washington, DC: The Catholic University of America Press).

Richfield, P. (2007), 'Robot Recon/Are Unmanned Systems Reducing Combat Risks?', *C4ISR Journal* [website], (updated 5 October 2007) <http://www.isrjournal.com/story.php?F=2958708>

Rifkin, J. (1996), *The End of Work* (New York: Putnam).

Rhea, J. (2000), 'The Next "New Frontier" of Artificial Intelligence', *Military & Aerospace Electronics* [website], (November 2000) <http://mae.pennnet.com/Articles/Article_Display.cfm>

Robinson, B. (2007), 'Robotic Evolution', *Defense Systems* [online], (updated June 2007) <http://www.defensesystems.com/issues/2_4/features/904-1.html>

Rochlin, G. I. (1997), *Trapped in the Net: The Unanticipated Consequences of Computerization* (Princeton, NJ: Princeton University Press).

Rogers, C. (2000), '"Military Revolutions" and "Revolutions in Military Affairs": A Historian's Perspective', in Thierry Gongorra and Harald von Riekhoff (eds), *Toward a Revolution in Military Affairs? Defense and Security at the Dawn of the Twenty-First Century* (Westport, CT: Greenwood Press).

Rogers, M. (1984), 'The Birth of the Killer Robots', *Newsweek* (25 June) 51–2.

Rogers, P. (2001), 'Towards an Ideal Weapon? The Military and Political Implications of the Airborne and Space-based Lasers', *Defense Analysis* 17:1, 73–88.

Ropp, T. (2000), *War in the Modern World* (Baltimore: The Johns Hopkins University Press).

Rosheim, M. E. (2006), *Leonardo's Lost Robots* (New York: Springer).

Saletan, W. (2006), 'Joystick vs. Jihad: The Temptation of Remote Controlled Killing', *Slate* [website], (updated 12 February 2006) <http://www.slate.com/id/2135969>

Sample, I. (2006), 'Now You See Him ... Scientists Are Taking Steps Closer to Making Invisible Cloak a Reality', *Guardian* [website], (updated 20 October 2006) <http://www.guardian.co.uk/technology/2006/oct/20/news.science>

Sandhana, L. (2002), 'The Drone Armies Are Coming', *Wired Blog* [website], (updated 30 August 2002) <http://www.wired.com/science/discoveries/news/2002/08/54728>

Schindler, D. and J. Toman (1988), *The Laws of Armed Conflict: A Collection of Conventions, Resolutions and Other Documents* (The Hague: Martinus Nihjof Publishers).

Schindlmayr, T. (2002), 'Future Personnel: Where Will They Come From?', *Defense & Security Analysis* 18:1, 85–8.

Schmitz-Elvenich, H. F. (2008), *Targeted Killing: Die völkerrechtliche Zulässigkeit der gezielten Tötung von Terroristen im Ausland* (Frankfurt a.M.: Peter Lang).

Schrader, E. (2003), 'U.S. Looks at Organizing Global Peacekeeping Force', *Los Angeles Times* [website], (updated 27 June 2003) <http://articles.latimes.com/2003/jun/27/world/fg-peace27>

Science Daily (2000), 'Robots Are Evolving, Population Is Booming Worldwide', [website], (updated 17 January 2000) <http://www.sciencedaily.com/releases/2000/01/000117071805.htm>

Scott, W. B. (1996), 'USSC Prepares for Future Combat Missions in Space', *Aviation Week & Space Technology* (5 August) 51.

Scully, M. (2007), 'Panel Earmarks $80 Million for High-Tech Battlefield Gear', *GovernmentExecutive.com* [website], (updated 22 June 2007) <http://govexec.com/dailyfed/0607/062207cdam1.htm?rss=getoday>

Searle, J. (1980), 'Minds, Brains, and Programs', *The Behavioral and Brain Sciences* 3:3, 417–57.

Shachtman, N. (2005), 'Attack of the Drones', *Wired Magazine* 13.06 [online], (June 2005) <http://www.wired.com/wired/archive/13.06/drones.html>

———(2006), 'The Supersonic Shape-Shifting Bomber', *Popular Science* (7 January).

———(2007a), 'Libya Caught in Jamming Sat-Phones', *Wired Blog* [online], (updated 09 April 2007) <http://blog.wired.com/defense/2007/04/if_youre_travel.html>

_____(2007b), 'Armed Robots Pushed to Police', *Wired Blog* [online], (updated 16 August 2007) <http://blog.wired.com/defense/2007/08/armed-robots-so.html>

_____(2007c), 'Marines: Give Us Exoskeletons, "Self-Aware" Robots', *Wired Blog* [website], (updated 26 November 2007) <http://blog.wired.com/defense/2007/11/marines-heart-e.html>

_____(2007d), 'Robot Cannon Kills Nine, Wounds 14', *Wired Blog* [website], (updated 18 October 2007) <http://blog.wired.com/defense/2007/10/robot-cannon-ki.html>

_____(2008a), 'Israel Eyes Thinking Machines to Fight "Doomsday" Missile Strikes', *Wired Blog* [website], (22 January 2008) <http://blog.wired.com/defense/2008/01/israel-thinking.html>

_____(2008b), '24 More Armed Robot Sentries for Base Patrol', *Wired Blog* [website], (updated 28 February 2008) <http://blog.wired.com/defense/2008/02/army-gets-more.html>

_____(2008c), 'Robot + Super Gun = "Crowd Control"', *Wired Blog* [website], (updated 27 May 2008) <http://blog.wired.com/defense/2008/05/metal-storm-iro.html>

Shah, A. (2005), 'Cebrowski Recommends Large Fleet of Small, Less Expensive Ship', *Inside the Navy* [website], (updated 4 February 2005) <http://www.comw.org/rma/fulltext/seapower.html>

Shaker, S. M. and A. R. Wise (1988), *War Without Men: Robots on the Future Battlefield* (Washington, DC: Pergamon-Brassey's).

Sharkey, N. (2007a), 'Robot Wars Are a Reality', *The Guardian* [website], (updated 18 August 2007) <http://www.guardian.co.uk/commentisfree/2007/aug/18/comment.military>

_____(2007b), 'Automated Killers and the Computing Profession', *IEEE Computer Society* [website], (November 2007) <http://www.computer.org/portal/site/computer/menuitem.5d61c1d591162e4b0ef1bd108bcd45f3/index.jsp?&pName=computer_level1_article&TheCat=1015&path=computer/homepage/Nov07&file=profession.xml&xsl=article.xsl&>

Shaw, M. (2005), *The New Western Way of War: Risk-Transfer War and its Crisis in Iraq* (Cambridge: Polity Press).

Shawcross, W. (2000), *Deliver Us From Evil: Warlords and Peacekeepers in a World of Endless Conflict* (London: Bloomsbury).

Shearer, D. (1998), *Private Armies and Military Intervention* (London: Adelphi Papers Routledge).

Shelley, T. (2006), *Nanotechnology: New Promises, New Dangers* (London: Zed Books).

Shore, J. (1987), 'Why I Never Met a Programmer I Could Trust', *Computer Professionals For Social Responsibility Newsletter* [website], (Fall 1987) <http://cpsr.org/prevsite/publications/newsletters/old/1980s/Fall1987.txt>

Shukman, D. (1996), *Tomorrow's War: The Threat of High-Technology Weapons* (New York: Harcourt Brace & Co).

Shurtleff, D. K. (2002), 'The Effects of Technology on Our Humanity', *Parameters* 32:2 (Spring) 100–12.

Sieff, M. (2008), 'Global Ballistic Missile Defense Systems in 2007', *Space Daily* [website], (updated 3 January 2008) <http://www.spacedaily.com/reports/Global_Ballistic_Missile_Defense_Systems_In_2007_999.html>

Silberglitt, R., P. S. Anton, D. R. Howell and A. Wong (2006), *The Global Technology Revolution 2020: In-Depth Analyses* (Santa Monica, CA: RAND).

Simms, A. (2008), 'Bear Necessities: Battlefield Extraction-Assist Robot', *Soldier Magazine* (September).

Simonite, T. (2007), '"Robotic Rampage" Unlikely Reason for Death', *NewScientist. com* [website], (updated 19 October 2007) <http://technology.newscientist.com/article/dn12812-robotic-rampage-unlikely-reason-for-deaths.html>

Singer, P. W. (2003), *Corporate Warriors: The Rise of the Privatized Military Industry* (Ithaca, NY: Cornell University Press).

_____(2008), 'How to Be All That You Can Be: A Look at the Pentagon's Five Step Plan for Making Iron Man Real', *The Brookings Institution* [website], (updated 2 May 2008) <http://www.brookings.edu/articles/2008/0502_iron_man_singer.aspx>

Sloan, E. C. (2002), *The Revolution in Military Affairs: Implications for Canada and NATO* (Montreal: Queen's University Press).

_____(2008), *Military Transformation and Modern Warfare* (Westport, CT: PRAEGER).

Smalley, R. E. (2001), 'Of Chemistry, Love, and Nanobots', *Scientific American* 285 (September) 76–7.

Sofge, E. (2008a), 'World War Bots, Love 2.0, Teleporting, Daytona Tech & More', *Popular Mechanics Podcast* [website], (15 February 2008) <http://www.popularmechanics.com/technology/military_law/4249618.html>

_____(2008b), 'America's Robot Army', *Popular Mechanics* [website], (March 2008) <http://www.popularmechanics.com/technology/military_law/4252643.html>

_____(2008c), 'The Inside Story of the SWORDS Armed Robot "Pullout" in Iraq', *Popular Mechanics* (15 April 2008) <http://www.popularmechanics.com/blogs/technology_news/4258963.html>

Southerland, R. (2007), 'Robots on the Job', *Securitysolutions.com* [website], (updated 1 February 2007) <http://securitysolutions.com/access_control/security_robots_job>

Space Daily (2003), 'Dupont Joins Effort to Use Nanotech to Enhance Safety of Soldiers', [website], (updated 27 May 2003) <http://www.spacedaily.com/news/nanotech-03zd.html>

_____(2006), 'IEDs Influencing Robotic Warfare Concepts', [website], (updated 6 June 2006) <http://www.spacewar.com/reports/IEDs_Influencing_Robotic_Warfare_Concepts.html>

Space War (2004), 'US Navy Awards Titan $22.5 Million Affordable Weapons System Contract', Space War [website], (updated 21 April 2004) <http://www.

spacewar.com/reports/US_Navy_Awards_Titan_$225_Million_Affordable_
Weapons_System_Contract.html>

Sparrow, R. (2007a), 'ABC interview with Robert Sparrow' [podcast], (updated
17 August 2007) <http://www.abc.net.au/triplej/hack/notes/s1717982.htm>

_____(2007b), 'Killer Robots', *Journal of Applied Philosophy* 24:1, 62–77.

Sparrow, R. and L. Sparrow (2006), 'In the Hands of Machines? The Future of
Aged Care', *Mind and Machines* 16:2 (May) 141–61.

Stanford Encyclopedia of Philosophy (2004), 'The Frame Problem' [website],
(updated 23 February 2004) <http://plato.stanford.edu/entries/frame-
problem>

Stanley-Mitchell, E. (2001), 'Technology's Double-Edged Sword: The Case of
Army Digitization', *Defense Analysis* 17:3, 267–88.

Strategic Comments (1999), 'The Future of Urban Warfare', *Strategic Comments*
5:2 (March) 1–2.

Sudia, F. W. (2001), 'A Jurisprudence of Artilects: A Blueprint for a Synthetic
Citizen', *KurzweilAI.net* [website], (updated 21 August 2001) <http://www.
kurzweilai.net/meme/frame.html?main=/articles/art0270.html>

Sukathorn, J., A. Cushing and G. Chirikjian (2003), 'An Autonomous Self-
Replicating Robotic System', presented at the 2003 IEEE/ASME *International
Conference on Advanced Intelligent Mechtronics*, [website], (2003) <http://
custer.me.jhu.edu/publication/pdf/auton.pdf>

Sullins, J. P. (2006), 'When Is a Robot a Moral Agent?', *International Review of
Information Ethics* 6 (December) 24–9.

Sutton, R. (undated), 'Should Artificially Intelligent Robots Have the Same Rights
As People?', [website], <http://rlai.cs.ualberta.ca/robotrightssutton.html>

Sweetman, B. (2007), 'Peek a Boo, I See You', *Aviation Week* [website], (updated
5 December 2007) <http://www.aviationweek.com/aw/blogs/defense/index.
jsp>

Swofford, A. (2003), *Jarhead* (London: Simon & Schuster).

Taylor, M. and E. Addley (2007), 'Undiagnosed Brain-Injury – The Legacy of
Iraq', *Guardian* [website], (updated 27 October 2007) <http://www.guardian.
co.uk/uk/2007/oct/27/politics.military>

Tesla, N. (1995), *My Inventions: Nikola Tesla's Autobiography*, first published
in: *Electrical Experimenter* (1919) <http://www.mcnabb.com/music/tesla/bio.
pdf> (accessed 10 July 2008).

Tesla, N. and A. Leland (1998), *Nikola Tesla: Guided Weapons & Computer
Technology* (Breckenridge, CO: Twenty-First Century Books).

The Economist (2006), 'Trust Me, I'm a Robot', *Economist.Com* [website],
(updated 8 June 2006) <http://www.economist.com/displaystory.cfm?story_
id=7001829>

_____(2007a), 'Unmanned Aircraft: The Fly's A Spy', *The Economist.
Com* [website], (updated 1 November 2007) <http://www.economist.com/
displaystory.cfm?story_id=10059596>

_____(2007b), 'Rise of the Machines', *The Economist.Com* [website], (updated 1 November 2007) <http://www.economist.com/opinion/displaystory.cfm?story_id=10063788>

The Star (2006), 'South Korea Considers Robots to Boost the Military', *The Star* [website], (updated 2 August 2006) <http://www.thestar.co.za/index.php?fArticleId=3372250>

Thomson, I. (2008), 'US Air Force Forms First Robot Fighter Air Wing', *vnunet.com* [website], (updated 13 August 2008) <http://www.vnunet.com/vnunet/news/2223782/air-force-forms-first-robot-fighter-wing>

Thompson, L. and D. Goure (2003), *Directed Energy Weapons: Technologies, Applications and Implications*, Research Report (Arlington, VA: Lexington Institute (February)).

Thompson, M. (2007), 'V-22 Osprey: A Flying Shame', *Time* [website], (updated 26 September 2007) <http://www.time.com/time/politics/article/0,8599,1665835,00.html>

Tiron, R. (2002), 'Unmanned Underwater Vehicles Not Quite There Yet, Navy Says', *National Defense Magazine* [website], (updated April 2002) <http://www.nationaldefensemagazine.org/issues/2002/Apr/Unmanned_Underwater.htm>

Tirpak, J. A. (1997), 'The Robotic Air Force', *Air Force Magazine* 80:9.

_____(2002), 'Send in the UCAVs', *AirForce Magazine Online* 84:8 [website], (updated August 2002) <http://www.afa.org/magazine/aug2001/0801ucav.asp>

_____(2005), 'Toward an Unmanned Bomber', *Air Force Magazine* 88:6 (June).

Toffler, A. and H. Toffler (1995), *War and Anti-War: Making Sense of Today's Global Chaos* (New York: Warner Books).

Toomey, C. (2003), 'Army Digitization: Making It Ready For Prime Time', *Parameters* 33:4 (Winter) 40–53.

Treder, M. (2006), 'Nano-Guns, Nano-Germs, and Nano-Steel', *KurzweilAI.net* [website], (29 March 2006) <http://www.kurzweilai.net/meme/frame.html?m=2>

Turse, N. (2008a), 'The Pentagon's Battle Bugs', *Mother Jones* (31 March).

_____(2008b), *The Complex: How the Military Invades Our Everyday Lives* (London: Faber & Faber).

Tuttle, R. (2003), 'DARPA, U.S. Air Force Seeks Input on Global Strike Project', *Aviation Week* [website], (updated 19 June 2003) <http://www.aviationweek.com/aw/generic/story_generic.jsp?channel=aerospacedaily&id=news/dar06193.xml>

Tvaryanas, A. P., N. Lopez, P. Hickey, C. DaLuz, W. Thompson and J. L. Caldwell (2006), *Effects of Shift Work and Sustained Operations: Operator Performance in Remotely Piloted Aircraft* (Brooks City-Base, TX: 311th Performance Enhancement Directorate, United States Air Force).

Tyler, R. (2008), 'War Against Robots: the New Entrepreneurial Frontier', *Daily Telegraph* [website], (updated 15 September 2008) <http://blogs. telegraph.co.uk/richard_tyler/blog/2008/09/15/war_against_robots_the_new_ entrepreneurial_frontier>

UK MoD (2001), 'Nanotechnology: Its Impact on Defence and the MoD', *Nanotechnology Panel* [online], (November 2001) <http://www.mod.uk/NR/ rdonlyres/63E7F0AE-3BBF-4ED9-8FD8-74A733CB40F0/0/nanotech.pdf>

———(2006), *The DCDC Global Strategic Trends Programme 2007–2036* (London: Development, Concepts and Doctrine Centre (December)).

Ulin, D. L. (2005), 'When Robots Do the Killing', *Los Angeles Times* [website], (updated 30 January 2005) <http://articles.latimes.com/2005/jan/30/opinion/oe-ulin30>

Ullman, H. K. and J. P. Wade (1996), *Shock and Awe: Achieving Rapid Dominance* (Washington, DC: National Defense University).

UN (2007), *State of the World Population: Unleashing the Potential of Urban Growth* (United Nations Population Fund).

US Army (2008), 'Future Combat Systems', [website] <http://www.fcs.army.mil/ systems/index.html> (accessed 8 October 2008).

US Congress (2001), *National Defense Authorization Act Fiscal Year 2001*.

———(2006), *Options for the Navy's Future Fleet* (Washington, DC: Congressional Budget Office (May)).

US DARPA, 'Hybrid Insect MEMS (HI-MEMS)', [website] <http://www.darpa. mil/MTO/Programs/himems/index.html>

———(2007a), 'DARPA Awards: DigitalTripwire: A Small, Automated Human-Detection System' [website], (updated 15 August 2007) <http://www.darpa. mil/sbir/2007STTRAwards.htm>

———(2007b), 'Urban Challenge', DARPA [website], (updated November 2007) <http://www.darpa.mil/grandchallenge>

———(2008), 'Blackswift Programme Solicitation 08-02', DARPA [website], (updated 29 February 2008) <http://www.darpa.mil/tto/solicit/PS08-02.pdf>

US DoD (1990), *The Air Force and U.S. National Security: Global Reach, Global Power* (Washington, DC: Department of the US Air Force (December)).

———(1992), *Forward ... From the Sea* (Washington, DC: Department of the Navy).

———(1997), *Vision for 2020* (Washington, DC: US Space Command (February)).

———(2000a), 'Joint Vision 2020', US Joint Chiefs of Staff [online], (June 2000) <www.dtic.mil/jointvision/jv2020.doc>

———(2000b), *Global Vigilance, Reach and Power/America's Air Force Vision 2020* (Washington, DC: Department of the US Air Force (December)).

———(2003), *US Air Force Transformation Flight Plan* (Washington, DC: Department of the US Air Force).

———(2005a), *U.S. Air Force Remotely Piloted Aircraft and Unmanned Aerial Vehicle Strategic Vision* (Washington, DC: Department of the US Air Force).

_____(2005b), *Unmanned Aircraft Systems Roadmap 2005–2030* (Washington, DC: Department of the US Air Force (August)).

_____(2006a), *Quadrennial Defense Review Report* (Washington, DC: U.S. Department of Defense).

_____(2006b), *U.S. Air Force Roadmap 2006–2025* (Washington, DC: Department of the US Air Force (June)).

_____(2007), *Unmanned Systems Roadmap 2007 to 2032* (Washington, DC: U.S. Department of Defense).

_____(2008), *U.S. Army Posture Statement 2008* (Washington, DC: Department of the U.S. Army (February)).

US Executive Office of the President (2008), 'National Nanotechnology Initiative FY 2009 Budget & Highlights' [website], (2008) <http://www.nano.gov/NNI_FY09_budget_summary.pdf>

US Joint Forces Command (2003), 'Military Robots of the Future', *About.Com* [website], (updated August 2003) <http://usmilitary.about.com/cs/weapons/a/robots.htm>

US Navy (2008), 'Aircraft Carriers – CVN-21 Program Fact File', [website], (updated 2008) <http://www.navy.mil/navydata/fact_display.asp?cid=4200&tid=250&ct=4>

US Navy and Marine Corps (2008), 'The Raven Revolution', *Navy & Marine Corps Small Unmanned Aerial Systems* [website], (30 May 2008) <http://www.navair.navy.mil/pma263>

Van Atta, R. H., M. J. Lippitz, J. C. Lupo, R. Mahoney and J. H. Nunn (2003), *Transformation and Transition: DARPA's Role in Fostering an Emerging Revolution in Military Affairs: Volume 1 Overall Assessment* (Washington, DC: Institute for Defense Analysis (April)).

Van Creveld, M. (1985), *Command in War* (Cambridge, MA: Harvard University Press).

_____(1989), *Technology and War: From 2000 B.C. to the Present* (New York: The Free Press).

_____(1991), *The Transformation of War* (New York: The Free Press).

Vassar, M. and R. A. Freitas (2006), 'Lifeboat Foundation Nanoshield', *KurzweilAI. net* [website], (updated 31 July 2006) <http://www.kurzweilai.net/meme/frame.html?main=/articles/art0685.html>

Versenyi, L. (1974), 'Can Robots Be Moral?', *Ethics* 84:3, 248–59.

Veruggio, G. (2005), 'The Birth of Roboethics', *IEEE International Conference on Automation and Robotics: Workshop on Roboethics*, Barcelona, 18 April 2005 [online] <http://www.roboethics.org/icra05/veruggio.pdf> (accessed 24 August 2008).

Vickers, M. G. and R. C. Martinage (2004), *The Revolution in War* (Washington, DC: Center for Strategic and Budgetary Assessments).

Vinge, V. (1993), 'The Coming Singularity', *Whole Earth Review* [online], (Winter) <http://www.frc.ri.cmu.edu/~hpm/book98/com.ch1/vinge.singularity.html>

Walker, F. (2006), 'Killer Robots US Military's New Vision', *The Sydney Morning Herald* [website], (updated 15 October 2006) <http://www.smh.com.au/news/world/killer-robots-us-militarys-new-vision/2006/10/14/1160246372617.html>

Wall, R. and D. A. Fulghum (2003), 'The Intel Battle', *Aviation Week & Space Technology* 158:19, 62–3.

Walzer, M. (2000), *Just and Unjust Wars: A Moral Argument with Historical Illustrations* (New York: Basic Books).

'WAR Defence' [website], (2008) <http://www.wardefence.com> accessed 16 September 2008.

Warden III, J. A. (1995), 'Air Theory for the Twenty-first Century', in Aerospace Power Chronicles, *Battlefield of the Future: Twenty-first Century Warfare Issues*.

Warren, P. (2006), 'Launching a New Kind of Warfare', *Guardian* [website], (updated 26 October 2006) <http://www.guardian.co.uk/technology/2006/oct/26/guardianweeklytechnologysection.robots>

Warwick, G. (2005), 'DARPA Seeks Oblique Wing Design', *Flight International* [website], (updated 9 June 2005) <www.flightglobal.com/articles/2005/09/06/201367/darpa-seeks-oblique-wing-design.html>

Warwick, K. (1997), *March of the Machines: Why the New Race of Robots Will Rule the World* (London: Century).

Waterman, S. (2006), 'U.S. Military Plans to Make Insect Cyborgs', *UPI* (16 March).

Weed, W. S. (2002), 'The Year in Ideas; Robotic Warfare', *The New York Times* (15 December).

Weinberger, S. (2008a), 'Charity Battles Imaginary Killing Machines', *Wired Blog* [website], (updated 28 March 2008) <http://blog.wired.com/defense/2008/03/charity-will-ba.html>

_____(2008b), 'Robot War Continues', *Wired Blog* (updated 31 March 2008) <http://blog.wired.com/defense/2008/03/the-robot-war-c.html>

_____(2008c), 'Armed Robots Still in Iraq, But Grounded (Updated)', *Wired Blog* [website], (updated 15 April 2008) <http://blog.wired.com/defense/2008/04/armed-robots-st.html>

Weiner, T. (2005a), 'New Model Army Soldier Rolls Closer to Battle', *New York Times* [website], (updated 16 February 2005) <http://www.nytimes.com/2005/02/16/technology/16robots.html?_r=1&oref=slogin>

_____(2005b), '"GI Robot" Rolls Toward the Battlefield', *International Herald Tribune* [website], (updated 17 February 2005) <http://www.iht.com/articles/2005/02/16/business/robot.php>

Weir, N. A., D. P. Sierra and J. F. Jones (2006), *A Review of Research in Nanorobotics* (Albuquerque, NM: Sandia Reports (October)).

Weizenbaum, J. (1977), *Computer Power and Human Reason: From Judgement to Calculation* (New York: W.H. Freeman & Company).

Werrell, K. P. (1985), *The Evolution of the Cruise Missile* (Maxwell AFB, AL: Air University Press).

West, B. (2005), *No True Glory: A Frontline Account of the Battle of Fallujah* (New York: Bantam Dell).

West, N. (1997), *The Secret War for the Falklands: The SAS, MI6, and the War Whitehall Nearly Lost* (London: Little, Brown and Co).

White, S. E. (2008), 'Brave New World: Neurowarfare and the Limits of International Humanitarian Law', *Cornell International Law Journal* 41 (February) 177–210.

Wiley, J.C. (1967), *Military Strategy: A General Theory of Power Control* (Annapolis, MD: Naval Institute Press).

Williams, M. (2006a), 'Technology and the Future of Warfare', *Technology Review* [website], (updated 23 March 2006) <http://www.technologyreview. com/Biztech/16620/page1>

_____(2006b), 'The Great Transformation', *Technology Review* [website], (updated May 2006) <http://www.technologyreview.com/Biztech/16817>

Williams, S. (2002), *Arguing A.I.: The Battle for Twenty-first Century Science* (New York: Random House).

Wilson, D. H. (2005), *How to Survive a Robot Uprising: Tips on Defending Yourself Against the Coming Rebellion* (London: Bloomsbury).

Winslow, L. (2007a), 'Unmanned Vehicle Robotic Warfare', *Online Think Tank* [website], (updated 18 May 2007) <http://www.worldthinktank.net/pdfs/ unmannedvehiclerobotic.pdf>

_____(2007b), 'Enemy UAV Defense Is Under Consideration', *Online Think Tank* [website], (updated 18 May 2007) <http://www.worldthinktank.net/pdfs/ unmannedvehiclerobotic.pdf>

Wirbel, L. (2004), *Star Wars: US Tools of Space Supremacy* (London: Pluto Press).

Worley, G. (2004), 'Robot Oppression: The Unethicality of the Three Laws', [website], (updated July 2004) <http://www.asimovlaws.com/articles/ archives/2004/07/robot_oppressio_2.html>

Yong, C. H. and R. Miikkulainen (2001), *Cooperative Coevolution of Multi-Agent Systems*, Technical Report (Austin, TX: University of Texas at Austin (February)).

Youngblood, N. (2006), *The Development of Mine Warfare: A Most Murderous and Barbarous Conduct* (London: PRAEGER).

Yudkowsky, E. (2003), *Creating Friendly AI 1.0.* [online], <http://www.singinst. org/CFAI/index.html>

Zaloga, S. (2005), *V-1 Flying Bomb 1942–1952: Hitler's Infamous 'Doodle Bug'* (Oxford: Osprey Publishing).

Zhongchang, S., Z. Haiyin and Z. Xinsheng (1998), '21st Century Naval Warfare', in Michael Pillsbury (ed.), *Chinese Views of Future Warfare* (Washington, DC: National Defense University).

Zimmer, C. (2004), 'Mind Over Machine', *Popular Science* 264:2 (February) 46.

Index